PELICAN BOOKS

A HISTORY OF INDIA

VOLUME TWO

Percival Spear was born in Bath, Somerset, in 1901, and educated at Monkton Combe School and at St Catharine's College, Cambridge, where he read History. He went to India in 1924 and for sixteen years was on the staff of St Stephen's College, Delhi. Here he taught European and English history and developed his interests in and study of Indian history. His first book on the subject, *The Nabobs*, was published in 1932. During the Second World War Dr Spear worked in the information department of the Government of India and afterwards returned to England to become Fellow and Bursar of Selwyn College, Cambridge; he then held a University lectureship there in South Asian History. Most of his books on Indian topics were written during this period and they include: *India, Pakistan and the West*; *The Twilight of the Mughals*; *India, a Modern History*; and Part III of the *Oxford History of India* (third edition). This period was diversified by a year spent in the University of California, at Berkeley, on a Visiting Professorship and visits to India and Pakistan.

Percival Spear died in December 1982.

PERCIVAL SPEAR

A HISTORY OF INDIA

VOLUME TWO

PENGUIN BOOKS

Penguin Books Ltd, 27 Wrights Lane, London w8 5tz (Publishing and Editorial)
and Harmondsworth, Middlesex, England (Distribution and Warehouse)
Viking Penguin Inc., 40 West 23rd Street, New York, New York 10010, USA
Penguin Books Australia Ltd, Ringwood, Victoria, Australia
Penguin Books Canada Ltd, 2801 John Street, Markham, Ontario, Canada l3r 1b4
Penguin Books (NZ) Ltd, 182–190 Wairau Road, Auckland 10, New Zealand

First published 1965
Reprinted 1968
Reprinted with Epilogue 1970
Reprinted 1971
Reprinted with revisions 1973
Reprinted 1975 (twice), 1977
Reprinted with revisions 1978
Reprinted 1979, 1981, 1982, 1983, 1984, 1985, 1986, 1987

Made and printed in Great Britain by
Hazell Watson & Viney Limited,
Member of the BPCC Group,
Aylesbury, Bucks
Set in Linotype Granjon

CONTENTS

MAPS

ACKNOWLEDGEMENTS

The publishers are grateful to the Indian Branch of the Oxford University Press for permission to print the maps on pp. 32–3 and 136–7, which are taken from the *Historical Atlas of the Indian Peninsula* by C. C. Davies.

INTRODUCTION

THE production of histories of India has become very frequent in recent years and may well call for some explanation. Why so many and why this one in particular? The reason is a twofold one : changes in the Indian scene requiring a re-interpretation of the facts and changes in the attitudes of historians about the essential elements of Indian history. These two considerations are in addition to the normal fact of fresh information, whether in the form of archaeological discoveries throwing fresh light on an obscure period or culture, or the revelations caused by the opening of archives or the release of private papers. The changes in the Indian scene are too obvious to need emphasis. Only two generations ago British rule seemed to most Indian as well as British observers likely to extend into an indefinite future; now there is a teenage generation which knows nothing of it. Changes in the attitudes of historians have occurred everywhere, changes in attitudes to the content of the subject as well as to particular countries, but in India there have been some special features. Prior to the British Indian historiographers were mostly Muslims who relied, like Sayyid Ghulam Hussain, on their own recollection of events and on information from friends and men of affairs. Only a few like Abu'l Fazl had access to official papers. They were personal narratives of events varying in value with the nature of the writer. The early British writers were officials. In the eighteenth century they were concerned with some aspect of the Company policy, or, like Robert Orme in his *Military Transactions*, gave a straight narrative in what was essentially a continuation of the Muslim tradition. In the early nineteenth century the writers were still, with two notable exceptions, officials, but they were now engaged in chronicling, in varying moods of zest, pride, and awe, the rise of the British power in India to supremacy. The two exceptions were James Mill, with his critical attitude to the Company and John Marshman, the Baptist missionary. But they, like the officials, were anglo-centric in their attitude, so that the history of modern

India in their hands came to be the history of the rise of the British in India.

The official school dominated the writing of Indian history until we get the first professional historian's approach, Ramsay Muir and P. E. Roberts in England and H. H. Dodwell in India. Then Indian historians trained in the English school joined in, of whom the most distinguished was Sir Jadunath Sarkar: and other notable writers; Surendranath Sen, Dr Radkakumud Mukerji, and Professor Nilakanta Sastri. These, it may be said, restored India to Indian history, but their bias was mainly political. Finally have come the nationalists who range from those who can find nothing good or true in the British to sophisticated historical philosophers like K. M. Panikkar.

Along with types of historians with their varying bias have gone changes in the attitude to the content of Indian history. Here Indian historians have been influenced both by their local situation and by changes of thought elsewhere. It is in this field that this book can claim some attention since it seeks to break new ground, or perhaps to deepen a freshly turned furrow in the field of Indian history. The early official historians were content with the glamour and drama of political history from Plassey to the Mutiny, from Dupleix to the Sikhs. But when the *raj* had settled down glamour departed from politics, and they turned to the less glorious but more solid ground of administration. Not how India was conquered but how it was governed was the theme of this school of historians. It found its archpriest in H. H. Dodwell, its priestess in Dame Lilian Penson, and its chief shrine in volume vi of the *Cambridge History of India*. Meanwhile in Britain other currents were moving, which led historical study into the economic and social fields. R. C. Dutt entered the first of these currents with his *Economic History of India* to be followed more recently by a whole group of Indian economic historians. W. E. Moreland extended these studies to the Mughal period. Social history is now being increasingly studied and there is also of course a school of nationalist historians who see modern Indian history in terms of the rise and fulfilment of the national movement.

All these approaches have value, but all share in the quality of being compartmental. It is not enough to remove political history from its pedestal of being the only kind of history worth having if it is merely to put other types of history in its place. Too exclusive an attention to economic, social, or administrative history can be as sterile and misleading as too much concentration on politics. A whole subject needs a whole treatment for understanding. A historian must dissect his subject into its elements and then fuse them together again into an integrated whole. The true history of a country must contain all the features just cited but must present them as parts of a single consistent theme. This has been the aim of this book.

The Mughal and British periods have been taken together because much misunderstanding has been caused in the past by their separate treatment. A concentration on the British period presents Indian régimes and institutions only in decay, leading easily to the assumption that this was the state that they were always in. Placing the Mughal period beside the British reveals to the reader that India had its going political concerns as viable as that of the British in India. In addition to this consideration, there is an organic connexion between the two which separate treatment misses. British India was deeply indebted to Mughal India on the one hand, and Mughal India was a characteristic Indian entity on the other in a way not realized by any other régime during the previous thousand years. In many ways British India saw the development of trends already existing in Mughal India and it is certain that British India would have been a very different place had the Mughals never ruled before them. The principle of continuity demands the twin treatment.

In the story itself I have endeavoured to weave the various strands of compartmentalized history into the single texture of the development of Indian society. We see at the turn of the sixteenth century a divided and uncertain society, impoverished in the north, embattled and brilliant in the south. We see the political and attempted spiritual integration of this society by the Mughals, its covering with the magic cloak of Persian culture. We note the disintegration of that society and the struggle to control the future which followed in the eighteenth century. Then we watch an outward re-integration by new and more alien foreigners, the British. But then, instead of a new cultural cloak for the few at the top, came an injection (in the form of the education policy) of new ideas into the ideological life-blood of Indian society. Thereafter the gradual transformation of Indian society, as it prepared antibodies against some forms of the western virus and modified itself under the influence of other forms, provided the inner meaning of modern Indian history, culminating in Gandhi and the national movement, independence, and the reign of Nehru. It is this inner meaning which the book endeavours to catch and transmit to the reader.

1

THE COMING OF THE MUGHALS

THE observer of the Indian scene in the early years of the sixteenth century might well have supposed that politically and
socially the country was in decline. Conflict, confusion, uncertainty were to be found nearly everywhere except in the extreme
south. The country was largely controlled by foreign members
of an alien religion, yet these were hopelessly divided amongst
themselves. The long reign of Hindu states had been broken at
the end of the twelfth century by the foreign rule of Muslim
Turks. Though alien and at first ferocious, these people were at
least united. For two centuries the Delhi empire or Sultanate
controlled the north and at times the centre of the country. The
rule was essentially military, and their régime something of an
armed camp, but they were open to cultural influences, they
employed Hindus largely in all the services, they built finely.
They settled in the country, their capital city of Delhi in the
mid fourteenth century was, on the testimony of the much-
travelled Ibu-Batuta, one of the leading cities of the contemporary world.

In 1398 the Turkish conqueror Taimur or Tamerlane ended
all this with his bloody raid on India and sack of Delhi. The
monuments of the next ten years still testify to the desolation and
despair which he left behind. It took nearly fifty years for the
Delhi kingdom to become more than a local chiefship, so that
the phrase was coined

> From Delhi to Palam (the modern New Delhi airport)
> Is the realm of Shah Alam.

Even then revival was slow and fitful. In the Deccan, or centre,
the Delhi empire had broken up into the succession state of the
Bahminis, a brilliant, brittle minority rule. But this state was
itself shattered in the late fifteenth century. The Muslim forces
were patently in disarray.

Nor were the Hindus in much better case. All over the north
they had lost sovereignty. Only in Rajasthan had they held out,

but here they were deeply divided by clan feeling and chiefs' rivalry, with new states flaking off from the old as the chisel of ambition worked on Rajput pride and obstinacy. In the Deccan they had given place to the Bahminis and their successors. In the deep south they appeared to be united and strong, but the union was precarious and the strength deceptive. A scene of divisions, tensions, and frustrated ambitions thus met the eye; the only redeeming feature which might have been noticed was the abounding energy everywhere. Each little state had its monuments as if intended for all time. Everyone had plans for enlargement which circumstances conspired to wreck. There was an energy, a turbulence, and a frustration abroad somewhat reminiscent of the early Italian Renaissance.

Let us now take a closer look at India as it was on the eve of Babur's invasion. The sceptre of the Turk in northern India, so rudely broken by Taimur, had now been grasped by the Afghans. These men were chiefs and adventurers who had migrated into India to take service with the Turks in the preceding two centuries, had received grants of land for their services, and had used the post-Timurid confusion to hoist themselves into political power. Their strength was energy, courage, and vigour; their weakness pride, clan spirit, and an inability to work together. Daulat Khan Lodi (1451–88) had gradually built up a new power at Delhi, but he was rather the President of a noble confederacy than an absolute monarch in the old style. His son Sikandar (1488–1516), who lived in Agra, followed in his footsteps, but, when the grandson Ibrahim tried to reassert the royal prerogatives, trouble began. His followers became restive and disloyal. The Lodi Afghans (their tombs and mosques may be seen in Delhi today), ruled from the banks of the Indus over the Punjab and Uttar Pradesh to the borders of Bengal. They stopped short at about the river Chambal to the south and had no hold over Rajasthan. Their empire had become impressive in size but it lacked inner strength. It had no independent source of authority and exercised no bureaucratic control. It was essentially a coalition of landed Afghans controlling other landholders, Muslim and Hindu, by virtue of their united military power. Disturb the sense of conformity, very easy in the case of Afghans, and the whole fabric became unstable. This was exactly what the luckless Ibrahim did. Bengal, once a province of the Delhi sultanate, was now an unstable splinter kingdom of Afghan chiefs.

The only other power in the north was the Rajputs of Rajasthan. By their heroism and constancy they had repulsed Muslim attacks in the fourteenth century. The Muslim dissensions in the fifteenth had encouraged them to emerge from their desert fastnesses but they remained divided into clans and petty states. A family quarrel or a disputed succession, and there were many such, was often the start of a new principality. This moment of time found the Rajputs of Rajasthan with an outstanding leader, Rana Sanga of Mewar. Without forming an empire he had succeeded in heading a confederation of chiefs which seemed to present a formidable if incalculable power and to be capable of challenging the Afghan power in Delhi. As often before and since, the Rajputs were an enigma, providing the politicians of the day with the current version of the query, what will they do next? It should be noted in passing that the term Rajput (literally son of a king) is a generic one for a warrior caste and in no way implies a particular physical race. In Rajasthan these warriors were a ruling race, but by no means all the inhabitants of Rajasthan were Rajputs. Rajputs of these and other clans were scattered all over northern and central India. Some had long genealogies but none can be traced back further than the fifth century A.D. Some clans like the Sisodias were probably formed from the chiefs of invading tribes, but others like the Rathors and Bundelas are neither foreign nor Aryan, but aboriginal in origin. The Rajputs collectively are not a race, but an example of how Hinduism can reconcile invasion, cultural and racial intermixture with itself by means of the pervasive concept of caste.

We now pass to central India and the Deccan, the area roughly between the rivers Chambal (south of Agra) and Kistna. To the west lay the fertile region of Gujarat, which had enjoyed firm government for a century. Its ruler Mahmud Begarha became a legend for his physical peculiarities. His beard descended to his waist, his immunity to poison caused the couplet to be coined:

> The King of Cambay's daily food
> Is asp and basilisk and toad.

Gujarat and the Rajputs were disputing the district of Malwa (between the rivers Chambal and Narbadda) between them. Further south in the Deccan the Bahmini Muslim kingdom, itself a successor state to the Delhi sultanate, had broken up in 1482. The area was now covered by the five splinter states of Bidar, Golkonda, Bijapur, Ahmadanagar, and Berar with the little hill state of Khandesh squeezed in between them and Gujarat. The rulers of these states spent their days fighting each other and the Hindus further south and any spare resources on poets for their courts and tombs for themselves. Their meteoric careers shoot across the pages of the chroniclers and violence is never far away. Their brilliance and turbulence passed the Hindu masses by but there must have been a modicum of prosperity and trade to enable their surviving monuments to be so substantial.

Beyond the dividing river of the Kistna came the Hindu empire of Vijayanagar, which controlled the rest of the peninsula except for a string of commercial principalities, headed by Calicut with its Zamorin, down the Malabar coast on the west side. Vijayanagar was the Hindu reply to the Muslim invasion of the south in the fourteenth century. It was the political expression of Hindu resilience to the Muslim menace and as such had been in existence for less than two centuries. It was not a national state but a political construction of two gifted Telugu or Andhra brothers. In essence it was a Telugu oligarchy ruling the Kannara, Tamil, and Malayali regions in the south represented today by the states of Mysore, Madras, and Kerala. Its focal point was Vijayanagar, a fortress capital looking towards the Muslim kingdoms to the north. The state was wealthy, for it controlled the spice trade of the south and the cotton industry of the south east. It had a bureaucracy to keep the chiefs in order, and a mercenary army, which included Muslim mounted archers, to defend itself from the Muslims to the north. Vijayanagar itself was a wonder city of the age as certified by both Muslim and European travellers. It must have been comparable to Delhi in the fourteenth century. It was reputed to have half a million inhabitants, as many as contemporary Renaissance Rome, to extend seven miles from north to south, and to have seven concentric city walls. Its culture was a hybrid of current Hinduism. The great gods Vishnu and Shiva were lavishly worshipped in orthodox style. Brahmins were privileged, suttee or the burning of widows was widely practised, and temple prostitution was common. But meat except beef was eaten by all and animal sacrifices in the Andhra manner were general.

One more element must be added to the Indian scene. These are the Portuguese. They arrived by sea with Vasco da Gama in 1497, coming, as they said, to seek Christians and spices. The Christians they were seeking were the subjects of the mysterious Prester John and were in reality the Abyssinians; the Christians they found were the 'Syrians' of Travancore, probably resident since the fourth century A.D., and unknown to Europe. The spices they wanted for themselves, but still more to deny them to the Muslim Egyptians who had a stranglehold on the supply to Europe. Their anti-Muslim attitude embroiled them, ironically enough, with the Hindu Zamorin, because he got his profits from the Arab traders plying between Calicut, South Arabia, and Egypt. In 1510 the Portuguese had established themselves at Goa half-way up the west coast and were seeking, by means of sea-fortress settlements, to control the maritime trade of the Indian ocean. Their methods, which included a cruelty unusual in the south and a perfidy, based on the doctrine that no faith need be kept with infidels, unusual even in the turbulent north of the day, made them generally detested.

On the surface the Indian scene thus appeared chaotic enough about 1520. Below were the agricultural Hindu masses who maintained by force of habit and power of devotion the Hindu religion and social system with its ever-proliferating sects and castes. Above were Brahmins of the temples and the schools and the nobles both Hindu and Muslim whose power came from landholding and who sought fame by serving the local state, or, if that was decrepit, setting up on their own. The Brahmins preserved Hindu thought and even developed it by means of commentaries, but they made no large impact because they mostly lacked royal patronage. Some Hindus, like Chaitanya in Bengal and the Maratha 'saints' in the west started popular religious movements, which remained local because of the condition of the country. On the Muslim side the *ulema* formed an intellectual *élite* in the cities, both as lawyers and theologians. Islam was carried to the people, and made converts, not by these rather arid legalists but by wandering preachers or holy men known generically as *sufis* or *pirs*. Some settled down like Nizam-ad-din of Delhi, where their centres became places of resort and, in course of time, of pilgrimage.

There remained the glittering if unstable life of the Muslim courts and of Hindu Vijayanagar. Here there was evidence of life and vigour, even if the general scene remained chaotic. Each Muslim provincial kingdom of the fifteenth and sixteenth centuries expressed itself in magnificent buildings which are part of India's artistic treasures today. In the north Hindu craftsmen and Muslim architects combined to produce a unique Hindu–Muslim style; in the Deccan was constructed a dome for a royal tomb only inferior in size to that of St Peter's, Rome. These buildings stand, as watchers of the past, in quiet country towns like Jaunpur and Kulbarga and Bijapur, as well as in busy modern cities like Agra and Ahmadabad. There was also much intellectual activity among Muslim poets and theologians for the princes, although so often violent in their deeds and ends, were liberal in their patronage of the arts. To preside over a *mushaira* or poetic competition had, in the value scale of Indian royalty, a place akin to attendance at Ascot or a Cup Final in that of British royalty. The cultural life of these courts was exotic and foreign, so that the activity it fostered was frail and isolated from the country as a whole. The main source of this culture was Persia, from which many of the invaders had come, and by whom nearly all, whether Turk, Arab, or Afghan, had been influenced to some extent. This influence, through lack of numbers and Hindu antagonism, was restricted to the courts and ruling classes, but it was to have a great significance for the future.

Given that India at this time was in a state of confusion and conflict, and that it was also bubbling with life and energy, we may ask whether there were any great forces moving the minds of men beneath the surface of events. Such forces I find difficult to see at this time. On the Muslim side the *élan* of Muslim pro-selytism had died away; the tendency was now, apart from moments of passion or fanaticism, to live and let live. The Turkish enthusiasm for conquest and empire-building had wilted under the hammer blows of Taimur. What was left was a general spirit of adventure. There were numbers of young men ready, in the unsettled conditions of north-west India and the Iranian plateau, to seek their fortunes in foreign parts. They would attach themselves to some great man in a distant kingdom and hope to achieve promotion and fame by their ability. Such a career was eminently open to talent, as the career of many dynasty founders shows. Everyone was in need of able young followers, and promotion, like disgrace, could be dazzling in its speed. This social fact meant that India contained many enterprising and relatively unattached men ready to take advantage of any twist of fortune and to rally to any outstanding leader. On the Hindu side we find no such tendency. The Hindu magnates were too busy trying to preserve what they still retained or to win back something that they had lost for their people to have time for adventuring. Within Hinduism there was intellectual and social activity but in both spheres the dominant interest was adjustment to the fact of Islam in their midst, with its strange and repugnant ideas, values, and practices. Hindu society was on the defensive and not ready for any large new constructive venture.

It was on this scene that the Mughal or Turkish chief Babur appeared in the year 1517. He himself was an adventurer, though not one of those who seek to gain fortune from nothing. Babur was trying to recover in one direction what he had lost in others. Babur's dynasty is entitled Mughal or Mongol but it should in fact be thought of as Turkish, which language they spoke. Turk and Mongol have been much intermixed in the ebb and flow of Central Asian intertribal warfare, and though some Mughals had decidedly Mongoloid features they were physically more Turkish than Mongolian. Babur was fifth in descent from the great Taimur. As a younger branch, however, his father's kingdom was reduced to the small principality of Farghana in Badakshan. Babur succeeded as a boy of eleven in 1494 but soon found himself threatened by the Uzbeg chief Shaibani Khan. He was soon a fugitive and spent the years between 1494 and 1513 trying to maintain himself in Farghana and recover Samarkand. As a descendant of Taimur, Babur considered he had a right to all Taimur's possessions. He was thus a king by profession and an adventurer by force of circumstances.

In 1504, in one of the turns of north-western politics, he gained control of Kabul and Kandahar. Gradually he welded these two districts with Badakshan over the mountains into a personal kingdom of his own, which he regarded as a compensation for the loss of his ancestral Samarkand, and which was to become the nucleus of modern Afghanistan. It was only from 1513, when he gave up hope of a northern kingdom, that he turned his gaze towards India. India was for him, as for the British East India merchants a century later, a second best as a field of activity. Babur's occasional raids gradually convinced him that all was not well with the Afghan Lodi régime at Delhi. Sultan Ibrahim was making pretensions, backed by executions, which his free-loving nobles resented. He heard reports of disaffection, the Afghan governor of the Panjab invited his intervention. It should not be thought that there was any element of national aggression or treachery in all this. It was a case, as they thought at the time, of a group of discontented chiefs asking another chief to replace their own as their nominal head. The only difference between this and many similar medieval intrigues was that the replacement happened to be a man of genius.

Babur took his cue with the two invasions of 1523–24 and 1525–26 leading up to the battle of Panipat on 21 April 1526. The battle was fought only fifty miles from Delhi, for so far had treachery and lukewarmness allowed Babur to penetrate already. In the fight he was heavily outnumbered by an army stiffened with a hundred elephants. On his side, however, he had the strength of loyalty in a compact group, cavalry which could manoeuvre skilfully on the wings, and the new artillery from Turkey commanded by a Turkish officer. It was these factors which proved decisive and the day ended with the death of Ibrahim on the field and the flight of his great army. There was no national rally, because the country was not interested in the fortunes of these alien aristocrats. Nor was there any rally to the dynasty, because it enjoyed no special divine or hereditary right and each Afghan chief thought himself in general as good as the temporary leader. Nor was there a rally to Babur, because the chiefs hoped that General Hot Weather would send him away leaving the field or fields of sovereignty to one of themselves. They watched and waited; there was a breathless interlude in north-Indian affairs.

Babur pushed on from Delhi to Agra where his first act was to lay out a garden in Persian style. He then had to face General Hot Weather, for his *begs* or chiefs objected to the heat and dust and demanded a return to the musk melons and cooling streams of the Afghan hills. This was Babur's most critical moment, which he finally overcame by a dramatic appeal to Mughal loyalty. Then came the Rajput threat. Rana Sanga at Mewar approached Agra with 100,000 Rajputs, an apparently far more formidable host than that of Ibrahim. Discouragement succeeded disgust among the *begs*, which Babur assuaged by a further appeal and the sensational breaking up of his loved drinking-cups.

In the battle of Kanwaha which followed (16 March 1527) the Rajput army proved to have weaknesses of its own. Clan jealousies undermined its resolution and the Rajputs had no answer to the wheeling tactics of the Mughal cavalry. It was the imperial swan song of the Rajputs. They have never since had any pretensions to north-Indian hegemony. Babur was now fairly secure and one more battle gave to him, by the time of his death at the end of 1530, a loosely-knit empire from Badakshan and Kabul through the Punjab to the borders of Bengal. It was a personal affair depending on the leadership of the man who built it up. None of his contemporaries could be blamed for supposing that such an empire might dissolve as quickly as it was formed. Consolidation required genius also, of a different kind, and no one could know that it would be provided in the person of his grandson.

Babur is one of the most attractive characters in Indian or any other history. He was not only a soldier–statesman of a familiar type, but a poet and man of letters, of sensibility and taste and humour as well. Wherever he went he laid out Persian gardens and his memoirs are dotted with references to natural beauties.

It was the absence of the hills and streams of his homeland that he felt so keenly in India. His memoirs, written in Turki and translated thence into Persian and English, are a masterpiece in their genre.* He had a zest for life which carried him cheerfully through the hardships of his early life when he was often a hunted man, and a sense of humour which could make even treachery look ridiculous.† His love of sport was infectious and spontaneous and he treated life as one long game of polo. He lacked the vindictiveness common at that time of fanaticism and intense power struggle and had a personal magnetism which could galvanize his followers as in those hot dusty days in Agra and in the camp before Rana Sanga's Rajputs. Any good soldier at that time could collect followers. Babur had the rarer gifts of retaining their loyalty, of inspiring them to further efforts, and of reconciling enemies as well as defeating them.

The state which Babur took over was an aristocratic confederation and had little bureaucratic machinery. Babur had therefore no ready-made apparatus of government, but he did have a free hand to shape new institutions. His genius was for personal government and he died before he had the chance or need to organize. The general state of north India at this time is much more difficult to determine because of lack of evidence. Such clues as we have suggest that the prosperity of the fourteenth century had not returned by the early sixteenth century. The agricultural Hindu mass remained at a subsistence level, punctuated by famines and floods. The upper classes, though better off than in 1400, were still relatively impoverished by constant wars and the reduced trade with a disturbed north-west. If the building of mosques, colleges, and tombs, acts of both piety and prestige, can be taken as a guide, it would appear that prosperity increased as one went south-eastwards, becoming pronounced in eastern Uttar Pradesh, where the Sharqi dynasty adorned Jaunpur. Babur himself took a poor view of the Delhi-Agra tract and

---

* *Memoirs of Babur*, transl. J. Leyden and W. Erskine, ed. L. King, Oxford University Press, 1921, 2 vols.

† When Daulat Khan of the Punjab twice changed sides, he had him brought into his presence with two swords hanging from his neck; one, as Babur remarked, for himself and one for his opponent, Ibrahim.

its inhabitants. We may conclude this chapter with an extract from his own description of Hindustan :

Hindustan is a country that has few pleasures to recommend it. The people are not handsome. They have no idea of the charms of friendly society, of frankly mixing together, or of familiar intercourse. They have no genius, no comprehension of mind, no politeness of manner, no kindness or fellow-feeling, no ingenuity or mechanical invention in planning or executing their handicraft works, no skill or knowledge in design or architecture; they have no horses, no good flesh, no grapes or musk melons, no good fruits, no ice or cold water, no good food or bread in their bazaars, no baths or colleges, no candles, no torches, not a candlestick.*

* op. cit., Vol. II, p. 241.

2

AKBAR

ONE of the things which has attracted to the Mughal period people without any special attunement to Islam, the Turks, or India itself, is the richness of the personalities it displays. The emperors led the way, but others jostle behind them and the interest extends behind the purdah curtain itself, in that age of secluded women, to the great Mughal ladies. Nur Jahan, Jahan-ara, and Zeb-un-nissa hold their own with Akbar and Shah Jahan. So great is the attraction that one has to beware of treating the period as a pageant of personalities, as a series of biographies of great men. It was much more than this both for its own time and ours; we should realize from the outset that these brilliant personalities were rather the jewels of the pavilion of Mughal India than the pavilion itself. Nevertheless, the two themes are closely intermixed, and as long as the more dazzling does not obscure the more solid each will serve to set off the other more clearly.

As the first lodgement of the Mughals in India is associated with the fascinating character of Babur, the struggle to consolidate is associated with the enigmatic figure of Homayun. Homayun is the problem child of the great Mughals. So loved by his father that he offered his life in exchange for his son when the latter was gravely ill, and, according to the chronicler, began to fail in health from that moment, Homayun seemed in 1530 to be an attractive and able youth with a bright future. But he was unstable and wayward as well as elegant, clever, and fascinating. He could charm and excite loyalty, achieve much in a burst of energy, and then throw all away through indolence and careless-ness. A Mughal Stuart perhaps, a fair and fatal king; yet with a streak of luck which carried him through his misfortunes. Homayun is of great interest as a person, but for us his signifi-cance is a hyphen which connects his great father Babur with his greater son Akbar.

Homayun succeeded to an uneasy realm extending from Kabul and Kandahar to the borders of Bengal. In its Indian portion it was filled with Hindu chiefs prone to local independence but not good at uniting against the outsider, and Turkish and Afghan Muslim chiefs all more or less resentful of the newly imposed *raj* and watchful for an opportunity to throw it off. The Afghans were not good at combining either, and it was perhaps this factor which finally tipped the scale on the Mughal side in the struggle which followed. It lasted for thirty years, from the accession of Homayun to the first years of Akbar's reign. The situation was politically fluid; the opposing forces were large but disunited and disorganized. An energetic ruler might build up a compact empire while the chiefs were nursing their grievances and looking for a leader. Delay and weakness were the great dangers since they would give time for the opposing forces to organize. Homayun gave both treatments in alternate doses, hence the agonies of fortune and dramatic interest of his reign. In 1534–35 Homayun took Malwa and Gujarat in a brilliant campaign but then 'took his pleasure' for a year at Agra and lost them both. This inactivity enabled the Afghan opposition to take shape and it now found a leader in the person of Sher Khan Sur, who had joined Babur in 1526 but now built up a power for himself in South Bihar. Only when Sher Khan moved against Bengal with its wealth and treasures did Homayun stir. In the campaign which followed from 1537–40 Homayun lost by indolence more than he gained by his bursts of activity. In 1540, after two resounding defeats, he found himself a fugitive. His brother Kamran closed Kabul and the Punjab to him, thinking, in the fashion of the time, that a brother's misfortune was his own opportunity. Homayun escaped to Persia with much difficulty, where Shah Ismail gave him asylum. On the way, at Umarkot in Sind on 23 November 1542, his son Akbar was born.

It seemed as though the Mughal inroad into India had come to an inglorious end. The impression was strengthened by the fact that Homayun's supplanter, Sher Shah, though an Afghan, was a talented organizer as well as a skilful general. The Lodis had ruled as heads of a feudal confederacy and Ibrahim's attempt to consolidate his power had cost him his throne. Sher Shah set up a bureaucratic organization while continuing his campaigns against Homayun's brother Kamran and the Rajputs. By the time of his death in 1545, before the Rajput fortress of Kalanjar from the effects of a cannon-ball shot, he had given his empire administrative form, established a vigorous centre, and embarked on that essential of traditional Indian government, a reassessment of the land-tax. Some of the inspiration came from the Turkish past of north India, and some, I think, from the contemporary Persian present, where the age-old imperial idea had again found form in the vigorous Safavid dynasty. Some scholars have gone so far as to claim Sher Shah as the virtual founder of the future Mughal empire on the ground that he provided the essential administrative framework. His achievement was certainly remarkable but it must be remembered that he only controlled northern India for five years, during the whole of which time he was carrying on campaigns as well. Thereafter there followed ten years of deepening confusion before the Mughals reappeared. It would therefore perhaps be truer to say that Sher Shah provided an administrative blue-print from which Akbar and his ministers later profited. Truer still to say would be, perhaps, that these ideas were in the air in any case, flowing in from a revivified Persia, and that Sher Shah was the first Indian ruler to try them out. That does not belittle a very remarkable achievement but places it in better perspective.

Sher Shah is the great might-have-been of Afghan history. He showed what the Afghans might have achieved if more than one at a time had possessed the capacity to rule and to organize as well as to fight and to raid. In the event, Sher Shah's Afghan empire collapsed almost as quickly as it arose. For eight years his son Islam Shah struggled against increasing opposition, and the empire then dissolved into warring factions. It was at this point that a revived and chastened Homayun reappeared in India. With the help of the Persian Shah Ismail, Homayun recovered Kandahar from his brother Kamran, and Kabul a little later. The fraternal drama ended in 1553 when Homayun, whose clemency towards Kamran in face of repeated treachery had been extraordinary for the time, was compelled by his nobles to blind him. After defeating one of the Afghan claimants in the Punjab, Homayun re-occupied Delhi and Agra, but within six months *

* January 1556.

died from the effects of a fall on the stairs of his library in Delhi.*

At this time the Mughal position was as insecure as Babur's had been on his occupation of Agra thirty years before. Several opposing forces were in being and one possessed a general of great ability in the Hindu Hemu. Nor could they claim the close unity of a foreign clan. Their former residence had given the Mughal *begs* connexions in India and as soon as Homayun entered India he had to take action against a chief in correspondence with the other side. The struggle was in no sense one of foreigners against natives; there was no tincture of nationalism to be seen. Essentially it was the rivalry of different aristocratic groups separated only partially by differences of clan and race. They shared the same Islamic religion, the same Persian cultural veneer, and the same personal ambition. The last was the strongest of the three, and it was this fact which made any noble liable to change sides at any moment. We have already seen that Homayun could not rely on his own family. Beyond that he could only count for certain on a small ring of personal followers, who had linked their fortunes with his.

The field was thus an open one and there was unusual scope for the exercise of leadership. It so happened that the leadership appeared at the precise moment in the Mughal camp, and that is why there is a Mughal period in Indian History. Babur was the founder only in the sense that he first came to India and inspired his successors by his achievement. Homayun is important in that he managed to maintain the claim just long enough for others to be able to take over. The work of both would have been in vain if his successor had not possessed genius on his own account.

At first the outlook was unpromising enough. Akbar was only thirteen years old and was at the time with his guardian, Bairam Khan. The first stroke of fortune was that this man, though not a Mughal, was loyal to the family, an able general, and a seasoned politician. His faithful guardianship of four years enabled the young Akbar to survive the initial crisis of the reign and handed to him a consolidated kingdom of north India. Bairam Khan successfully met the challenge of the Hindu

* Now known as the Sher Mandal in the Purana Qila.

general Hemu at the second battle of Panipat. He recovered
Gwalior, and Jaunpur in the eastern half of what is now Uttar
Pradesh. In 1560, Akbar, now in his eighteenth year, dismissed
him rather in the manner of Kaiser William II dropping the
pilot Bismarck. Difference in age and incompatability of temper
boiled up in mutual suspicions. Akbar had yet to master Bairam's
successors. This was accomplished when Adham Khan, who had
murdered the Prime Minister in a palace conspiracy, was per-
sonally felled by Akbar and then hurled over the palace walls on
his orders. Henceforth, for over forty years, the government was
Akbar's own.

It is in this period that the Mughal empire became a political
fact over half of India and a factor in the life of India which has
influenced her ever since. It was not the mere existence of empire
so much which was important but the shape which it took, and
this it owed to Akbar more than to any other man. In some
respects, indeed, he was conventional enough. He was a matter-
of-fact imperialist on the question of territory. Like the English
Dalhousie in the nineteenth century with regard to British rule,
he believed quite simply that the more of India to come under
his rule the better for all concerned. In this he was neither in
advance of nor behind his time. His distinction lay in the fact
that he was more successful than others. His generalship was
outstanding. He possessed both personal magnetism, the ability
to manoeuvre and to judge situations, and the Napoleonic gift of
rapid movement. In 1573, on news of a revolt in Gujarat, he
marched from his capital Fatehpur-Sikri to Ahmadabad, a distance of 600 miles, with 3,000 horsemen in nine days' travelling.
He defeated a large but astonished army of insurgents on the
eleventh day from his departure and was back in his capital
again in another thirty-two days. This feat secured Gujarat for
the Mughals for a hundred and eighty-five years. His first and
hardest campaigns were against the Rajputs, who remained
formidable though divided as ever. Until subdued they presented a permanent threat on the flank of the Mughal bases of
Delhi and Agra. The nearest state of Jaipur was first won over,
and in 1568–69 the two great fortresses of Chitor and Ranthambor were captured. Udaipur or Mewar maintained independence

in its rocky desert fastnesses, but the rest of Rajputana accepted the Mughal supremacy. This was the hinge of Akbar's fortune both military and political, as will be noted later.

From this period, conquests followed in steady succession. Fertile Gujarat with its cotton and indigo was first secured in 1572, bringing with it the port of Surat with its trade with Arabia, the Persian gulf, and Egypt. Bengal, the richest province in the north with its abundance of rice, silk, and saltpetre, was acquired in 1574–76. Down to the time of Clive it was providing the sinews of government to Delhi. Kashmir followed in 1586, Orissa in 1592, and Sind in 1595. Then began the attack on the Deccan kingdoms which by Akbar's death had absorbed Berar, Khandesh, and part of Ahmadnagar. By the time of his death in 1605 Akbar controlled a broad sweep of territory from the Bay of Bengal to Kandahar and Badakshan. He touched the western sea in Sind and at Surat and was well astride Central India. He had the richest and most vigorous as well as the largest territorial share of India and the north-west. The empire was knit together by waterways from Bengal to Delhi and by imperial highways elsewhere. His empire was balanced by the Persian empire on the Iranian plateau, itself preoccupied with the Ottoman Turkish empire beyond, and there was no one else whose power was comparable. He had a ready-made supply of hardy recruits from the north-west, attracted by the hope of fame and their own poverty; he had the resources of Bengal and the profits of the middle-eastern trade to sustain him and a central organization to maintain his control. This was the foundation of the century of stable government which followed.

But if Akbar's rule had rested on a foreign minority only it would have been brittle, however outwardly brilliant. This brings us to the second feature of his work which raises him from the class of military conquerors to that of great leaders. Leadership, however inspired, is not enough; it has to be creative leadership if it is to charm a mixed people to cooperate in goodwill rather than acquiesce through fear. Akbar's stroke was to raise himself from the position of a leader of a minority Indo-foreign group (the Muslims) to the accepted ruler of all Hindustan. The previous sultans of Delhi had, it is true, employed

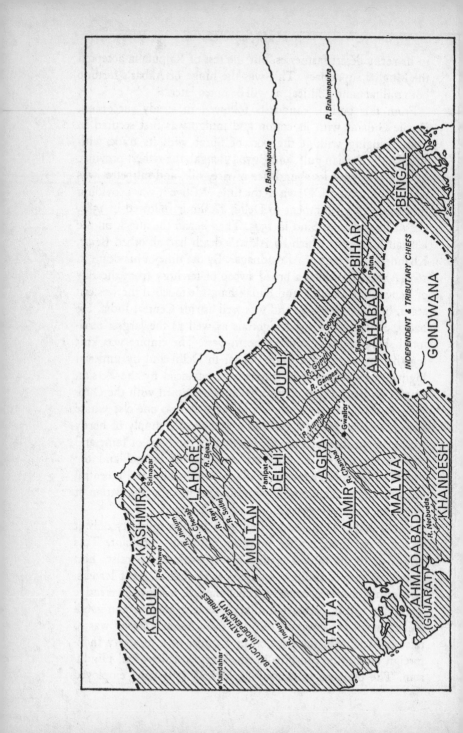

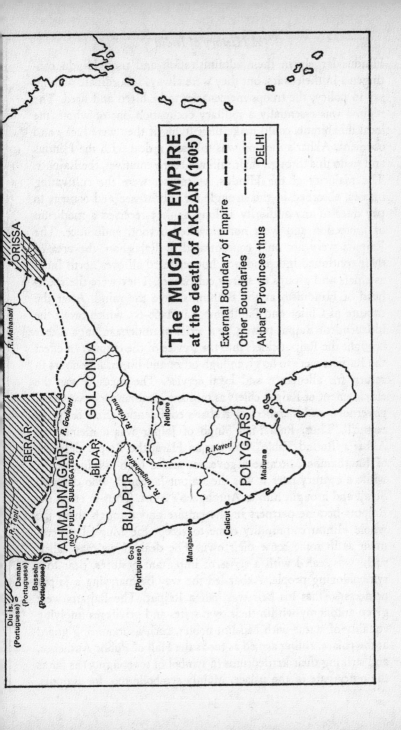

The **MUGHAL EMPIRE**
at the death of AKBAR (1605)

External Boundary of Empire — - — - —
Other Boundaries · — · — · — ·
Akbar's Provinces thus **DELHI**

R. Mahanadi

ORISSA

BERAR

R. Tapti

Daman
(Portuguese)

Bassein
(Portuguese)

Diu Is.
(Portuguese)

AHMADNAGAR
(NOT FULLY SUBJUGATED)

R. Godavari

GOLCONDA

BIDAR

R. Krishna

BIJAPUR

Goa
(Portuguese)

R. Tungabhadra

Nellore

R. Kaveri

POLYGARS

Madura

Mangalore

Calicut

Hindus largely in their administration and used Hindu contingents in their wars, but they were always subordinate with no say in policy, the troops mercenaries to be hired and fired. The régime was essentially a military occupation out of whom the local inhabitants could make their living if they were lucky and obedient. Akbar's method was to make a deal with the Hindus and to do this through their militant representatives, the Rajputs. The majority of the Hindus, of course, were the cultivating masses, absorbed in the struggle for subsistence and content to pay dues to any authority so long as they received a modicum of protection and were not provoked beyond endurance. The Rajputs were not only concentrated in Rajasthan, the area of their continued independence, but scattered all over north India as chiefs and groups of sturdy cultivators. They were the spearhead of Hinduism as the Brahmins were the mind. After the capture of Chitor and Ranthambor in 1568–69, which broke the independent Rajput power, by a series of understandings Akbar brought the Rajput chiefs into the service of the empire. In effect the Rajputs were to be given high office and imperial honours in return for allegiance and loyal service. The method was the employment of Rajput chiefs as military commanders, provincial governors, and members of Akbar's confidential circle or 'privy council'. Thus, Raja Man Singh of Jaipur was a member of Akbar's 'Round Table', Rao Surjan Hara, the Rajput defender of Ranthambor, became a governor and a high-ranking noble, while a century later it was the Rajput Jai Singh who defeated Sivaji and brought him to Aurangzeb's court. Thus in effect the Rajputs became partners in the empire and through them the whole Hindu community came to accept the Mughal government as in some sense their own. The deal, if we may call it such, was sealed with a series of important gestures, dear to a symbol-loving people. Akbar led the way by marrying a Jaipur princess so that his heir was half a Rajput. The Rajputs were given autonomy within their own states and privileges implying equality of status with Muslim nobles, such as mounting guard at the palace, riding armed as far as the Hall of Public Audience, and striking their kettledrums (a symbol of sovereignty) as far as the outer gate of the palace. Mainly symbolic too, for Rajputs, though important for others, was the abolition of the *jizya* or poll-tax exacted in Muslim countries on non-Muslims.

Akbar's third achievement was the organization of a bureaucratic administration and an imperial service. The administration will be described briefly in the next chapter but the imperial service, the steel frame, as it were, of the Mughal edifice and eminently Akbar's work, is worth mention here. The system continued in being till the mid eighteenth century, and the grades, as titles of honour, lasted in the Nizam's Hyderabad until the Indian take-over in 1948. The officers were known as *mansabdars* or holders of commands. They were arranged in thirty-three grades from the commander of ten to a commander of 5,000 (in the first instance). A *panch-hazari*, or commander of 5,000, was a great officer of state and noble combined. The title was not hereditary, appointment and promotion were by imperial favour, and rank did not in itself confer office. The members were essentially a service forming a pool of officers available for civil or military employment. Those holding titles of 500 upwards were known as *amir* or collectively *omrah*.* They were bound to maintain for imperial service the number of troops indicated by their command and were liberally paid for this purpose. Akbar added the condition that they should be paid in cash and his administrative arrangements were such that this was achieved during his lifetime. In Akbar's time the service was largely foreign; seventy per cent were born outside India, while the remaining thirty were equally divided between Hindus and Muslims. The Hindu disparity was not as great as the figures suggest, because the Hindu names were to be found in the higher ranks rather than the lower. In other words, they were Rajput chiefs with a sprinkling of other Hindus sharing on a rough fifty-fifty basis with Indian-born Muslims in the higher direction of the empire. Two features common to later British practice may here be noted : a reliance on foreign personnel, and the practice of nomination. The *mansabdar* system provided a career open to talent to the ambitious young nobleman, or, indeed, any young man of parts. Instead of seeking fame in obscure

---

* This is the Arabic plural. English writers added their own plural and called them 'omrahs'.

local independence, in insurrection, or in gang robbery, such youths could find both distinction and an outlet for energy in the constructive service of the state.

The last major achievement of Akbar may be described as the re-creation of the imperial idea in India. The early Hindu emperors had surrounded themselves with an aura of sanctity, perhaps derived from ancient Persia and certainly in tune with Hindu ideas. The Muslim sultans were venerated by their followers no more than by their subjects; each dynasty was forgotten within a generation of its overthrow. Akbar restored this concept of imperial sanctity, the symbol of success being the addition of the *nimbus* or halo to the imperial head in Mughal paintings from Akbar's time onwards. The orthodox Aurangzeb's head is so adorned equally with the heretic Akbar. It is this purpose which, in my belief, lies behind the otherwise strange episode of Akbar's 'Divine Faith' or *Din Illahi*. This episode, the subject of more description and speculation than almost anything else about Akbar, sprang from his undoubted interest in religion and tendency to free thought and mysticism. It was publicized in Europe because it aroused the hopes of the Jesuit fathers whom he called to Agra that he was about to become a Christian, and in India for opposite reasons by the rival free-thinking and orthodox factions in his court. Akbar was always liberal-minded; as early as 1562 he abolished the pilgrim-tax at the holy Hindu city of Mathura. There followed marriage with Rajput princesses, the Rajput partnership, and the abolition of the *jizya*. About 1575 Akbar seems to have undergone a mystical experience, a time when he spent whole days and nights in prayer. There followed a period of religious discussions into which were brought Portuguese fathers from Goa, Hindu Brahmins, Jains, and Zoroastrians. This period culminated about 1580 in a break with Islam and a revolt organized by the orthodox who used his brother Muhammad Hakim in Kabul as a figurehead. It was the crisis of the reign, both political and religious. With the revolt crushed in 1581 Akbar was unchallenged for the rest of his life. He used the next twenty-four years to develop an eclectic cult much influenced by Zoroastrianism and centred on himself. He drew in a number of

Muslim intellectuals like Abul Fazl (the philosopher of the cult), his brother Faizi, the poet, and some Hindus like Raja Birbal. The cult never spread beyond this circle and its details are not now of import, but we may note two significant facts. The first is that Akbar was himself treated as a superhuman or semi-divine person, and the second that his son Jahangir retained some details which tended to glorify the monarch while he discarded the cult as a whole. Most writers treat the story as the eccentricity of a great man in his later years. But in fact the cult was proclaimed when he was aged forty and in full vigour. Of Akbar's eclecticism there need be no dispute. But all other evidence suggests that he was far too shrewd to allow such a thing to endanger his policies. In fact he turned it into a policy. The problem of every all-Indian ruler in the past has been to find a basis for loyalty to the throne on the part of all classes. Akbar knew as well as anyone else that you could neither draw Hindus and Muslims into a new religion nor induce one permanently to submit to the other. He therefore set out to establish a cult of the monarch, to present him as a semi-divine personage whom it was a religious duty to obey and sacrilege to oppose. In doing this he used fragments of Persian tradition and ideas current at the time. Hence the aura, hence the religious prostrations.* And I think that, broadly speaking, he succeeded. In Indian estimation the Mughals rose above the general run of kings and princes; they had a divine right, a something which set them apart from all others. Loyalty to the dynasty was a factor in the Mutiny of 1857, a hundred years after its loss of effective power. Akbar succeeded in re-growing the divinity that doth hedge a king. He provided India with the first Muslim dynasty to receive the free allegiance of Hindus as well as Muslims and whose claim to rule was accepted for reasons other than the possession of superior force. The obverse side of the medal was that he deeply offended the orthodox Muslims in the process.

There seems no doubt that Akbar was a remarkable personality. Though formally illiterate he had a prodigious memory and a keen intellect; he made up for writing by dictation and for

* e.g. the *sijdah* or complete prostration to the monarch as to a divinity.

reading by readers. He had great physical strength and personal courage which was seen in the feats of his early years and in his conduct in battle. He had the magic of magnetic leadership which excited devotion from his followers and extorted admiration from his enemies. He was the natural centre of every group he entered. His values were those of his age which counted duplicity and harshness as statesmen's tools. But in some respects he led the way. He was more humane and more generous than most men of his time and more tolerant. Above all he possessed creative imagination which can use success to transform a situation rather than humiliate an opponent and can use the ordinary motives of the average man for constructive purposes. All in all, I think that Akbar makes good the claim to be with Asoka, the two Indian statesmen of world rank before the twentieth century. This is how his son described him :

He was of middle height, of a wheat-coloured complexion, with black eyes and eyebrows. His beauty was of form rather than of face, with a broad chest and long arms. On his left nostril was a fleshy mole, very becoming, of the size of a split pea, which physiognomists understood to be an augury of great wealth and glory. His voice was extremely loud, and in discourse and narration he was witty and animated. His whole air and appearance had little of the worldly being but exhibited rather divine majesty.

In concentrating upon Akbar's achievement in north and central India the rest of the country has been neglected. The excuse must be that it was in the north that the shape of India for the next two centuries was being determined. There is, however, one event in the south which cannot go unmentioned, because it also had significance for the future. This is the fate of the Hindu empire of Vijayanagar, which controlled India from the Kistna and Tungabhadra rivers to the sea at Cape Comorin. Its rise was described in the previous volume and we must now record its fall. Its recurrent struggles with the Muslim Deccan kingdoms culminated in the disastrous battle of Talikota in 1565 which was followed by capture and sack of the capital city. The empire lingered on for many years but never recovered its strength. The Muslim kings gradually encroached in the south, thus preparing the way for the Mughals in the seventeenth and eighteenth centuries. Had the result of Talikota been different, the British and French in the eighteenth century might have found a Hindu empire in the south balancing a Mughal empire in the north.

3

THE MUGHAL EMPIRE

THE Mughal Empire became a legend in contemporary Europe through travellers' accounts of its magnificence and its wars. Aurangzeb's bloody rise to power and the splendour of his court was one of the things every educated person knew in the late seventeenth century. It has remained a legend in India because it lasted long enough to be part of the accepted order of things and because, though not Hindu, it was generally felt to be Indian. Its traces are to be found throughout the country except along the Malabar coast and in the extreme south. It was an independent or semi-independent interlude between the rule of the very foreign British and the very alien central Asian Turk. As such it retains value for the nationalist Indian of today though, if he has strong Hindu feelings, he may make an exception in the case of Aurangzeb. Yet Mughal India was perhaps as different from the India of the Hindu emperors as Kublai Khan's China in the fourteenth century, as described by Marco Polo, was from classical China a thousand years before. Each had a foreign cultural veneer which was the temporary effect of particular circumstances but which observers took to be a permanent part of the scene. This fact should be remembered in looking at Mughal India. The period is important to us because of its relationship to the future and to the mind of India. But it was neither a revival nor a continuation of past régimes; it had its own characteristics and mystique.

The first impression which visitors received was of a gorgeous centre of power, filled with the panoply of state and supplied with all known luxuries. The next, for the more observant like ambassador Sir Thomas Roe, was of the abject poverty of the masses. Both these impressions had truth, but they were far from the whole picture. The fact was that the country held together under the Mughals for nearly two centuries and was relatively happy and prosperous. How was it done? The first answer lies in the personalities of the great Mughals. In the seven figures who ruled between 1526 and 1712, from Babur to Bahadur Shah, we have two of undoubted genius, two falling only just outside this category, and two highly competent sovereigns. Only Homayun remains to be accounted for, and he lacked neither talents or virtues.

The empire could not have continued so long without such heads but Mughal India was much more than a series of talented rulers. Its next element was the central bureaucracy, controlled by the monarch but spreading its tentacles throughout the empire. It was largely the creation of Akbar, but it was maintained by his successors. A vital part of this was the *mansabdars*, who have already been mentioned. They acted as, as it were, the emperor's eyes and ears, the oil which caused the bureaucratic wheels to revolve. The emperor controlled them in a number of ways. Akbar paid them their large salaries in cash, so that they lacked a territorial basis for revolt. His successor found this system too arduous to maintain, and gave them assignments on the land revenue, in other words tracts of land from which they collected the revenue in lieu of a salary. The obvious danger of this practice was countered in two ways. The first was rotation of office; Mughal officers rarely held high appointments, such as governorships, for more than three or four years at a time. The second was the resumption of their property at death. The assignments of land were for life only; the next generation had to start from the bottom with an official appointment. During life, payments were always in arrears so that they were only able to make ends meet by means of advances from the Treasury. At death, the great man's property was sealed and nothing was released until the advances had been recovered. The process amounted to death-duties of about a hundred per cent. Aware of the fate which hung over them the Mughal lords accentuated the situation by heavy spending. Why not get the glory to be derived from ostentation and public works when you could pass nothing on to your family? Thus the Mughal nobles were notable for their ostentation, their crowds of retainers with even more than the average insolence of office, their works of piety in the shape of mosques, wells, and rest houses, of ease like their gardens and summerhouses, and of remembrance like their great domed tombs. The Mughal nobility was thus an official aristocracy which was hereditary as a class but not as individuals, which was landholding but not feudal.

This class was spread over the country to work the administrative machine. Akbar divided the empire into twelve *subahs* or provinces, which later grew to eighteen. These in turn were subdivided into *sarkars*, the ancestor of the British district, and further into *parganas*, the ancestor of the sub-district. Throughout this system the principle of division of authority prevailed. From the *subah* downwards there were two sets of officers, the magisterial and the revenue. The former controlled the armed forces and were responsible for law and order, while the latter collected revenue and were responsible for the land assessment. The former had the greater dignity, but since the land was the main source of government revenue the latter was also indispensable. The fact of interdependence was clinched by the fact that the *diwan* or revenue officer sent his collections to Delhi which in turn supplied the *subadar* with cash for his followers. As long as the system was in working order the *diwan* could not revolt because he had supplies without troops while the *subadar* could not because he had troops without supplies.

The government appeared to the people in the countryside mainly as a revenue-collecting agency. The cultivated land was recorded, the value of the crops assessed, and the share of the government fixed. The revenue dues were actually collected directly by government officers called *amils* or by deputies such as the mansabdars, grantholders (*jagirdars*), or local chiefs who had been left undisturbed. Whoever the agents might be, the actual collection took the form of a bargaining match with the agents, the one pleading poverty, the other state necessity. In unsettled times villages would fortify themselves with mud walls or scrub hedges and sometimes go forth to battle with the collectors. The distinguishing feature of the Mughal period was that the assessment was on the whole fairer and more accurate than for long before, thanks to the work of Akbar's revenue minister, the Hindu Todar Mal. The collection was also on the whole more steady and controlled than previously, though he would be a bold man who said that there was no abuse or injustice. These things are matters of relativity and it was relativity of experience which determined the feelings of the peasants. In general, the proportion of the gross produce or its value taken was one third; high enough, but a figure which compares favourably with the half currently demanded in the Deccan, and elsewhere previously. The steady application of authority from the centre gave time for the new revenue arrangements to take root, so that 'Todar Mal's *bandobast*' was still a legend in the Indian countryside two centuries after it had been made.

There was no elaborate system of judicial courts such as the British later introduced. Criminal cases in the towns were dealt with by government-appointed Muslim *qazis* or law officers administering the Muslim code. But each community had its own personal law which it administered through its own agents. There were the *qazis* for the Muslims and the pandits and caste or village *panchayats* for the Hindu. In the countryside, government courts only existed at the district headquarters or other small towns; the imperial officers were only concerned with large-scale crime such as gang robbery. Order was maintained in the villages largely by the village elders themselves, whose arrangements were fascinating and intricate, or else by agents of a local landholder. Thus the villager saw the government mainly in the guise of a revenue-collecting agent, who fleeced him occasionally, as a judge in a dispute, or as an army which plundered him. It did not matter much who ruled in Delhi – Mughal, Maratha, or Englishman. His concern was with his crops, with the next monsoon, and with the annual visitation of the collecting officer.

The government thus had a network of authority spread, as it were, over the surface of Indo-Muslim society, a wiring system of political electricity. We have now to note the energy it possessed to vitalize this system, and if necessary to defend it. We have already noted the *mansabdars*, who manned all the higher provincial posts and were the major instruments of the imperial will. Below them were the subordinate officials all over the country who were mainly Hindus. If a Muslim showed promise, he had good chances of promotion; if he was incompetent a Hindu was preferred. Thus the day-to-day administration was largely in the hands of Hindus of the clerical castes

(Brahmins and Kayasthas). This had been the case even under the belligerent Turks (though not in such a recognized way) and was to be under the British after them. Much depended on these subordinate officials because they possessed an inner independent cohesion of their own. Their public ethic was loyalty to their superiors whoever they might be. But there were degrees of loyalty according to the superior's behaviour, and the groups, both by position and talent, owned great resources of obstruction and subtle sabotage. It has been recently suggested that the decline of both Mughal and British authority was connected by the failure of both to retain their positive loyalty through overt acts of policy. In general it can be said that these men responded readily to leadership and sympathetic handling and that during most of the Mughal period they were loyal servants of the régime.

Apart from these agents, imperial and otherwise, there was the army. The bulk consisted of the *mansabdars'* contingents, but their possible use against the government was restricted by the mansabdar's habitual absence from the assigned lands which supplied his income, the lack of any hereditary tie between these lands and his family, and his tendency to save money on maintaining troops to use in display and furthering his interests at court. But the Mughals also had other resources. Akbar had 12,000 horsemen in direct pay and readiness for any emergency. In addition there was a body of 7,000 young noblemen (*ahadis*) who had something of the status of a-d-cs. A large troop of elephants was maintained, who were, however, perhaps more useful for transporting artillery and display than actual fighting. Finally and most important they monopolized the newly-introduced artillery. Cumbrous and inefficient as it then was, it could nevertheless still deal quickly with the average rebel stronghold and breach the walls of the strongest castles.

We have thus a picture of a great area studded with villages mainly concerned with sowing and reaping and the next monsoon, diversified by a few large centres of political power, where display, luxury, and teeming life was the rule. It was in fact a mainly subsistence economy. But this was not the whole of the story for there was also much commercial activity and important industries. Relative to the economy as a whole they were small but they were important in themselves and provided much of the economic surplus used to run the government and support its wars. The movement of trade was severely limited by transport difficulties; bulk articles could only be transported down the rivers or overseas. Such were sugar from Bengal and Madras, saltpetre from Bengal. Intermediate articles such as indigo, opium, tobacco, and cotton goods could be transported at a price which meant that they went by water or became luxury goods through expense. Luxuries such as gold, silver, and ivory, fine silks and muslins were carried by camels over the north-west passes and by bullock wagons elsewhere. The size of the trade can be gauged from W. E. Moreland's * calculation that while 30,000 tons of merchandise went annually by sea only 500 tons came over the passes on the backs of 3,000 camels. The main industry for which India had been famous from classical times, and of which she was a supplier to both east and west, was cotton. In the south the spice trade was important, though the actual industry was limited to the Malabar coast. India had an active trade with the Middle East and Europe, the main articles of export being textiles, indigo, saltpetre, and spices. In return she received luxuries like wines and novelties and metals, specially silver bullion. This constituted the Indian silver drain which was the bugbear of English mercantilists.

The opinion of economic historians is that the effects of this trade were marginal rather than general. They increased the prosperity of their area of concentration rather than the country as a whole. Thus Gujarat benefited from the indigo industry and Malabar from the spice trade. The peasant of the interior was little affected, while artisans like the weavers of the Coromandel coast had little advantage over the fellows save a stable and skilled employment. The profit went to the merchants who employed them.

While the individual worker was little better off than the ordinary peasants, there is no doubt that these industries enhanced perceptibly the total wealth of India. There was not enough increment to increase the general standard but there was

* W. E. Moreland, *India at the death of Akbar*, pp. 220–21, 236–7.

more for the select few. The question then arises as to how the whole national income was spent. There seems little doubt that most of it was gathered up, in one way or another, by the administration. The surplus of agricultural production was creamed off by the land tax, the government, central or provincial, taking the major share and the rest going to the local landholders with a small residue to the villages collectively from which the corporate village life and its services were maintained. The actual cultivator was left with just enough to subsist on and no reserve against famine. The surplus of industry went largely to the administration through port, provincial and town duties. The sums paid to evade duties or propitiate hard pressed officials were all a part of the same system. Something was kept back by the merchants which formed a reserve of capital upon which princes drew at times of war or stress. The only other item which escaped was a proportion of the silver bullion, imported annually into the country, which vanished underground. Some of this became rustic working capital, in the form of bangles and jewellery, for wedding expenses, temple offerings, and security for advances to purchase seed etc., while the rest went to small or large hoards in the absence of banks.

The surplus which went to the government in one form or another was paid out to support the central administration and its officers. The salaries of the *mansabdars* were in our terms enormous but it must remembered that they included the upkeep of their prescribed military contingents. Thus a commander of 5,000 (the highest rank in the earlier days) had a salary equivalent to £24,000 of Elizabethan or Stuart purchasing power, at a time when the total revenue of England was something less than a million pounds. Two hundred years later the Governor-General's salary was £25,000 a year. When all this had been allowed for there still remained a considerable margin for productive work. But in fact relatively little went in that direction. A prudent monarch like Shah Jahan would build up a bullion reserve which a successor would dissipate in war or show. Prestige dictated display in the form of personal pomp or magnificent buildings. To this we owe the Mughal architectural heritage from the Taj Mahal downwards. They were the Mughal equivalent of Marie Antoinette's chocolate cake for the peasants. You could look at but not subsist on them. The nobles followed the imperial example and were further impelled to display by the official system which virtually confiscated their fortunes at death. When all these drafts had been made upon the annual national surplus but little remained for productive works. The list is short and, in relation to the size of the problem, unimpressive. A few fine bridges and sarais, a few trunk roads and the repair of Feroz Shah's canal to Delhi leave little else to be added. The Mughals preferred a garden to a canal and their officers a tomb to a well. So the great opportunity of spending the concentrated national surplus on productive work was missed; India was the scene of much economic activity but little economic progress.

The question has been much canvassed as to the relative prosperity of the Indian under the Mughals and the British. It would be better at this stage to consider the Indian with the contemporary European. There seems to be good ground for thinking that the average peasant had more to eat than his European counterpart,* and suffered no more oppression from the lords. It is possible that the strength of custom and the intricacies of the caste system gave him greater protection. On the other hand he was more liable to the disaster of flood and famine, when his rulers could not help him much even if they would. The professional classes in both societies had a modest but assured position, perhaps slightly better in India than Europe. The mercantile class, on the other hand, was constricted by authority, by caste and class prejudice. They did not dare to display their wealth like the merchants of London or Amsterdam; they appeared at court more often as victims of a 'squeeze' than as respected financial advisers. Taking it all in all Mughal India, with an estimated hundred million inhabitants, had for about a century and a half a standard of life roughly comparable with that of contemporary Europe, though arranged on a different social and economic pattern. The peasant had a little more to eat, the merchant less opportunity of spending. Most European travellers commented on the dire poverty of the countryside but

* See W. E. Moreland, op. cit., ch. 8.

we must remember that before the agricultural revolution there was also dire poverty in the European countryside. The big advantage which Europe then possessed over India was capital accumulation and investment by the merchants and more productive spending by the governments.

An observer who visited only the cities of Mughal India might have supposed that India was mainly a Muslim country with a few pagan hangers-on and that Persian was the current language. Mosques, Muslim tombs, palaces, and troops would everywhere meet his eye and Persian or something like it would ring in his ears. The former impression would be dispelled as soon as he ventured into the Indian hinterland, but the latter would follow him to the seats of power all over India. It was part of the Persian cultural mantle which the Mughals cast over the whole of India and which is their distinctive contribution to the country. This influence almost amounted to what Professor Toynbee would call an abortive civilization. The Mughals themselves were Turks. The first generations spoke Turkish so that Persian was only a second language. They brought with them sundry signs of their nomadic origin such as the Turkish title *Khan*, the horse-tail switch, the love of horseflesh and the chase, their drinking bouts, and the architecture of their public halls, which were tents frozen into stone. But they came under the charm of the radiating Persian culture and adopted it so thoroughly that it was this that they passed on to India. They had the zeal of the convert for his new faith. For them things Persian *were* civilization so that their attitudes carried with them the force of assured conviction. Students of culture may study in future (none has done so yet) the contrast in the development of the Mughal and Ottoman Turks in India and Turkey respectively, the one imbued with Persian culture which they carried with them like an infectious disease, the other trying to live on their own, unresponsive to both Persian and Greek ideas.

It is true that Persian was known in India long before the Mughals. It was used by the Turks of the Sultanate for business and literature and Delhi was in the thirteenth and fourteenth centuries a Persian literary centre. But these people were too few in number, their influence too limited in scope, and their outlook too far removed from the Hindu population for Persian to make any impact on the country as a whole. Rulers collected poets as American millionaires do pictures; with them Persian had no more general influence than Norman-French in Norman England. By the time of the Mughals the whole climate of feeling and relations had changed. Within, the two communities were beginning to integrate, so that one was far more ready to borrow from the other than previously; without, Persia had revived from the agony of Mongol conquest; she was a great empire in her own right, and had the prestige of power as well as of letters. From civilizing her conquerors she had passed to conquering her barbarians.

The first strand in this mantle was the Persian language. It was a government language, used widely through the country because of the wide Mughal administrative web. Its cultural prestige caused it to be studied by aspiring youth everywhere as a symbol of culture as well as a careerist tool. The beauty and range of its literature captivated the most utilitarian of its pupils, while its pre-Muslim background gave it an attraction for Hindus which Arabic could never have. The big step in Persian influence was the use of Persian by the Hindu nobility and the Hindu ministerial class. This was cemented by Akbar's Rajput partnership. From that time Persian became the diplomatic language throughout India, the language of the Rajput courts like French in Henry III's England and the stock-in-trade of the clerical Hindu. When the missionary Swartz went on a mission to the Hindu raja of Tanjore in the extreme south of India in the eighteenth century, they conversed in Persian. Hindu students in Delhi commonly took Persian as one of their degree subjects to the outbreak of the Second World War.

The next sign of Persian influence was in the arts. Mughal architecture can be followed from its early almost pure Persian phase in a building like Homayun's tomb (1560) through the Indo-Muslim style of Akbar's day to its apotheosis in the Taj Mahal, which could have been built nowhere else but in India and not there without the background of Persian influence. In painting, Persian ideas combined with the local Indian tradition to produce the Mughal miniatures which continued into the nineteenth century. The Persian love of water and flowers found expression in the Mughal formal garden. One of Babur's first acts on reaching Agra was to lay out a garden; one of the last acts of the last emperor was to do the same. The story continues with the decorative arts; Persian styles and conventions can be seen equally in Hindu palaces and garden houses with Muslim. The dress of the Mughals was originally Turkish but it was much influenced by Persian refinements. Eventually it provided a standard for the nobility everywhere. The Indian dress of Mr Nehru traced ultimately to Persian origins. The Persian love of poetry and song found a ready response in Indian hearts, but it was the Mughal example which fixed this taste into a social convention, so that a *mushaira* or public assembly of poets to recite poems to a critical audience is as important an event in north India as a Test Match is in England. Finally we may note that Persia, through the Mughals, became the school of manners for Hindustan. Hindu forms were set aside as rustic and in this respect Mughal influence has persisted till today.

We may ask, in conclusion, whether Persian influence penetrated into the world of ideas and what its permanent influence upon India has been. The mystical and freethinking ideas of the *sufis* were carried into Hindu and Muslim India through the medium of the great Persian poets. On the religious side these were easily equated with the *bhakti* or devotional school of Hindu saints; they illustrated existing concepts rather than modified them. But they certainly encouraged an eclecticism between the two bodies and some mutual understanding. The movement of comprehension on the Muslim side, which lasted for a century from Akbar's day, was a Persian product. Related to religious ideas was the Persian idea, dating back to the pre-Muslim past, of monarchy as a divine institution. We have seen how this was used by Akbar and can say that the notion, though not Akbar's form of it, was truly naturalized. Queen Victoria inherited some of its mystique when she was proclaimed direct ruler of the country in 1858.

Persian tastes, ideas, and attitudes are so imbedded in north India that they are often thought to be local products. Though Persian is no longer spoken, its daughter language of Urdu through Hindi continues its influence and is widely spoken in India as well as being one of the official languages of Pakistan. Hindustani, the everyday language of the north, is deeply indebted to it. But perhaps the most lasting of Persian influences was the administrative. Persia gave to – or revived in – India the imperial idea with a semi-sacred head and with it an imperial apparatus of government. Persian nomenclature and administrative concepts were so pervasive that they were found among the fighting Marathas when struggling to be free of the Mughals. The Mughals re-acclimatized in India the idea of an all-pervading ordered administration. The British could not have organized India as they did if the people had not already been, as it were, apprenticed to the idea of unity. Nor, in consequence, could independent India have grown so quickly in unity and strength. Mr Nehru was sometimes called a great Mughal; he was their heir in a truer sense than perhaps he himself realized. The united India of today would not have been possible without them.

4

THE GREAT MUGHALS

THE seventeenth century was the great age of the Mughals. To contemporary Europe India was the land of 'the Great Mogul', on a level with the great Sophy of Constantinople and the grand Cham of Persia. Their pomp and luxury intrigued and their power impressed foreigners. Bernier's description of the empire at its height was something of a best-seller and so popularized Mughal politics as to move Dryden to write his Tragedy of Aurungzebe. China, then in transition from the native Ming to the foreign or Manchu Ching dynasty, was relatively little regarded.

The empire at this time may be said to have rested upon four main pillars. These were the personalities of the emperor, the Rajput alliance or understanding, the policy of toleration, and the balance of power. All four were inherited from Akbar's day, the second and third being his deliberate creation and the fourth the situation he left to his successors. Though cracked and dented in various ways, broadly speaking these pillars stood throughout the period so that the empire seemed majestic and secure at the end of it. In 1700, indeed, it covered an area larger than British India without Burma, and this without later aids such as the telegraph, railways, or supplies from abroad. Aurangzeb's word was effective from beyond Madras in the south, to Bengal in the east, and Kabul and Badakshan in the north-west. The Rajput alliance and Hindu tolerance are assumptions which underlie the period; it is the other two pillars which provide, as it were, the *motifs* for the action of the period. The phrase 'balance of power' may sound odd in view of our recent assertion that Akbar never recognized it. This is true; Akbar, like most of his predecessors and his successors down to the present day, regarded India as one and indivisible. The extension of power to the geographical limits was not aggression to their minds but an expression of natural law. Nevertheless there was in fact a power situation in 1600 which might be described as one of balance. This balance took two forms, external and internal. The external balance was with the Safavid dynasty with whom the Mughals shared (with the possession of Kabul, Kandahar, and Badakshan) the control of the Iranian plateau. The symbol of their rivalry was the varied fortunes of Kandahar, finally captured by the Persians in 1649. But neither side wanted to overthrow the other, for the existence of each had advantages for the other. For India the Persian power was a safeguard against nomad invasion from central Asia; while it stood, schemes of southern conquest could be pursued in comparative security. For Persia the Mughals kept the restless Afghans in order, and gave them comparative security for dealing with the Ottoman Turks to the west, still in an expansive mood.

But apart from this external and relatively stable balance (as long as the two empires held together) and one tacitly accepted by both sides, there was an internal and unstable balance which the Mughals never accepted as more than a temporary state of affairs. This was formed by the independent states, mostly Muslim, of central and south India. The Muslim states were successors of the Bahmini kingdom, which in turn was a splinter of the Delhi sultanate, and so could be legalistically described as rebels. But the real reason for aggression was the dogma of Indian indivisibility. The most orthodox of the emperors, Aurangzeb, was the most implacable of annexers. It took nearly to the end of the century to extinguish the last Deccan Muslim kingdom, by which time a new Hindu power had arisen on the Mughal western flank. It was the existence of Persia which stimulated Mughal activity in the north-west and of the Deccan kingdoms in the south which provided both a focus of imperial activity and a drain of surplus military energy. Without this balance of power, unacceptable to the Mughals and gradually overturned, as it was, the empire might have broken up in internal dissensions in the mid seventeenth instead of the mid eighteenth century. A few dates in the calendar of imperialism will illustrate the point. On the Persian front Kandahar was lost in 1622, recovered in 1638, and finally lost in 1649. In the Deccan Ahmadnagar was captured in 1616 and the rest of the kingdom in 1632. Bijapur and Golkonda, though hard pressed in the sixteen fifties, were not extinguished until 1686 and 1687 respectively. Thereafter Aurangzeb campaigned against the Marathas until his death in 1707.

If the pillar of balance was one which the Mughals did not recognize and did their best to overturn, that of personality is one for which they must be given full credit. Akbar's long reign of forty-nine years and his overpowering personality might be thought likely to crush out all initiative from his sons. Nevertheless his successor Jahangir (1605–27), though drunken and cruel, proved to have the ability to hold his own and extend the empire, and to possess a personality in his own right. He was saved from a war of succession by the pre-decease of his brother and had only to deal with a short-lived revolt of his eldest son Khusrau. Along with his vices of drink, temper, and cruelty he proved to have a keen artistic sense so that he became a kind of life-president of Indian artists, an attractive love of nature, and a sense of humour. His attachment to the empress Nur Jahan is well known and commemorated by a special issue of gold *mohurs*. He wrote his own memoirs and he and his court are vividly portrayed by the English ambassador Sir Thomas Roe who spent nearly four years (1615–19) in following the Mughal court from camp to camp in search of commercial privileges.*

Shah Jahan was a man of greater mark, though in my view less attractive than Jahangir, in spite of his obvious faults. Shah Jahan was a man of great executive ability, to which he added a love for the magnificent and a refined artistic sense, specially for architecture. He was in a special sense the architectural director of his day and there seems to be little doubt that the great buildings of his reign, the Taj Mahal, the Delhi Fort, and Jama Masjid, and the reconstruction of the Agra Fort, would not have been what they are without his personal inspiration and direction. To these great gifts he added a capacity for affection revealed in his marriage with Mumtaz Mahal. Here the catalogue often ends, but there is another side. His romantic love did not hesitate to expose Mumtaz to the rigours of travel in all states of health so that she died at the age of 39 after giving birth to her fourteenth child. In his youth he was not only ambitious but cruel and vindictive to an unnecessary degree. A more controlled

* *The Embassy of Sir T. Roe to India*, ed. Sir W. Foster, O.U.P., 1926.

man than his father he was also more ruthless. At his succession he executed all the male Mughal collaterals, the descendants of his brothers and uncles, although at that time they had little political significance. In his later years he became sensual and self-indulgent to an extent remarked upon even in that far from critical age. The sorrows of his later days were to a large extent a direct reflection of the acts of his early ones. The pathetic prisoner of the Agra Fort gazing romantically across the Jumna to the Taj was in fact an old man who had gained power by ruthlessness and lost it through self-indulgence. As a ruler he governed India firmly for thirty years and left behind him a legend of magnificence, rough justice, and prosperity.

If Shah Jahan has been over-romanticized his son and successor Aurangzeb has been unduly denigrated. His rise to power through a dramatic civil war with the imprisonment of his father and the destruction of brothers, son, and nephew provided his European portrait through the publication of Bernier's Travels in 1670. Later writers contrasted his bigotry with Akbar's tolerance, his failure against the Marathas with Akbar's success with the Rajputs. He provided the reverse to the Akbarian medal of genius and this in general is the current picture of him today except in Pakistan, where many proclaim him the greatest Muslim ruler of India. It is forgotten that he governed India for nearly as long as Akbar (over forty-eight years) and that he left the empire larger than he found it. In fact, though Aurangzeb's rise to power was ruthless as well as dramatic, it was not more so than that of others of his race. Aurangzeb succeeded not because he was more cruel but because he was more efficient and more skilled in the current game of statecraft with its background of dissimulation. He never shed unnecessary blood; he spared his father and made away only with those who 'touched the sceptre'. Once established he showed himself a firm and capable administrator who retained his grip of power until his death at the age of eighty-eight. He lacked the magnetism of his father and great-grandfather but inspired an awe and even terror of his own. In his private life he was simple and austere in striking contrast to the rest of the great Mughals. In religion he was an orthodox Sunni Muslim who thought of himself as a model Muslim ruler. He differed from Akbar in consciously tolerating Hindus rather than treating them as equals, but his supposed intolerance is little more than a hostile legend based on isolated acts such as the erection of a mosque on a temple site in Benares.

Aurangzeb's reign really divides into two almost equal portions. The first twenty-three years were largely a continuation of Shah Jahan's administration with an added note of austerity. Marathas, Jats, tribesmen in the far north-west were all kept in order. The emperor sat in pomp in Delhi or progressed in state to Kashmir. From 1681 he virtually transferred his capital to the Deccan where he spent the rest of his life in camp, superintending the overthrow of the two remaining Deccan kingdoms in 1686-7 and trying fruitlessly to crush the Maratha rebellion. The assured administrator of the first period became the embattled old man of the second. Along with change of occupation went change of character. The subtle and ruthless politician became an ascetic and a sage, a saint according to Muslim estimation, spending long hours in prayer, fasting, and copying the Koran, and pouring out his soul in agonized letters. Yet he never lost his grip of power; it was said that his eldest surviving son in far Kabul never received a letter from his father without trembling. The Mughal ogre of popular historians was in fact both a most able statesman and a subtle and highly complex character.

The gallery of the great Mughals is completed by Aurangzeb's son Bahadur Shah, commonly neglected because his reign lasted barely five years. He was an old man (by contemporary standards) of sixty-three when he acceded yet his achievements in the time would have done credit to most men in their prime. He waged the usual war of succession with resolution, skill, and unusual humanity. He made a settlement with implacable Marathas, tranquillized the Rajputs, decisively defeated the Sikhs in the Panjab, and took their last Guru into his service. He was travelling throughout his reign and only came to rest at Lahore in the last few months of his life.

It was during the seventeenth century that certain developments occurred which were to have a decisive result in the eighteenth century and later. There was first what may be called a Muslim intellectual movement which sowed the first seeds of the Pakistan of the future. The first Mughals were 'kings by profession' and Muslim by birth or circumstance. Like their central Asian forbears they regarded the ruled as a flock or herd to be tended and exploited rather than converted or persecuted. With Akbar Persian *sufi* or liberal ideas came in. There was an emphasis on inner religion and a tendency to find common spiritual principles beneath different outward forms. In spite of the collapse of Akbar's cult this trend of syncretist thought continued and found another royal patron in Shah Jahan's Crown Prince Dara Shikoh. Aurangzeb represented the reaction from this trend which stemmed in the seventeenth century from the thinker Sheikh Ahmad Sirhindi. Sirhindi sought to reconcile Sunni legalism with the religion of the spirit and so to repel the tendency to syncretism with Hinduism. He emphasized the aspect of Islam as a body of believers as well as belief. In this way he provided for the Indian Muslim an alternative sheet anchor with which to face the coming storm. When the Commander of the Faithful in India (the emperor) failed to command and the temporal power collapsed, he could fall back on the sovereignty of God and the congregation of the faithful. The Mughal concept of empire was an all India one; Sirhindi provided the germ for a Muslim state in India.

In Hindu India there were also developments, little noticed at the time but pregnant for the future. The *bhakti* movement, or religion of the heart directed to a particular deity, spread from western India among the Marathas into the Punjab where Guru Nanak (1469-1539) founded the sect later to be known as the Sikhs. In the sixteenth century Chaitanya, a devotee of the Lord Krishna, extended the movement to Bengal and carried it up country with the restoration of Krishna's holy city of Brindaban on the Jumna. These movements led to some loosening of caste bonds though they also tended to crystallize into new ones. But they all used the vernacular as their medium and were thus influential in developing the modern Indian languages like Marathi and Bengali. As far as these had passed the dialect stage and acquired linguistic personality by the nineteenth century it was due to the influence of these cults. Hindi owes much to Tulsi Das of Benares (1534-1623) whose version in that language of the

Ramayana, the Sanskrit epic of Rama and Sita and almost, one might say, the Bible of the north Indian people, laid the foundation of modern Hindi.

To these religious and literary developments, modifying the outlook of the people and casting shadows into the future, must be added the more obvious ones which were both religious and political. In the north there occurred the rise and transformation of the Sikhs. At first they were a syncretist sect seeking to unite the two great communities. Guru Nanak was a man of peace who borrowed such ideas from Islam as monotheism and brotherhood. His successors became gradually enmeshed in local politics and acted like local chiefs. The first clash with the Mughals came when the Guru backed the wrong side at Jahangir's accession by supporting his misguided son Khusrau. A total breach came when Aurangzeb executed Guru Tegh Bahadur in 1675. His successor, Guru Gobind, completed the transformation of the sect into a militant religious body distinct from both Hinduism and Islam. Though he submitted to Bahadur Shah shortly before his death, the conflict had been too bitter for reconciliation and the new community had a notable anti-Muslim bias. His loans from Islam, taken in the midst of conflict, were no less notable. The Islamic prohibition of alcohol was matched by a ban on tobacco; meat was added to the permitted Sikh diet. The new Sikhs had a holy book like the Koran in the Granth Sahib, they eschewed idolatry and caste like the Muslims, they had their holy warriors in the *Akalis* like the Muslim *ghazis*) and their idea of martyrdom in battle matched the Muslim concept of *jehad* or holy war. The Sikhs have for nearly three centuries alternately disrupted and ruled the Panjab.

The biggest movement of all, which has attracted the major share of historical attention, was that of the Marathas. This hardy, capable, and rough-hewn people stretched along the Western Ghats, spilling over into the narrow coastal plain of the Konkan and across the Deccan towards central India. They consisted mainly of a minority of highly intelligent and exclusive Brahmins and a majority of the Sudra or cultivator class. They were short and stocky, unhandsome in appearance but wiry and enduring, tenacious, enterprising, and persevering. They lived in a poor country, had few monuments of the past and little taste for the graces of life. Hitherto they had had no history, but they had a sense of belonging which is one of the prerequisites of national feeling. It is difficult to say why they burst forth with such brilliance in the seventeenth century unless one surrenders to the great man doctrine and attributes it all to Sivaji. Nor can one say that Muslim intolerance or invasion touched off a national Hindu movement. If this were so, why did they not rise against the Muslim Bahminis in the fourteenth and fifteenth centuries, who were much more active than Bijapur in the sixteenth and no more tolerant than the Mughals? The rise of the Marathas remains, to my mind, one of the many historical mysteries of Indian history. The solutions so far offered are really evasions, and we must concentrate on the fact of their emergence. In the seventeenth century Maratha chiefs took service with the local Muslim states, and one of them, Shahji, was a fiefholder of Bijapur. The decrepitude of this state tempted his son Sivaji to add to his father's holding on his own account. Irregularity led to rebellion which the general Afzal Khan was sent to put down. Sivaji disposed of him (in 1659) in a private parley by embracing him with steel claws attached to his fingers. This incident still lives in the minds of both Marathas and Muslims. Sivaji was now independent, too strong for the feeble Bijapur government, too distant and insignificant for the Mughals. He remedied this by sacking the great Mughal port of Surat in 1664 when only the English merchants successfully defended themselves in their warehouses. Set Mughal campaigns followed and Sivaji was brought to book by the Rajput Jai Singh. A settlement was attempted on the lines of Akbar's deal with the Rajputs and Sivaji journeyed to Aurangzeb's court at Agra. But it broke down because of the mutual suspicions of both parties. A romantic escape, a daring journey, a genius for leadership found Sivaji at the time of his death in 1680 the master of a compact and well-organized kingdom in western India. His genius lay not only in outwitting the Mughals with guerilla tactics, but also in welding the people, caste-conscious Brahmin and independent Sudra, into a harmonious whole. The defence of cow and country, of religion and the homeland, was the warcry. It was both Maratha nationalism and Maratha Hinduism, an embryonic regional national state.

The struggle which recommenced when Aurangzeb went to the Deccan in 1681 and intensified after the fall of the Deccan kingdoms lasted for twenty-six years until the emperor's death. It ranged over the whole of the Deccan and over the far south. It is usually said that it exhausted the empire and ruined its morale; in fact, that it broke the empire as well as the emperor's heart. This is a gross exaggeration, for we have already noted how far Bahadur Shah went to restoring the empire's vigour in barely five years. It is true that it absorbed resources and reduced morale, but there is another equally important fact commonly overlooked. In the course of the struggle Sivaji's well-knit Maratha kingdom was broken up. The hardy patriots noted for their moderation towards their foes and restraint towards civilians * had become toughened raiders notorious for their rapacity and ruthlessness as much as for their daring. They were to spread this reputation all over India until their name was as much dreaded by other Hindus as by Muslims. Maratha independence survived but at the price of the soul of Maratha nationalism. What emerged was a species of Maratha imperialism which regarded the rest of India as its legitimate sphere of operations. Maratha leadership was not accepted by India because the Marathas had made themselves hated. They were hated because the iron had entered into their souls in the Mughal struggle. The Maratha bid for Indian empire was in effect defeated before it began by the octogenarian Aurangzeb. They became too bitter and aggressive to be acceptable as national leaders and they lacked the power to impose themselves permanently on the whole country.

* We have the Muslim historian Khafi Khan's testimony for this.

5

EUROPEANS AND MUGHAL INDIA

As European historians of ancient India have been apt to over-estimate the influence of the Greeks upon India because of their natural interest and the convenient Greek habit of leaving records, the modern historian has been tempted to overplay the part played by Europeans in Mughal India before 1700. And the reason is much the same. They naturally interested their own writers, they left numerous and excellent records far easier to study than the Persian of India itself. Jesuit missionaries and professional travellers made careful and searching reports, while the merchants built up great collections of detailed records. There was one motive for the modern historian lacked. by the ancient; the European in Mughal India could always be regarded as the shadow of the future whereas the Greeks and their influence vanished into the mists of legend and speculation.

European interest in India has persisted since classical times and for very cogent reasons. India had much to give Europe in the practical form of spices, textiles, and other oriental products. The best classical accounts are in fact the commercial ones. When direct contact was lost with the fall of Rome and the rise of the Muslim Arabs the trade was carried on through middle-men. In the late Middle Ages it increased with the increasing prosperity of Europe. It should be remembered that the spice trade was not solely a luxury trade at that time. Spices were needed to preserve meat through the winter (cattle had to be slaughtered in late autumn through lack of winter fodder) and to combat the taste of decay. Wine, in the absence of ancient or modern methods of maturing, had to be 'mulled' with spices. This trade suffered two threats in the later Middle Ages. There was the threat of Mongol and Turkish invasion which interfered with the land routes and threatened to engulf the sea route through Egypt, and there was the threat of monopoly shared be-tween Venetians and Egyptians. Crusading zeal against the

Muslim and commercial zeal against spice monopólists were the motives which sent Columbus to America in 1492 and Vasco da Gama to Calicut in 1498.

There followed the episode of the Portuguese empire in India. Vasco da Gama told the first Indians he met on the Malabar coast that he came to seek 'Christians and spices'. The Christians he had in mind were a legendary people to be rescued from Muslim encirclement who would help him in his crusades; they were in fact probably the Abyssinians whom da Gama never met. But the Portuguese did meet Christians in Malabar itself, descendants of Christians settled since at least the fourth century A.D. The Portuguese soon found that Malabar was as important a centre for re-export of spices from the East Indies as for the sale of its own limited range of pepper and cardamom. They also found that the trade with Egypt and so with Europe was in the hands of Arab merchants. So a double strategy was developed. A series of strong points was established so as to dominate both the East Indies and the Arabian sea. The object of the former measure was to control the spice trade at its principal sources from Java to the Mulucca Islands (home of the clove) and of the latter to cut off the Arabian-managed spice trade from south India to Egypt and the Persian Gulf. In this way the European spice trade would be diverted to Portuguese ships and toll could be taken (by a system of licences) of all the remaining maritime trade of the Indian ocean. The Portuguese were largely successful in their venture because of the superior power of their ships, whose guns could blow most 'country ships' of the time out of the water, of the daring and endurance of their captains and men, and of the genius of Affonso de Albuquerque.* It was he who in 1510 captured Goa on the west coast of India from the Sultan of Bijapur and made it the capital of the Portuguese eastern empire. Its strong points besides Goa were Socotra off the Red Sea (he could not take Aden), Ormuz in the Persian Gulf, Diu in Gujarat, Malacca, the entrepôt for the Far East and the spice trade in the East Indies, and Macao in China. The function of Goa was to supervise Malabar, of the next three to control the pilgrim traffic to Mecca as well as the general trade

* Captain General 1509–15.

to Egypt, Iraq, and Persia, and of Malacca to control the East Indian spices at their source.

The system worked, considering the distances and resources involved, with remarkable success for about a century and then broke down because of events in Europe. We are here concerned with its effects in India. The Portuguese never attempted large-scale conquest but they did impinge on Indian affairs and they carried their culture with them. Politically their control of the sea irked Mughal and preceding Muslim rulers because of the toll they took of the trade from the port of Surat and the pilgrim traffic. In seizing and retaining their strong points they acquired a reputation for cruelty and perfidy because their practice on both these points was below the current Indian standard. They were deeply impregnated with the idea that no faith need be kept with an infidel. It was from this period that the word *feringi* (lit. *farangi*, frank) acquired the opprobrium of which echoes may still be heard today. In religion they were intolerant to the extent of allowing no Hindu temples in Goa and introducing the Inquisition (1560), both measures which can be regarded as substandard from the Indian standpoint, and they advertised this trait in their rough handling of the Syrian Christians of Malabar to secure their submission to Roman supremacy.

Socially the policy of Albuquerque in encouraging mixed marriages had important results. His object was to rear a population possessing Portuguese blood and imbued with Portuguese Catholic culture who would be committed by race and taste to the Portuguese settlements and so form a permanent self-perpetuating garrison. The result was the race long known as Luso-Indians and now as Goanese or Goans. They are mainly Indian in blood, Catholic in religion, and partly western in outlook. In recent times they have spread all over India as traders and professionals, a less successful version of the Parsis. From early times they spilled over from the Portuguese settlements and formed communities of their own which tended towards disorder and piracy. One such at Hughli was suppressed by Shah Jahan in 1632. These activities, again, did not add to the Feringi reputation.

The Portuguese who sailed with da Gama were men of the

Catholic renaissance and their successors were under the influence of the Counter-Reformation. Culture and religion for them were inextricably mixed and it was impossible to say where Catholic stopped and Renaissance Portuguese began. Thus the west which first contacted India in modern times did so in its Iberian Catholic vesture which had a strange similarity in texture with the Indo-Islamic culture which it encountered. In both religion and culture formed something of a seamless garment; both were clear-cut in their beliefs, dogmatic in their expression, and inclined to intolerance. This is perhaps the reason why all the rich gifts of Renaissance Europe, as imported by the Portuguese, made so little impression on India as a whole. Jahangir admired their pictures and had them copied. The halo, taken by Europe from the Buddhists, was returned to India by the Portuguese. Akbar listened with interest to the Jesuit Fathers' discourses. The New Testament was translated into Persian. But this was virtually all. The west, though mingling its Portuguese blood with the Indian, remained culturally alien and sterile. The legacy of Portugal and sixteenth-century Europe to India was the Goans, the Catholic community in India with its missions begun by the enthusiastic St Francis Xavier, a *lingua franca* of which traces still linger in the ports, and a faint odour of intolerance. The first western cultural assault on India had failed.

The next European incursion into India was a strictly commercial one from the Protestant north. In 1580 Portugal was taken over by Spain and a load thereby added to the burden of empire which Portugal was already finding too heavy to bear. The new mixed population were brave and loyal but they were attached to their eastern homes and disinclined to risk all in new adventures. Success had brought wealth, and wealth in the oriental style including the debilitating institution of slavery on a large scale. Spain was deeply engaged in Europe and the New World and inclined to leave the Portuguese possessions to themselves. In Europe it was now the Portuguese Spanish who were the spice monopolists, with their depots at Lisbon and Antwerp. The Dutch in successful revolt against the Spaniards and the English, with fresh self-confidence after the Armada in 1588, were disinclined to put up with this. This was the origin of the trading ventures which summarize European contact with India in the seventeenth century.

The Dutch sent their first fleet to the East in 1595. Being commercial realists they went straight to the source of the spice trade in the East Indies, established themselves at Batavia (now as previous to their arrival called Jakarta), and proceeded to oust the Portuguese. Then they established a chain of posts through Ceylon and Capetown to connect themselves with their home base and proceeded to develop a great Asian network of trade by which they planned to earn the resources needed to purchase spices without drawing on the silver bullion which was in chronic short supply in northern Europe. India came within their purview only as a link in their great commercial chain. It was a source of textiles for sale in the East Indies in exchange for spices while the extreme south and Ceylon were valuable for their own supplies of pepper, cardamom, and cinnamon. The Dutch had 'factories' or warehouses as far north as Agra but they took no part in politics or cultural contacts. Their eccentric tombs at Surat and their factories at Cochin and Negapatam are their principal memorials in India. Only in Ceylon did they exercise dominion in the plains from Colombo and leave a living memorial in the Burgher community.

The English formed their East India Company on the last day of 1600. They had the same commercial vision as the Dutch and they began by sailing to the same destination. But there they found a bleak reception. No sooner had the Dutch got the better of the common foe, the Portuguese, than they showed jealousy of the English traders. Their object was monopoly, not co-existence, and to them fellow-Protestants were just as much interlopers or intruders as Catholics. The capital of the English company was only a tenth of that of the Dutch * at this time so that the struggle was unequal. The friction culminated in what is known as the Massacre of Amboyna in 1623, when the Dutch seized the English factory there and executed the occupants. No redress was ever obtained and the English had thereafter to be content with a minor role in the East Indies. It was this Dutch success in preserving their East Indian market that drove the

* £50,000 to £540,000.

English to concentrate on India as a second-best. Without it there might well have been no British Empire in India.

India was a second-best because there were no spices except in the extreme south where no one was able to seize a monopoly over other Europeans or the local Indian rulers. Spices were small in bulk, in short supply in Europe, and therefore highly profitable; the first Dutch 'clove' ship produced a profit of 2,500 per cent. The main Indian products like textiles, saltpetre, and sugar were more bulky and so more expensive to carry, and produced under more competitive conditions. The margin of profit was therefore much less and the labour of winning it greater. The Dutch came to control the production of spices as well as their marketing, so that they could buy at their own price in the East Indies as well as sell on their terms in Europe. In India, on the other hand, the merchants had to compete both with other Europeans and local merchants for their goods in highly competitive conditions, and had to deal with usually strong governments who could not be bullied and had often to be expensively propitiated.

In India the English merchants at once met Portuguese opposition. But here they were helped by three factors – the unpopularity of the Portuguese, whose control of the Arabian sea and the pilgrim traffic was resented by the Mughals, the waning Portuguese resources, tied as they were to Spain and hard pressed by the Dutch in the east and the north, and their own maritime prowess. The English went first to Surat and applied to the Mughal court for privileges. But they could do nothing so long as the Portuguese held the sea. For this reason the efforts of Captain Hawkins between 1607–11, in spite of his becoming a boon companion of Jahangir and being given a *mansab* of 400, came to nothing. The first turning-point came in 1612 when the Company's ships defeated the Portuguese in the Swally estuary off Surat. The Mughals were then willing to talk and there followed the embassy of Sir Thomas Roe, a peppery and insular but far more weighty person than Hawkins. The second turning-point was his agreement with the Mughals in 1618 whereby the Company obtained important privileges in return for the protection of the commercial and pilgrim sea traffic from the Portuguese. The Company tacitly became the maritime auxiliary of the empire. This agreement covered the Company's relations with the Mughals throughout the seventeenth century. The third turning-point was the siege of Ormuz in the Persian Gulf jointly with the Persians and its capture in 1622 from the Portuguese after a heroic resistance. The Portuguese were overborne, but must be given the credit for going down fighting.

From this time the company steadily developed its activities. Its first headquarters (from 1612) was at Surat which was moved to Bombay in 1674 (a wedding gift of Charles II's Portuguese queen Catherine transferred to the company). In 1640 a factory was established at Madras on a plot of land leased from one of the last Vijayanagar rulers. By 1700, however, they too were subjects of the Mughal. In Bengal, attractive for saltpetre and silks, a factory was set up at Hughli, to be replaced in 1690 by Calcutta, a malarial swamp redeemed by a deep water anchorage. Relations in general were harmonious except for a time when Sir Josiah Child, an ambitious Company chairman, thought that the time had come to 'lay the foundation of a large, well-grounded, sure English dominion in India for all time to come'. His expedition to Chittagong was a failure; the English merchants were expelled by Aurangzeb's officers from Bengal and Surat. The Calcutta factory with its fortified factory of Fort William, was one result of this episode. Thereafter a chastened company took care not to challenge the empire again until there was hardly anything left to challenge in 1756. For a time it was convulsed by a struggle with a rival company till the union of the two in the United Company in 1708. Their further efforts to obtain privileges was by the respectful method of Surman's embassy to the Mughal Court (1714–17).

The pattern of trade which developed was one of steady rather than spectacular returns. And it presupposed reasonable tranquillity in the country. In the west the main articles were cotton piece-goods, cotton yarn, and indigo from Gujarat; from the Malabar coast pepper and such other spices as could be bought second-hand from Ceylon and the East Indies; from Madras and the south-east coast again piece-goods, and yarn and sugar; from Bengal specially silks and saltpetre. The opium trade was to come later. In return India bought metals such as tin, lead, and quicksilver, novelties, specially mechanical ones, tapestries, and ivories. But these purchases never equalled the Company's payments. India would take little of England's staple product of broadcloth so that the balance had to be made up with silver bullion. The drain on silver made the Company a target for attack at home which in turn spurred them to seeking alternative means of payment through inter-Asian trade. These difficult and competitive conditions caused the English merchants to study local conditions, markets, and tempers far more closely than the Dutch with their monopolies. By giving them a detailed knowledge of Indian conditions and an insight into Indian character they provided an unconscious preparation for their later debut on the Indian political stage. The English merchants would have been monopolists if they could, as some of their later proceedings in Malabar testify; but their enforced acceptance of competitive methods in fact proved an excellent preparation for later developments. They were schooled in the current methods of negotiations with its bargaining, its promises and evasions, its covert understandings and secret pressures. In the process they acquired a skill in dealing with the Indians that even the French, with their more attractive manners, never achieved.

The only other European traders of importance were the French. Their company was founded by Colbert in 1664 but it was so closely tied to the state that its fortunes rose and fell with the careers of ministers and turns of politics. It was not until after 1720, with Dumas at Pondicherry and Dupleix at Chandernagar, that its fortunes revived rapidly. The Danes had settlements at Tranquebar, but they were more important for the missionary activities carried on there than for commerce. This was, perhaps, the first perceptible cultural impingement of the Protestant west on India. It gave to the south of India the singularly attractive figure of Frederick Christian Swartz but otherwise made so little impression that few Indians were probably even aware of it. The Emperor also tried his hand from the Low Countries, but his Ostend Company was both short-lived and ill-fated.

However, the organized companies were by no means the only

Europeans in Mughal India. There was a sprinkling of them throughout the country in various guises. There were the travellers who came on their lawful occasions. Some took service in the country as did the greatest of them, François Bernier, with the Mughal 'Omrah' Danishmand Khan. Some practised their professions like the jeweller Travernier who has left us an expert's description of the Peacock throne, or Dr Gemelli-Carreri who has given a classic description of Aurangzeb in later life. Some were craftsmen like Austin of Bordeaux who was responsible for the inlaid work on the throne portico at Delhi, or Geronimo Verroneo who was connected with the Taj. The Mughals welcomed foreign artists and craftsmen as they welcomed foreign poets, as tending to enhance their glory. Then there were the adventurers pure and simple. The type of these was the Venetian Niccolao Manucci who went to India at the age of sixteen. He

began a colourful career as an artilleryman with Dara Shekoh; on his defeat took up doctoring (because Aurangzeb insisted that European artillerymen should load as well as aim the guns) and continued as a quack till he died in the south in the eighteenth century, leaving lengthy memoirs full of amusing and unreliable anecdotes.*

Mughal India was thus not unacquainted with Europeans. It traded with them, occasionally fought them. It employed them, did its best to outwit them, and thought it understood them. There was no mystique about them. India thought she had their measure and regarded them as pawns in the never-ending games of politics and commerce. Of cultural influence there was little or none, not even permitting a comparison with the Portuguese influence in the sixteenth century. India had most to do with the northern Europeans, and to her they seemed to be heavy, shrewd, and dull, and in no context dangerous.

* *Storia do Mogor*, ed. W. Irvine, 3 vols.

6

DECLINE, COLLAPSE, AND CONFUSION

THE first half of the eighteenth century in India is occupied by the collapse of the Mughal empire and a struggle for power by its would-be successors. The Mughals had never succeeded in really integrating the country. Their Indo-Persian cultural plant may be described as an abortive aristocratic civilization whose roots did not penetrate deep enough into the Indian soil to enable it to withstand the storms which tore down the overshadowing imperial umbrella. The Mughals had provided an idea but not a sufficiently strong belief in a way of life. The weakening of imperial power was therefore followed, not by a revival under some other leaders, but by a release of elemental forces. As respect for the empire waned, willingness to compromise and let live waned too. Concessions and attitudes on the part of the emperors which formerly would have been greeted with gratitude and hailed as masterstrokes now met with no response and finally with contempt. The British were to have something of this experience themselves, for the pressure of power tends to bend the mirror of judgement and so distort the image of public opinion. Of what use was it to abolish the *jizya* or poll-tax on unbelievers, when one no longer had the power to enforce it?

The visible decline of the empire can be dated from 1712, the year of the death of Bahadur Shah I. But it remained an apparently imposing institution until the 1750s, and few thought its doom inevitable before then. The first stage in the process was succession wars which left a puppet in the hands of kingmakers. The kingmakers overreached themselves when the third choice proved a clever youth who disposed of them in the course of two years. This youth was Muhammad Shah, who reigned for twenty-nine years until 1748. He was one of those rulers like Louis XV who had the cleverness to divide his opponents but not the vigour to rule himself, who could preside but not inspire. Under him the empire did not founder but drifted ever nearer the rocks. With him it was truly a case of 'après moi le déluge'.

The twenties saw the next stage when the empire was virtually

divided into two. Asaf Jah, Nizam-ul-mulk, baulked in his reforming intentions as chief minister in Delhi, retired to his
Deccan provinces and became the virtually independent ruler
of the southern half of the empire from Hyderabad. Though
there were never co-emperors the division may be compared with
that between the eastern and western halves of the Roman empire. They were allies rather than rivals, and, as in the case of
Byzantium, the newer foundation long outlasted the collapse of
the older. The empire had crushed the Sikhs in 1716 for a
generation but it found itself helpless against the Marathas. In
1738 the Marathas plundered the suburbs of Delhi and dictated
a peace which divided the two halves of the empire by the cession of the province of Malwa. In 1739 came the humiliation of
the Persian King Nadir Shah's invasion. Neglect, ineptitude,
divided counsels, and treachery led to military debacle at Karnal,
the occupation of Delhi, massacre, and wholesale plunder.
Nevertheless, when Nadir Shah's back was turned, with the
Peacock Throne in his train, the empire seemed to recover and
even repelled the first of the Afghan incursions in 1748. With
Muhammad Shah's death on the morrow of the victory the
collapse began. A civil war between rival ministers left a headlong and ruthless youth in power, who murdered two emperors
and called in the Marathas before vanishing into obscurity. The
south was already the Nizam's domain. Kabul was lost to Nadir
Shah in 1739. Sind and fertile Gujarat with Surat went in 1750,
prosperous Oudh in 1754 with the defeated chief minister, and
the martial Panjab to the Afghans in the same year. Bengal still
sent tribute but was virtually independent.

The cause of this collapse is usually put down to the effeteness
of the emperors. This was certainly one cause since personality
was one of the main imperial pillars. But it was not the only
cause or necessarily the vital one. Another was Aurangzeb's
policy of treating the empire as a Muslim state instead of an
Indian state with Islam as the state religion. He was far too
cautious to outrage Hindus as a whole, in spite of particular acts
of intolerance, but their previous passive support and even pride
turned into indifference and disdain. Martial groups like the
Sikhs and the Jats were encouraged to open revolt. The Rajputs

no longer felt themselves to be partners in the empire and though some states like Jaipur continued as allies they no longer did so with enthusiasm. The declining empire became an affair of the Muslims, which it was not the business of the Hindus to prop up. Then there was the loss of the steady stream of adventurers from Afghanistan, Persia, and Turkestan which had supplied the empire with vigour, loyalty, and ability. The Afghans were busy adventuring in Persia where they overthrew the Safavid monarchy in 1722, and then in setting up on their own. The Persians were occupied in coping with the Afghans, and, after Nadir Shah's death in 1746 with further dissensions of their own. The Turks were experiencing one of those periods of contraction in Central Asia following expansion for which no satisfactory explanation has yet been given.

All these causes had their effect, yet it may be doubted if they provide the whole explanation. In addition there was, as I see it, an inner malaise, a kind of general loss of nerve on the part of the Muslim community. The Mughals themselves had lost their sense of mission to rule. The Muslims had no sense of purpose and valued the empire only as a stepping-stone to personal power. The so called 'reformers' were elders like the Nizam who stood for the 'good old days' and the stricter ways of Aurangzeb. They had no vision for the future; nothing is ever saved by looking backwards. So the ablest men, instead of cooperating for the common good, carved out kingdoms for themselves to the general confusion. And the most thoughtful theologians like Shah Wali-ullah, instead of calling on Muslims to rally round the throne, took refuge in the concept of the community of the faithful looking only to God. In this atmosphere the bravery of a young Shah Alam or the skill of a Mirza Najaf Khan were lost in the general run of cynicism, opportunism, and indulgence.

If the Mughal hold on the sceptre was weakening there was no lack of applicants for its reversion. The most spectacular of these were the Persians with their dramatic swoop on Delhi in 1738–39. But as so often with oriental historians, and specially European historians of the orient, love of drama has distorted historical perspective. The Persian invasion was a flash in the pan, a prestige blow with few after effects. The real competitors were elsewhere. The first of these were the Marathas, whose hardihood and staunchness had survived the Mughal onset and gathered strength and confidence in the process. Aurangzeb had, it is true, broken up the compact Maratha kingdom beyond repair. But the Mughal struggle had also done much else. It had confirmed the Marathas in a belief in guerilla warfare and a taste for plunder; their mobility and the slowness of their adversaries had made them feel that all India was their field. In Sivaji's time the land was divided into *swarajya*, or the homeland, where settled administration prevailed, and *mughlai*, or foreign land, the legitimate object of raids. To these lands were applied, according to Maratha military success, the exactions of *Chauth* (one fourth of the land revenue) and *sar-deshmukhi* (one tenth). Later Maratha writers have suggested that these demands included protection of the areas concerned from others or from further demands but little trace can be found of this in practice. It was, in fact, a share of the revenue taken by the strong hand and used to make that hand stronger. The system involved endless disputes, much uncertainty, and oppression. It is easy to see why the Marathas were loved nowhere in India outside Maharashtra and in Hindu districts like west Bengal and Rajasthan least of all.

The years after Aurangzeb's death saw a rapid transformation of Sivaji's kingdom into a confederacy headed by a hereditary minister styled the Peshwa. Sivaji's grandson Shahu returned to Satara with Mughal manners and outlook. In 1714 he confided power to the Brahmin Bhat family whose members ruled the Maratha homeland. Maharashtra was still poor and barren, but the rest of India seemed open, so the decision was made to expand. By deciding to go north instead of south Shahu made the fortunes of the Peshwa, for in the south other ministers were his equals while in the north the generals were his subordinates. The decision once taken the expansion was so rapid that the problem arose of controlling the generals. Until the battle of Panipat in 1761 this was achieved by such devices as causing the generals to send part of the *chauth* to the Peshwa at Poona and giving them lands in the homeland which could be confiscated on misbehaviour. By this means the Marathas by 1750 spread right across central India to Orissa (which they occupied) and Bengal, which they attacked. They were under the general control of the Peshwa but were becoming more and more distinctly divided into five sections. The Peshwa himself controlled Maharashtra from Poona, the Gaekwar most of Gujarat from Baroda, the Bhonsla central India from Nagpur, while the two most enterprising officers, Holkar and Sindia, established their headquarters respectively at Indore and Gwalior. All these officers passed on their power, like the Peshwas, to their descendants, so that what began by being, as it were, five army commands, developed steadily into a mother state and four largely autonomous dependencies.

The event which turned the Maratha power from the status of an empire *in* India to that of a competitor for the empire *of* India was the cession of Malwa by the Mughals in 1738. Through the gap thus created between Delhi and Hyderabad they poured eastward to the sea at Orissa and threatened Bengal. To the north they began the harrying of the perennially brave but tradition-bound Rajputs. By 1750 they were ready to move to the north should Delhi collapse.

Delhi did collapse, but the actually fatal blows came once more from the north-west in the shape of the Afghans. Throughout the main Mughal period what is now Afghanistan on the map was divided between the Persian and Mughal empires. Persia had Herat, India Kabul, and Kandahar was disputed. The tribesmen then as later were a nuisance, but the main routes were kept open by a mixture of subsidies to chiefs and punitive expeditions. In the early eighteenth century an Afghan revolt overthrew the Persian monarchy, and though it was quelled for a time by Nadir Shah its end was an independent Afghan power, at times swelling to imperial dimensions and at times little more than a number of chiefships. In Ahmad Shah Abdali the Afghans found a soldier of genius. Undeterred by his repulse in 1748 at Sirhind he gradually secured the Punjab and then took and sacked Delhi in 1756–57. The distracted Mughal minister then called in the Marathas, already deeply involved in imperial politics. From this moment the triangular power struggle be-

tween Mughals, Marathas, and Afghans became a duel between
Marathas and Afghans. The Marathas saw the control of the
empire opening before them. The Peshwa accepted the challenge,
drove back the Afghans, and talked of 'leaping over the walls of
Attock'. When the Afghans rallied with Indian support he sent
his cousin, the Bhao Sahib, with a formidable armament. He
was, however, outmanoeuvred by Ahmad Shah and brought to
decisive battle at Panipat in unfavourable conditions. On
13 January 1761 he and the Peshwa's heir were killed and his
army destroyed so completely that the Marathas did not re-enter
the north for another decade. The Peshwa followed his cousin
in a few months from vexation of spirit.

The battle of Panipat was decisive, but it was decisive in a
negative sense. The empire seemed to lie within the grasp of
Ahmad Shah. But at this moment his followers mutinied for
their two-years arrears of pay and compelled him to retire to
Afghanistan. Thus the imperial sceptre was denied to both
Afghan and Maratha. North India was left in a power vacuum
which various adventurers tried vainly to fill during the next
forty years. Ahmad Shah and his successors themselves never got
further than Lahore, and the Punjab gradually slipped from
their grasp. The other main competitor recovered indeed, but
never completely. The Peshwa-controlled confederacy now dissolved into five virtually independent states, and it was these,
and not the old confederacy, with whom the British had to deal.
The Peshwa's government in Poona was distracted with internal
dissensions while the other four spent their time alternately
enlarging their borders and contending for supremacy. The two
northern chiefs, Sindia and Holkar, were the most prominent
and of these Madhu Rao Sindia showed signs of genius. But
after gaining control of Delhi, defeating the Rajputs and his
rival Holkar, and seizing power at Poona, he died in 1794 just
when it seemed that he might be the destined empire-builder.
Delhi and the region around passed to the nominal deputy of
Ahmad Shah who ruled on behalf of the wandering emperor
Shah Alam. From this arose the kingdom of Delhi, a kind of
sunset reflection of Mughal power. Its independence ended when
Shah Alam called in Sindia in 1785. After he was blinded by a

half-mad Afghan chief in 1788 he became a pensionary, first of Sindia and then of the British.

There remains the Punjab. The Sikhs, who from a devotional religious sect had been transformed into a militant anti-Muslim brotherhood in the seventeenth century, had been savagely repressed by the Mughals in the early eighteenth century and finally driven into the foothills (where their hill refuge forts may still be seen) in 1716. As Mughal authority waned in the Punjab from 1750 they reappeared on the plains in small roving bands. Active, aggressive, and sustained by a militant faith they were soon operating all over the Punjab from the Salt Range to the neighbourhood of Delhi. They were divided into twelve fraternities or *misls* and gradually set up a number of petty states, some of which, like Patiala, lasted until independence in 1947. By the end of the century they had produced a leader of genius in Ranjit Singh, who, having secured Lahore in 1799, set about the reintegration of the Panjab.

Thus the aftermath of Panipat left India like a swirling sea at high tide, angry and tumultuous but divided and lacking direction. The *idea* of unity and imperial authority persisted but its Mughal embodiment had all but vanished. It is interesting to speculate as to what might have happened if the great anarchy of forty years had been prolonged indefinitely without foreign intervention. The period threw up some remarkable leaders who in other circumstances might each have founded an empire and dynasty. As it was, however, they tended to cancel each other out and thus leave the way for a third party with special advantages from another world. In the north we may hazard that a Maratha dominion under Sindia controlling Delhi, Rajasthan, and much of central India would have been faced by a determined Sikh power in the Punjab. Oudh and Bengal might have continued under the Muslim rule to fall victims to the winner of the former struggle. Those areas showed little sign of energy or revival in this period. In the south the brilliant Mysorean adventurer Haidar Ali and his almost equally able son Tipu would have had no British wars to hinder them. They might well have built up a Muslim Vijayanagar empire and absorbed the ex-Mughal state of Hyderabad. By a complete reversal of the earlier struggle they would then have faced the Maratha Peshwa in central and western India. It is difficult to see an end to the wars which would have ensued or to measure the poverty and misery which would have accompanied them, because it is difficult to envisage any one of the leaders triumphing over the rest. In the absence of a definite decision western intervention must have come in some form in the nineteenth century, because India was too valuable an economic prize to be left to herself in a rapidly shrinking world.

India was not left to herself, but it is important to realize that conditions favouring intervention existed before it actually occurred and that these conditions were self-induced. Before either British or French actually intervened, there were a great many people in India on the look-out for help either to further their ambitions or to save their possessions. The actual onset of intervention arose from Anglo-French commercial and political rivalry in India and political rivalry in Europe. In the late seventeenth and early eighteenth century the French stake in India was not great enough to be worth the despatch of an English armament. The two companies therefore declared neutrality and went on trading. But between 1720 and 1740 the French Company's trade increased ten times in value until it was nearly half that of the old-established English company at about £880,000. The stake of both countries in India was now considerable. The British were deeply involved with indigo, saltpetre, cottons, silk, and spices; they had a growing trade with China and a strong vested interest in England itself in the form of shipping and stores brokers. The value of the trade was more than ten per cent of the public revenue of Great Britain at that time.

The occasion for intervention arose with Frederick the Great of Prussia's seizure of Silesia in 1740. In the War of the Austrian Succession which followed (1740-48) Britain and France were on opposite sides in the rival coalitions. In the repeat performance of the Seven Years War (1756-63) the alliances were reversed so that Britain, though supporting the opposite party, was again opposed to France. It is these two wars, of wholly European origin, which provided the political turning-point in the history of modern India. In the first war there was a simple contest between the two companies backed by their respective states. In 1746 a French fleet made possible the capture of Madras but quarrels prevented the taking of the subordinate Fort St David. In 1748 a British fleet returned and Pondicherry in its turn was unsuccessfully attacked. By the treaty of Aix-la-Chapelle in the same year Madras was exchanged with the French for Cape Breton Island in North America. In appearance the *status quo* was restored, but in fact two important things had happened. Both sides had noted the power of the guns landed from the fleets for the sieges and Dupleix, the French governor, had conceived the possibility of using this power to gain support within the country itself. He was a man of remarkable energy and diplomatic skill with a piercing vision into the realities of local politics, though hampered by lack of military knowledge and by a nervous sensibility which made it difficult for him to work with colleagues. It happened that at this moment a breakdown occurred in the authority of the Nizam of whose dominions the Carnatic with its European settlements formed a part. This provided the opportunity for the second phase of the struggle, which may be termed Dupleix's private war. In 1748 the old Nizam, a man of the Aurangzeb school, died and there was also rivalry for the governorship of the Carnatic. French help secured the defeat of the new Nizam's nominee so easily that Dupleix was tempted to go further. On the murder of the new Nizam he was able to place his own nominee on the Hyderabad throne supported by a body of French troops under the gifted officer de Bussy. The object of all this was to squeeze Madras by surrounding it with hostile territory. As the plan developed the English Company of necessity supported Muhammad Ali, the son of the governor defeated in 1749. He held out in the rock fortress of Trichinopoly and his ejection became the key factor in the struggle between the two companies. But here the struggle took an unexpected turn with the appearance of Robert Clive, a problem-child transplanted to Madras to be a discontented 'Writer' or clerk who turned out to have a genius for irregular warfare. His seizure of Arcot in 1751 with 210 men and retention of it in a fifty-day siege led to a reversal of fortune and finally to the surrender of the French forces at Trichinopoly and the death of their candidate Chanda Sahib. Dupleix's policy was in ruins and he was recalled two years later.

The third and final phase was again an open struggle brought on by the Seven Years War. The English were first in the field but their force was diverted to Bengal. When the French forces arrived in 1758 they were crippled by jealousies and bad leadership. They failed to take Madras and were decisively defeated at Wandiwash in 1760, where de Bussy was taken prisoner. Brave to the last the wayward Lally endured an agonizing siege in Pondicherry for eight months until its fall. This was the real end of the French bid for Indian power. Their reappearance in 1782 was a passing phase only made notable by the genius of their admiral de Suffren.

In this struggle the English owed their success to the successful assertion of sea-power, greater resources, and steadier support from Europe. Both sides had striking leaders such as Dupleix and de Bussy for the French, Clive, Pigot, Lawrence, and Coote for the English. But the English had more competent subordinates and were better at working together. Though less attractive to the Indians than the French they also in fact handled them better because of their long experience. But the result of the struggle, which is now apt to seem local and limited in scope (all the actions were in fact on a very small scale), was not merely to clear the Indian field for the British. Its course wove several patterns which greatly influenced their behaviour in the more vital field of Bengal. One was Indian readiness to call in European help as providing what they believed to be a decisive factor in any dispute. Another was the new European confidence in the superiority of their armed forces in Indian conditions. This was based on the effect of disciplined troops against undisciplined ones, and on the superior fire-power of their muskets and cannons which made it possible to break up a cavalry charge before it could reach an infantry line. Thus the power of the main Indian arm was neutralized and the balance restored, as in classical times, to small numbers of highly trained infantry. A third pattern was that of the European-sponsored Indian state. This was Dupleix's concept, worked out by de Bussy in Hyderabad. His object was to use Indian authority to ruin English trade; his method to make his support vital to an Indian ruler so that he could dictate policy. This method was practised by de Bussy with great skill in Hyderabad with little apparent harm to the state. Its success presupposed, however, a highly competent operator, a fairly stable state, and the absence of strong European commercial interests to sway policy. It was this example which Clive had in mind when he sailed for Bengal, but the state he found there proved very different from that of Hyderabad.

7

THE ENGLISH IN BENGAL

WHEN the Seven Years War was seen to be impending the British government sent troops to Madras with the object of attacking de Bussy in Hyderabad. Clive went with them with the reversion of the government of Fort St David in his pocket. But before he could move a crisis had arisen in Bengal. The company's trade in Bengal was much younger than in Madras, dating only from the latter part of the seventeenth century. But it had prospered and had made Calcutta, centred on Fort William (erected by Mughal permission), a prosperous and growing city. Bengal was still ruled by Mughal viceroys or *subadars*, now styled Nawabs.* While the empire at Delhi was in its death throes, the system went on in Bihar and Bengal and an annual tribute was regularly despatched. Since 1740 the ruler of Bengal had been the virtually self-appointed Alivardi Khan. He had proved an able ruler and had repelled with difficulty a prolonged Maratha attack. He regarded the European merchants with a mixture of suspicion and wariness, and maintained a running controversy with them over dues, privileges, and the interpretation of Mughal *farmans*. But though he seemed outwardly strong his position had elements of weakness. He headed a Muslim aristocracy in a Hindu countryside. He lacked the recruits from up-country necessary to maintain an army in an unwarlike area. He was increasingly dependent on Hindu bankers and entrepreneurs for his administration. The aristocracy itself was divided, lacking in morale and fresh recruits. With a strong ruler these weaknesses remained concealed, but with a weak one they were serious handicaps.

Alivardi died in April 1756 and was succeeded by his grandson Siraj-ad-daula, a youth of twenty. He was vacillating and headstrong; we shall never know whether age and experience would have added balance to his nature because he was beset by crises from the moment of his accession. He found himself the

---

* The plural of na'ib (Ar) a deputy. The deputy referred to the emperor, the plural form was adopted as an honorific.

ruler of a virtually independent state, for the Delhi government was disappearing between contending Afghans and Marathas. In Bengal itself the situation was confused; two relatives opposed his accession and Hindu notables were becoming increasingly restless under a Muslim minority government. Further, the English and French companies were palpably preparing for a renewal of hostilities between themselves. Like the Afghans in the north they were an unknown quantity who excited more alarm than their local resources justified. The English Company, for its part, had a considerable stake in Bengal by this time. The Mughal *farman* of 1717 had given the Company virtual free trade for its goods; the network of Bengal waterways gave easy access to the interior and the resources of the area provided rich opportunities. To a flourishing trade in cotton and silk goods and yarn and sugar was added a growing trade in saltpetre for gunpowder in the European wars. The obverse side of this prospect was continual disputes with the Bengal government as to what constituted free trade. The disputes were often bitter, but never led to an open breach because both sides reaped enough advantage from the trade to make compromise worth while. A more delicate point was fortification for this 'touched the sceptre'. The Company had its fortified factory Fort William in 1696; but it did not complete it until 1716 and then soon cluttered it with warehouses and houses close to the walls. There is no doubt that the company's servants, while commercially contentious and aggressive, were very unwarlike, nor had they much political sense. Not for them the planning of empire.

It was this lack of political sense, along with Siraj-ad-daula's headstrong nature, which precipitated the crisis. As the Seven Years War approached both French and English began fortifying their settlements. The French desisted at Alivardi's insistence. The English prevaricated but failed to push on their defences. They thus got the worst of both worlds by arousing the suspicions of the Nawab before they had any serious means of defence. There followed the Nawab's march on Calcutta in June, the flight of the governor and most of the council downstream to Fulta, and the capture of the city. This episode might well have ended with one more compromise as in Aurangzeb's day if it had occurred in isolation. But it so happened that the force intended to deal with de Bussy in Hyderabad had just arrived in Madras; it also happened that the senior royal officer refused the command which was then entrusted to Clive. The expedition was intended to recover Calcutta and return for its orginal purpose. That this did not happen was almost entirely due to the personality and talents of Clive. Like most men of his situation he was an opportunist not overburdened with scruple, but unlike the others he had diplomatic as well as military qualities of a high order. He carried with him from Madras not only 900 Europeans and 1,500 Indian troops in five transports with five men-o'-war but a determination to make the most of his opportunities and an idea of de Bussy's success in sponsoring the Hyderabad state in the French interest.

Events played into his hands. Calcutta was retaken in January 1757 and the Nawab brought to peace and an alliance in February. There the episode should have ended with Clive's return to Madras with his men. But there were the French to be dealt with. The Nawab's alarm at Ahmad Shah's capture of Delhi secured his consent to the capture of French Chandernagar and thus to his own isolation. Clive then became aware of plots to dethrone Siraja. He was moved by ambition, cupidity (forty millions sterling were said to lie in the treasury of Murshidabad), and the example of de Bussy (could not rich Bengal be run in the interest of the Company's trade). It was thought that the whole annual investment of the Company could be met from the revenue surplus leaving the whole proceeds of trade for profit, with, of course, corresponding advantages for the Company's servants. He selected the most eligible pretender in the person of the elderly general Mir Jafar and then, helped again by the Nawab's mingled rashness and timidity, placed him on the throne after a few anxious moments of indecision and the cannonade of Plassey in June 1757. In these events Clive showed qualities of a high order, since he moved with deftness and resolution through a maze of uncertainty and intrigue. But they were diplomatic rather than military, for the actual fighting was slight.

To Clive the guerilla leader and diplomatist we now have to

add Clive the kingmaker and plunderer. Overnight he found himself, as he thought, the de Bussy of wealthy Bengal and Bihar who could dispose of their riches to the Company and his followers. But the experiment which began on Hyderabad lines with the displacement of one ruler by another and his maintenance by the European force of the kingmaker ended very differently. After de Bussy there remained Mughal Hyderabad; after Clive there was never an independent Bengal. In external affairs Clive equalled his model. He was able to break up a Dutch armament and take Dutch Chinsura, he repulsed the Mughal heir-apparent (later Shah Alam) when he tried to reassert his rights, and he protected the provincial governors from the longing financial glances of Mir Jafar. He even obtained a Mughal title from Delhi.* It was in internal matters that the experiment went wrong. The trouble here was the presence of European merchants and their's and the Company's commercial interests, factors both largely absent in Hyderabad. With thoughts of Alivardi's treasure-hoard in mind private payments of more than a million sterling were stipulated in addition to the official compensation of which Clive's share was £234,000 and a land grant worth about £30,000 a year. When the fabled forty millions turned out to be only one and a half these payments were still insisted on. Mir Jafar found himself in constant want of money and involved in endless financial disputes with people who possessed irresistible force and believed he still had a secret hoard somewhere. The financial bleeding of Bengal had begun. As appetite grows by what it feeds on these *douceurs* led to further demands. Mir Kasim on his accession in 1760 paid £200,000 to the Council and his successor three years later another £139,000 to the same council. The returned merchants demanded their share and were rewarded with the abolition of duties on their personal or private trade in Bengal. They were thus able to undercut their Bengali competitors at every turn. They could do more, and here we come to another vital difference from Hyderabad. Once the Company's forces had established their superiority over the Nawab's the whole countryside lay at the mercy of its agents because of its unwarlike nature.

* *Sabat Jung* – the tried in battle.

Any merchant who could hire a few followers could browbeat the Nawabi officers and intimidate the villagers as they could never have done with the chiefs and tougher peasants in the Deccan. This process was made the more easy by the fact that the Company at this time had no direct ruling powers and could plead that it had no responsibility for the actions of its merchants in the interior.

After 1757 there thus grew up a state of Bengal administered by the Nawab but where the military power was in the hands of the Company who used it to help themselves to the revenue and to give their merchants a free run of the country's internal trade. The sponsored state became a plundered state. In a few years Bengal was ruined and the Company brought to the verge of bankruptcy. The situation could develop without outside interference because of the distracted state of the more vigorous parts of the country. It was from this unpromising start that the first Company's dominion grew to become the basis for the later hegemony. It is this dominion of Bengal which may be described as the Company Bahadur.*

Clive, though he had himself opened the floodgates, kept the merchants within bounds, until his return to Britain in 1760. Within a year the Calcutta Council displaced Mir Jafar for a supposedly more pliant nawab, and, when they found that in fact he was more resolute and was organizing an army, replaced him in turn after a severe campaign. The bone of contention was again free private trade. Alarmed by this news and that of a renewed invasion of Shah Alam, and perhaps still more by a reduction in profits (for fighting costs money), the Company sent Clive back to Calcutta in 1765 as a kind of poacher turned gamekeeper. Acting with extraordinary vigour in two years he transformed the situation and laid the foundation of the Company's Indian dominion. He first dealt with the internal situation. Shah Alam and Shuja-ad-daula of Oudh had already been defeated at Baksar, but Clive had to decide where to limit his authority. It was tempting to march to Delhi and administer the whole Jumna-Ganges valley as the imperial deputy. There was

* The popular honorific for the Company. Literally, the valiant or brave company.

no physical obstacle but Clive realized that the Company was not then fitted to play an imperial role in India and decided to limit his commitments. It was not the least of his achievements. Shuja was restored to Oudh, with a subsidiary force and guarantee of defence, the emperor Shah Alam solaced with Allahabad and a tribute and the frontier drawn at the boundary of Bihar. In Bengal itself he took a decisive step. In return for restoring Shah Alam to Allahabad he received the imperial grant of the *diwani* or revenue authority in Bengal and Bihar to the Company. This had hitherto been enjoyed by the nawab, so that now there was a double government, the nawab retaining judicial and police functions, the Company exercising the revenue power. The Company was acclimatized, as it were, into the Indian scene by becoming the Mughal revenue agent for Bengal and Bihar. There was as yet no thought of direct administration, and the revenue was collected by a Company-appointed deputy-nawab, one Muhammad Reza Khan. But this arrangement made the Company the virtual ruler of Bengal since it already possessed decisive military power. All that was left to the nawab was the control of the judicial administration. But he was now persuaded to hand this over to the Company's deputy-nawab, so that its control was virtually complete. The machine of administration remained Indian, with Mughal trappings and titles, but the control was that of the Company.

Clive's third task was his hardest : the disciplining of the Company's servants. He came armed with powers to restrain present-taking and regulate internal private trade but few expected him to implement his instructions. He took a high line from the first so that the alternative was submission or return to England. The value of presents receivable was sharply limited. Private trade was forbidden and instead a Society of Trade set up which distributed the profits of the salt monopoly in fixed proportions according to rank. Though disavowed by the Company later it was the starting-point of a system of graded salaries. He finally reduced military allowances or *batta* and quelled with characteristic vigour a 'White mutiny' organized by one of the brigadiers.

After two years of this tempestuous activity Clive returned to England to become enmeshed in the webs of Company intrigues and English politics, and to die by his own hand seven years later. Affairs in Bengal slipped back while the Company counted on profits which never actually materialized and slipped towards bankruptcy. Nevertheless, Clive's work was not wholly undone. The outline of a Company's state in India had been traced and a rough shape had been given to its organization. If still more rapacious than an average Indian state or Mughal *subah*, in that a larger proportion of the national income was creamed off by the rulers and less returned to the ruled, at least the open plunder of the early sixties had been stopped. The great blunder of the Company (and Clive) at this time was the belief that the surplus Bengal revenue could pay for the Company's annual investment; a belief whose fallacy rested on their failure to prevent their servants from syphoning off the major part of this surplus into their own pockets or those of their friends at home.

The threatened bankruptcy of the Company stirred them to a fresh effort at reform. On the one hand Warren Hastings was appointed with a mandate for reform, on the other an appeal was made to the State for a loan. The result was the beginnings of state control of the Company and the thirteen-year governorship of Warren Hastings. The cross currents of state interference with the Regulating Act, of company intrigues and of political rancour as India became a subject of personal and party politics, have made this period the most colourful in British Indian history. The drama was heightened by the personality of Warren Hastings himself, which, like an inflatable lifeboat in a stormy sea, seemed to grow larger as the waves grew higher. His subtle and flexible personality, concealing an implacable will and unbending purpose, came so to dominate the scene that the study of the period became largely a question of pro- or anti-Hastings. His latest biographer is no exception to this rule.* But here we are concerned with Warren Hastings's relevance to India and we must leave the personal controversies and psychological studies to the standard works.

Broadly speaking, it may be said that Hastings provided a coherent shape to a state of which Clive had only sketched an outline, and he successfully defended that state almost single-

* Keith Feiling, *Warren Hastings*, London, 1954.

handed with hardly any help from home against a concerted Indian attack. When he left India the Company Bahadur of Bengal, with its branches or bridgeheads in Madras and Bombay, was one of the recognized great powers of India. An adventurer's *tour de force* had become a solid political fact. The greatness of the achievement may be measured by the size and number of the obstacles; the shortcomings of his agents, still largely corrupt and more mercantile than political in outlook; divided counsels and jealousies in Bombay, Madras, and London; personal animosities on his council and perpetual intrigues at home. His greatness lay in the fact that he won through in spite of them without loss of vision; the price was a certain souring of temper which transformed the resilient governor of 1772 into the suspicious, secretive, self-justifying, and relentless ruler of the seventeen-eighties. In a sense, both sides in the great controversy were right, for both greatness and meanness are to be found in him. But seen in the context of his times Hastings becomes neither a monster nor a martyr. His study becomes the fascinating one of a man of great powers under enormous strains both from within and without, never sure of his position for long and always compelled to act as if he was.

Hastings's first important work was that of an organizer. In the two and a half years before the Regulating Act came into force he put in order the whole Bengal administration. The Indian deputies who had collected the revenue on behalf of the Company were deposed and their places taken by a Board of Revenue in Calcutta and English collectors in the districts. This was the real beginning of British administration in India. It was by no means direct rule but it did introduce a new principle in the idea of European superintendence of Indian agency. In the actual control of the revenue administration Hastings was not so happy, achieving little more than a series of abortive experiments. But it must be remembered that not only had he little experience of revenue matters himself but that he lacked reliable colleagues and that most of those from whom information could be collected were interested in concealing the truth. Hastings was much more successful in his commercial reforms. The *dastaks* or free passes for the private trade of the Company's servants were

finally abolished in 1773. Duties on all goods except the monopoly articles of salt, betel-nut, and tobacco were lowered to a
uniform rate of two and a half per cent and the flow of trade
stimulated by the limitation of customs houses to five main
centres. Measures which ten years before had led to the outvoting
of the governor and a sharply-contested war were carried through
by Hastings's dexterity virtually without protest or opposition.

The next theme of Hastings's time was his struggles with his
Council. These were precipitated by the passing of the Regulating Act in 1773, which not only made Hastings Governor-General with supervisory authority over Madras and Bombay but
named three members of a Council of four from the public men
of England of whom at least one, Philip Francis, thought that
he would make a much better Governor-General than Hastings
himself. The details of these struggles have proved fascinating
for those who love drama and personalities, but we are here concerned with their relevance for India. Their first result was to
make any consistent internal policy difficult, so that the real organization of the British Indian or Bengali dominion was postponed for a decade. Their next consequence was to spread
faction throughout the Company's service in Bengal and back
in Leadenhall Street and Westminster. As the struggle proceeded
you were either a Hastings or a Francis man, and later just pro-
or anti- Hastings. As a result every settlement was provisional,
every action open to revision. The harmony and order which
Hastings had introduced in his first two years were lost and the
new morale which he had begun to build could not be maintained. He himself had to use some of the old methods to maintain his support both in Bengal and London. The cleansing of
the administration also had to wait a decade. A third result was
the gradual souring of Hastings's temper as well as the steady
expansion of his personality. Hastings came to dominate the
British Indian scene as no man had done before or after him and
his record has fascinated men's minds and bedevilled their judgement ever since. It was the strains of this struggle which led him
to the acts about which controversy lingers. The Rohilla campaign of 1774 was an act of state against which criticism was not
sustained. But his acquiescence in the judicial murder of Nand

Kumar, his goading of the Raja of Benares into revolt in 1781 by repeating exactions, and the harassment of the Begams of Oudh for the same reason were incidents foreign to the nature of the younger and more genial Hastings of 1772-74. Francis had his revenge in inveigling Burke to undertake the impeachment of Hastings, but the court of posterity has found for Hastings against both.

Hastings's supreme work was the preservation of the British dominion from Indian assault while one hand was, so to speak, tied behind his back by these internal dissensions. Apart from this his difficulties were briefly the jealousy of Madras and Bombay, the existence of two restless and expanding Indian powers in the Marathas and Haidar Ali of Mysore, and his isolation from Britain itself, begun by the outbreak of the American War of Independence in 1775 and made almost complete by the addition of France and the European coalition in 1778. Hastings's dauntless spirit and undeviating statecraft shone at its brightest when, menaced by an Indian coalition and cut off from Britain by the American–European war, he heard successively of the surrender of Burgoyne at Saratoga and of Cornwallis at Yorktown.

Madras and Bombay were jealous because they had been independent governments responsible only to London until the Regulating Act came into force in 1774. It happened that the one faced the able and expansive Muslim adventurer, Haidar Ali of Mysore, and the other the heart of the formidable Maratha power at Poona. The object of Hastings's policy was the simple one of maintaining the existing Bengal dominion intact and avoiding entanglements with Indian powers. The Company's primary object was still trade and trade required peace. Hastings's first venture was to lend a brigade to enable the ruler of Oudh to subdue in 1774 the unruly Rohillas to the west of his dominions. The object was to protect the buffer state of Oudh from Maratha attack; the method laid Hastings open to the charge that he was interfering in the affairs of an Indian state and condoning the behaviour of the Nawab of Oudh's troops. His next problem was the Marathas and for this he had to thank the Bombay government. The Maratha power was now reviving after the catas-

trophe of Panipat. But in 1772 the promising young Peshwa
died and the Poona government was plunged into a series of
succession struggles. In 1774 the Peshwa's brother was murdered
with the connivance of his uncle, Raghunath Rao who was, however, driven away by a party supporting the Peshwa's posthu-
mous son. Bombay supported Raghunath and was overruled by
Hastings who was in turn overruled by the Directors. They
capped their former censures of interference in weak states by
now authorizing interference in a strong one. Before a force
from Bengal could reach Bombay after a brilliant march across
India the Bombay army had been trapped and forced to surrender on its way to Poona at Wadgaon in 1779. The war
dragged on for three more years until Hastings, having detached
the ablest chief Sindia by his diplomacy, was able to make peace
at Salbai in 1782.

. While the Maratha war was in progress a fresh crisis arose in
the south as the result of the follies of the Madras government.
The affairs of Madras had long been in disorder; one unnecessary war with Mysore had been provoked in 1769. In 1776 Lord
Pigot, the defender of Madras against the French, who had been
sent back to carry out reforms, was arrested by his own Council
and died in captivity the following year. The Madras government by its tactlessness then induced a coalition of the usually
hostile Marathas, the Nizam of Hyderabad, and Haidar Ali of
Mysore, without preparing any means for meeting it. In 1780
the Carnatic was overrun to the walls at Madras and two armies
defeated. Hastings then rose to his full stature. With the Bombay
war still on his hands he suspended the Madras governor, poured
in supplies and troops with his best general. In a year he restored
the situation and then detached first the Nizam and then the
Marathas. Thus strengthened he was able to meet the threat of
the French fleet under the gallant de Suffren and the landing of
a French force under de Bussy. Haidar died in 1782 and peace
was concluded with his son Tipu at Mangalore in 1784.

Hastings's work was to show that the Company's territories
could be defended against the strongest available union of Indian powers single-handed and without help from Europe. He
also showed that, given sufficient resolution, one man could con-

trol the distant and factious governments of Madras and Bombay. Henceforth there were not three Company's governments in India but one. Henceforth the British dominion in India was not only established in the country but recognized as one of its great powers. As there were no such things in India at that time as historic frontiers or a recognized balance of power, that dominion had to grow greater if it was not to become smaller. In this sense Hastings can be called the real founder of the British dominion in India. He found a revenue administration and he left a state.

8

THE BENGAL STATE AND HEGEMONY

IF Clive founded the British Indian state (though in rather the style of a robber baron) and Warren Hastings gave it coherence (though sorely hindered by his enemies in Bengal and in London) and made it politically viable, it was Cornwallis who gave it definite form and stamped on it characteristics of its own. The Company's dominion in India became a distinct state both Indian and English, for which it is convenient to use the label 'Company Bahadur'.* This state was of the type which any other conqueror might have established, though of course it had characteristic English features. In itself it presaged no revolution or transformation of India, but only the first stages of a new cycle of conquest, consolidation, prosperity, and decline. But since the administrative measures then taken radically affected the form of later Indian public life, it is worth looking at it as a whole.

The appointment of Cornwallis as Governor-General in 1786 was the direct result of the controversies aroused by the acts of Clive and the régime of Hastings. The near bankruptcy of the Company brought on intervention by the state which reversed the natural order of events by eventually entirely replacing the child by the parent. The Company's appeal led to a series of parliamentary inquiries and the facts then revealed gave ample ammunition to all those jealous of the Company's monopoly as well as to those with a feeling for the public good. Controversy ranged in effect from the inquiries of 1772 through the discussions of the India bills in the eighties to Warren Hastings's impeachment, which did not end until 1795. By a process of prolonged discussion, which included the passionate partisanship of Burke, of trial and error, of often clumsy manoeuvres and ungracious actions with some downright injustice as well, certain broad principles of the relationship of India with Britain were worked out. There was to be no private mercantile British dominion in India. The actions of officials in India were to be accountable in England. The Company as an Indian ruler was

* *Bahadur* – brave or valiant. A common honorific for the Company.

responsible for the welfare of its Indian subjects. The first of these objects was achieved by parliamentary legislation; the other two were clinched by Warren Hastings's impeachment. The attack on Hastings began as a private vendetta by Sir Philip Francis. It became a national project when the sympathy and passions of Burke were aroused and the support of the Whig party secured. The impeachment was permitted to continue by Pitt very possibly to divert Whig energies and Burkean passions into a political side-channel. It ran its dreary nine-years course because no one had the courage to stop it. The net result was to ruin the career of Hastings, who was shown in the course of the proceedings to have saved British India. This discreditable episode yet had important results. The charges were political, but the background was the suggestion of irresponsible tyranny. The political ruin of the most distinguished Indian statesman the Company had produced, even though he was finally acquitted, underlined the determination of Parliament to enforce the principles already laid down by the Regulating and India Acts. Henceforth no one could act irresponsibly or tyrannically in India and hope to get away with it.

The legal links were the Regulating Act of 1773 and Pitt's India Act of 1784. The Regulating Act bound Bombay and Madras to Hastings in Bengal in unwilling subordination and Hastings himself to a vindictive council in Calcutta. Only a man of supreme talent could have carried a state through ten years of crisis and war in such circumstances. The India Act set up a double government by which the Company was overseen in London by a minister known as the President of the Board of Control and in Calcutta by a Governor-General in whose appointment the state had the dominant voice. Thus British India broadly came under national control and was subject to the parliamentary directives of non-aggression, clean administration, and attention to the welfare of the people. In some hands much of the act might have been a dead letter. It worked because its creators were Pitt, then at the beginning of his long ministry, and his working partner Dundas, who for seventeen years was left to 'run in' the machine.

Cornwallis enjoyed more authority in British India than anyone before and few after him. Like Dundas he was one of Pitt's inner circle and he also was a landed magnate in his own right and a soldier whose reputation had survived Yorktown. He was Pitt's agent in India and he ruled for seven years. He was beyond the reach of Company opposition in India or of undermining operations at home; he could firmly refuse even the Prince of Wales's requests for patronage.

Cornwallis's first act was to reassert the authority of the state and cleanse the administration. He called his predecessor Macpherson's government 'a system of the dirtiest jobbing'. He suspended the whole Board of Revenue for irregularities and sent many servants home. He enforced the new rules against private trade and insisted on the Company providing generous salaries in its place. He then reorganized the whole administration. Hitherto a 'factor' might in turn hold commercial, political, and administrative posts. The Company was essentially still a commercial body administering a state as a side-line. It was only natural that many companies' servants should consider that their main business was still to make a fortune with public spirit as a desirable extra. Cornwallis altered all this. The service was divided into commercial and political branches, into one or other of which you had to opt. Henceforth you were either a merchant or an administrator, but not both. As a merchant you could still trade on your own but as an official you had to be content with a large salary. This was the beginning of the Civil Service as known in the nineteenth century and the beginning of the end of the Company's commercial activities. Government in its world was now more important than trade.

Cornwallis's next major measure was the Europeanization of the services. Previously, large use had been made of Indian agency up to the use of a deputy nawab for revenue and judicial purposes. Cornwallis had a strong sense of Indian shortcomings. 'Every native of India, I verily believe,' he wrote, 'is corrupt.' His view of his own countrymen in India was not very different, but whereas he saw a cure for them he could see none at the time for Indians. So, with the exception of Ali Ibrahim Khan, 'the incorruptible judge of Benares', all high Indian officials were dismissed and all posts worth more than £500 a year reserved for the Company's civil service which was in return reserved for Europeans. This measure marked the Company's service with an indelibly foreign stamp, and its effects were felt right down to 1947.

Cornwallis's third great measure was the settlement of the revenue and land system of Bengal. Here again, his work lasted into the twentieth century. In Bengal and Bihar the revenue had previously been collected through hereditary *zamindars*. The word *zamindar* means literally a landholder, which can cover the meanings of owner, tax-collector, and some kind of mixture between the two. The *zamindars* of Bengal were really the rural agents of the government. What they paid was subject to an annual wrangle with the government officers, and, while they might be beaten and maltreated to make them pay more, they were rarely actually dispossessed. What the villages could actually pay was the *zamindar*'s secret; the difference between what they could squeeze from the village and what the government could squeeze from them was their living. Thus settlements of land tax were annual, though the measurements on which the assessments were made traditional ones were based on the great survey made in the time of Akbar. In addition to this function they had police and magisterial powers in their jurisdictions. Raja Chait Singh of Banaras, who was browbeaten by Hastings, was one of the biggest men of this class. Below the *zamindars* came the cultivating peasants. They were exposed to the rods of the *zamindars* as the *zamindars* were liable to the rods of the government officers, but like the *zamindars* themselves they had a traditional hereditary right and were rarely dispossessed.

The great difficulty of the Company was to know how much the countryside could safely pay. This was the *zamindars'* secret which they were disinclined to share since their living depended on its exploitation. At first, the Company's demand together with its servants' derangement of the local economy led to over-collection. The hardships of this were heightened by the great famine of 1769–70 when the Company tried to collect the revenue as usual. Bengal sank from a state of fabled prosperity to rural misery. Hastings made several attempts to regularize the situation but he never succeeded in penetrating the *zamindars'* secret. Cornwallis had the advantage of Hastings's experience and of the services of one of the ablest of the Company's servants in John Shore, who was to succeed him as Governor-General. Cornwallis was himself an English landlord of the better sort, and a strong believer in authority, fair-play, and stability. Given these premises, it is easy to understand what happened. Settlements were made with the *zamindars* for a term of years, fixed at ten in 1789 and finally made permanent. Cornwallis in fact looked on them as landlords. They were to be the government agents for keeping the countryside quiet and in return were to be given security of tenure as long as they paid their dues and the un-earned increment of the land arising from rising revenue of increased cultivation. But there are certain features which pre-vented the idyllic results of Cornwallis's hopes from being real-ized. The cultivator was to be secure as long as he paid *his* dues to the *zamindar*. But there was no way of determining exactly what these were and the means of redress lay in the new English courts which were in effect out of his reach and beyond his un-derstanding. So the peasant became in effect a tenant-at-will of the *zamindar*. The *zamindar* was to make a fixed annual pay-ment to the government, retaining one tenth of his collection as his fee. But at first the rates were high and prices did not rise, so that he could not pay even by squeezing the peasant. Then he was sold up in a civilized British way instead of being beaten up but left where he was in the Mughal way. The result was a big change in *zamindari* personnel and the appearance of new men from Calcutta who bought estates as financial speculations. The new landlords were often absentees with no local connexions. The Bengal peasantry became a rustic proletariat and Corn-wallis's benevolent, improving landlord a Calcutta rentier. A final touch was the removal of police powers from the *zamindars* and with them their last direct touch with the peasants. The net result was stability at the price of justice and good relationships.

Cornwallis's final work was in the legal sphere. Hastings had organized a system of courts and the Regulating Act had brought in a Supreme Court which administered English law to the confusion of Indian litigants. Cornwallis took over crim-

inal administration from the deputy-nawab, and by pruning the
Muslim criminal code of some barbaric features produced a code
much more humane than that of contemporary England and
one of the most enlightened in the world. He formed civil district courts in each of twenty-three districts with four courts of
appeal. These courts were too remote, expensive, and dilatory to
be of much value to the people at the time. But Cornwallis added
two features which were eventually proved to be of great significance and to be regarded as the sheet-anchors of liberty by the
middle class to be. These were the separation of judicial and
executive powers in the district courts and the rule of law. This
latter, now a keystone in the Indian legal arch, is so important
that the regulation is worth quoting in full.

The collectors of revenue and their officers, and indeed all officers
the Government, shall be amenable to the courts for acts done in
their official capacities, and Government itself, in cases in which it
may be a party in matters of property shall submit its rights to be
tried in these courts under the existing laws and regulations.*

When Cornwallis handed over to his lieutenant Shore in 1793
he left him an Indian state which now had a visible shape and
form. It covered Bengal and Bihar as far as Benares and had, as
it were, two reluctant dependencies in Madras and Bombay.
Cornwallis is often thought of as an anglicizer and the new state
as an aggressively western one. In fact it was much more in the
Indian than the English tradition, as a closer examination will
show. At the top stood the Governor-General, now supreme in
his council and subject only to the authority of the Directors and
the President of the Board of Control in London. In fact he was
secure so long as he had the support of the President and the
cabinet. He had direct control over the Bengal presidency, which
was the main block of the Company's state, and supervisory and
over-ruling powers in Madras and Bombay. The supports of his
authority were the army and the services. The Company's army
had Indian regiments with European officers and some European troops; there were also royal troops which were augmented
in times of crisis. The services were now Europeanized in the

* *Cornwallis Correspondence*, Vol. II, p. 558.

middle and upper cadres and divided into the revenue, judicial, and commercial branches. The members were regularly paid and had begun to acquire standards of integrity and an *esprit de corps* of their own. The country was divided into twenty-three districts in which a new police force maintained law and order, a judge administered the law, and a collector was responsible for revenue collection. He worked, as had been noted, mainly through local magnates. The state was pledged to non-aggression but in fact Cornwallis waged one major war and even the pacific Shore forcibly replaced the unfriendly ruler of a neighbouring state. The land revenue, which most closely affected the life of the people, was collected along traditional lines, though with new personnel at the top and enhanced power for the *zamindars*. For the rest customary life pursued its way largely untouched, religious and social observances and occasions continued as before, commerce and industry ran in the normal channels. The ordinary Bengali might have felt that, after the troubles of the sixties and seventies, life was once more following its accustomed course. The chief difference was that the rulers were new. They were perhaps less compatible than their predecessors, but that was partly because they were strange whereas the Muslims were familiar. They were both foreign and both impure as they had been for over five hundred years. True, there had been some displacement of classes. The old Muslim governing class was now in retirement with broken fortunes and the mainly Hindu *zamindars* were about to follow them. A new class of monied men had arisen in the towns, acting as the go-betweens of the new rulers. There was a lack of such patronage of religion and art as even the late government had practised, a rush of wealth and disregard for piety which all lovers of the old ways deplored. But these things mainly affected the towns and the great ones. In the vast countryside the essential pattern of life was unchanged, nor were its ideas or customs challenged.

The new state was in fact in the framework of the Indian tradition, for all Cornwallis's calculated Englishry. It had little in common with English institutions; the checks and balances of eighteenth-century England were in fact the very things which had been cast aside in the previous twenty years. A 'constitutional' governor became a virtually absolute governor-general, independent presidencies became subordinate. But when a comparison is made with the Mughal and *nawabi* régimes which preceded it the story is quite different. We find the head of the state comparable to the emperor or the *subahdar*. Each had his great show of authority, his inner ring of advisers, the public opinion of his own officials to consider. The governor-general, it is true was subordinate to London, but London was distant and pre-occupied and he had in practice a large latitude of action. His position resembled that of a Bengal *subahdar* nearly a century before, who, while subject in a very real sense to the Emperor Aurangzeb in the distant Deccan, could enjoy a large liberty of action so long as he obeyed orders, collected the revenue, and transmitted the tribute. The pattern of the state followed broadly Mughal lines down to the division of authority between the military and revenue branches. Both were essentially foreign, in personnel as well as in culture. It must be remembered that through most of the Mughal period seventy per cent of the higher officers were foreign born and only half the remainder Hindus. A Muslim Pathan was quite as foreign to a Bengali, though more familiar perhaps, than an Englishman or a Scotsman. In both régimes a foreign culture was cultivated by those at the top expressed in a foreign language (Persian and English). These languages were cultivated as a matter of business by all those who wanted to 'get on' in government circles. Both governments were what may be called police states, or, more politely perhaps, law and order states. That is, they were not concerned with promoting any special order of society, social, religious, political, or economic. They were content to provide a framework for society within which traditional cultures could pursue their ways, commerce and agriculture proceed unmolested. Hindu and Muslim agreed in this, that it was the ruler's duty to preserve society, not to destroy it or transform it. The Company Bahadur, though more aloof from the local cultures because alien to both, adopted essentially the same attitude.

If the correspondence of the two states was so close, must it be said that new Company was but old Mughal writ large? The argument has been that the new state, as Cornwallis left it, did not differ in kind from the old, though there were many differences in detail such as a new personnel, a new system of courts, and a much more efficient army. But there were certain changes which, though they may have seemed to have made little difference at the time, proved to be significant in the light of later developments which could not then be foreseen. Warren Hastings, who never ceased speculating in the midst of his cares, believed in what might be called the strictly Mughal pattern. The English as foreigners would rule Indians on Indian lines, largely through Indian agency. Their governmental rule was supervision rather than detailed administration. They were the guardians of an ancient society and as such they would protect and foster it; they would patronize its religions, its arts, its literature. Cornwallis, who left others to consider the implications of his acts, proceeded on a different plan. He thought of the English as ruling Indians for their good, but on European rather than Indian lines. And since what he saw of Indian culture did not impress him he would patronize it as little as possible. But he would not interfere with it either. To the contemporary Indian his attitude meant more foreigners and more aloofness, but no revolutionary change. It was in the future that this seed was to bear unexpected fruit. Apart from this Cornwallis introduced two features into Indian society, neither of which was much regarded at the time because neither was fully understood. One was the rule of law which was outside current Indian experience and related to newfangled courts and therefore not taken seriously. The class which was to benefit by it had not yet arisen. The other was the introduction of English landlordism. This had, in fact, a large impact on the cultivator, but its implications were not realized at once. And it was, after all, an adjustment of relationships rather than a revolution in them.

Within twenty-five years of Cornwallis's departure, leaving behind as he thought, an unaggressive and stable state within the complex of the Indian political system, the state had swallowed up its rivals to become the ruler of most of India and overlord of the remainder. The process was dramatic and colourful, an epic for the imperialist Anglo-Indian historian; so much was gained in so short a time against such odds and in the face of such difficulties at home. The details of the process are the proper province of larger histories; here we can only mention its principal features since it was a necessary prelude to the next step in Anglo-Indian relations. Cornwallis left India in peace and this was in general maintained by Shore.

With the arrival of Lord Mornington (better known as Lord Wellesley) a dramatic change occurred. There had been a change in the climate of opinion in England, for Pitt and Dundas were now faced with an embattled revolutionary France and the rising young general Bonaparte. He was even then conducting his army to Egypt with its implied threat to India. In India itself the Company had a declared enemy in the brilliant if erratic Tipu Sultan of Mysore, and the Marathas, for all their divisions, might yield to French blandishments. Prudence therefore seemed to dictate some forward move. In Company circles, also, there was increasing pressure to advance as the cheapest way, in the long run, of securing satisfactory conditions of trade. To these spurs to action must be added the personality of Wellesley himself, then only thirty-seven years old, full of ambition and energy, and a convinced imperialist. He at once seized on the injudicious reception by Tipu of a stranded French party and the even more injudicious advertisement of the fact by the French governor of Mauritius (then the Île de France) to stage a campaign against him. Wellesley organized this himself and showed that his ability matched both his energy and ambition. In May 1799 Tipu fell fighting bravely in the breach of his fortress capital of Seringapatam. Half his state was annexed and the rest restored to the child heir of the dispossessed rajahs of Mysore. This was the real beginning of British territorial dominion in South India.

The destruction of Tipu provided a release for British energies. It removed a bogey which had overshadowed all their activities in South India for thirty years and which seemed to show that even brilliant men of fortune, relying only on mercenaries, could still withstand and on occasion humiliate the Company's forces. Now the rest of India lay open before them, a scene of division, decay, and ineptitude. Divisions afflicted the Marathas, decay the Nizam, and ineptitude the Rajputs. The effect on Wellesley was no less electric. He had crushed the Company's best organized and most resolute foe. He would now see how far he could go before the opposition solidified again. He gathered round him a group of able and ardent men who were later to finish his work and, as the organizers of the new British India, to look with something like awe at the magnitude of their achievement. At home, the government, faced with the still rising power of Napoleon, was content to give him a free hand so long as he was successful. Only the Directors queried the expense and resented the arrogance of their agent.

Wellesley then proceeded to acquire lands from certain helpless states. On the pretext of discovered correspondence with Tipu the Carnatic, or coastal strip from the river Kistna to Cape Comorin on which Madras stood, was annexed. The Nawab was pensioned off, a sufficient reward, Wellesley considered, for an alliance of over fifty-years standing. The Nawab of Oudh was brought to the point of offering to abdicate and then penalized for retracting by the loss of half his state. The commercially useful Mughal fragment of Surat on the west coast was absorbed. Wellesley now sought to take advantage of the acute divisions and jealousies of the remaining Indian states. For this purpose he employed the device of the subsidiary treaty. He would guarantee the independence of a threatened state in return for control of its external relations. The method was to station a force of the Company's troops in the capital, available to deal with any attack. These were under the control of a British Resident and were paid for by the state itself. Thus, should the state fall out with the Company, it would find the Company's hand already at its heart. The financial arrangement made internal interference possible at any time on the ground of non-payment of the subsidy for the force. In the then circumstances the whole arrangement meant for any state freedom from Indian conquest at the price of subjection to the British.

Wellesley's first great success with this weapon was with Hyderabad in 1798. The Nizam was old and discouraged and harassed by the Marathas. For him it was an easy way out, for his successors the end of free action. A decisive moment came when the Peshwa Baji Rao, hard pressed by his own chiefs, bought security by the Treaty of Bassein in December 1802. He was the head of the Maratha confederacy and his action was a shattering blow to Maratha pride. In 1803 the Maratha chiefs went to war, to be defeated by Arthur Wellesley and Lord Lake. All seemed set for a British *raj* up to the Sutlej when next year the chief Holkar staged a spectacular recovery. It became clear that the Company had overstrained its strength. Britain, then faced with invasion by Napoleon, was in no position to send reinforcements. Wellesley was recalled in 1805.

There followed eight years of marking time while the Napoleonic empire rose and fell in Europe. The Company stood its ground in the north from the Ganges to the Sutlej but withdrew from Rajasthan and the centre. Lord Minto preferred embassies to armies and limited his conquests to the seizure of Mauritius and France's Dutch satellite's island of Java. It was hoped that the remaining Indian powers would somehow sort themselves out and achieve a stable state system. But they did no such thing. Instead the situation was aggravated by the growth of marauding robber bands called Pindaris. They were recruited from disbanded armies and displaced villagers and it was nobody's interest to suppress them. The chaos which they wrought in central India and their raids on British India provided a powerful pretext for the final British intervention. Independent India, as then constituted, was filling the cup of anarchy in readiness for the Company. Apart from Ranjit Singh in the Panjab, who was blocked from the rest of India by the Sind and Rajasthan deserts and the British on the Sutlej, it contained no personality of power and no element of political hope.

In 1815 Napoleon was finally defeated. Already, in 1813, when the Company was given a new charter, commercial interests in England had grown strong enough to break the Company's trade monopoly. The feeling was now strong that India contained great potential wealth and that, according to free trade principles, monopoly would hinder rather than encourage its exploitation. The corollary of this view was the completion of British supremacy as a commercial necessity and a practical, economical way of arranging for this development. It would be far cheaper to keep your armies on the Sutlej and police the rest of India than to maintain a circle of forces around an anarchical centre as well as man far longer and more complicated frontiers. The benefit of supremacy for the internal flow of trade is too obvious to need stressing. The Indian situation and British opinion were thus ready for action; the clearing of European skies provided the opportunity. The final phase fell to the Marquess of Hastings (he came to India as the Earl of Moira), a one time friend of the Prince Regent and manager of Warren Hastings's impeachment, who turned out to be a capable planner and a seasoned statesman. He first waged a frontier war with the Gurkhas (1815–16) from which both sides emerged with a mutual respect which has continued to this day. He then drew up a master plan for the extirpation of the Pindaris in their central Indian lairs with the cooperation of the Maratha chiefs on pain of war. The Marathas were too spirited to submit and too divided to unite. The result was a straggling, disorganized war with inevitable disaster to their cause. Sindia submitted in time to save his state at the price of his loss of control of Rajasthan. The freebooter Amir Khan was made respectable as the ruler of Tonk. The Peshwa in Poona, the Bhonsla in Nagpur, and Holkar's forces took arms at different times and were defeated in detail. The Pindaris were hunted hither and thither until their bands broke up and their leaders scattered. By mid 1818 all was over. The chief political casualty was the Peshwa's territories which were annexed to Bombay, the Peshwa himself being pensioned off near Kanpur. The big political result was the establishment of British hegemony in India up to the banks of the Sutlej. The surviving Maratha states now entered the orbit of the British system, having lost their own sun in the person of the Peshwa. The Rajput states, freed from Maratha control, hastened to conclude subsidiary treaties with the British. Desolated and depressed by Maratha domination, they were happy to resume their traditional position of Mughal times as feudatories of the paramount power.

9

SUPREMACY – WHY AND WHEREFORE

THE officers who now organized the new British dominion of India had in many cases started their careers as ardent members of Lord Wellesley's 'nursery'. Now, prematurely aged and with experience beyond their years, they looked with surprise and awe at the magnitude of their achievement.* They thought that their dominion was precarious, that underground forces, particularly religious, might at any time break out and overwhelm them. The thought that Indians, as the result of 'improving' or westernizing measures, might eventually take over their own government, was to occur to them. But even Mountstuart Elphinstone, who thought it 'the most desirable death for us to die', and Charles Metcalfe, who acquiesced in the possibility, thought any such development 'at an immeasurable distance'. They would both have been much surprised to see the Indian flag hoisted in Delhi only a hundred and twenty-nine years later.

When we consider that it took less than eighty years for a foreign mercantile body from a distant country to gain control over a whole sub-continent containing an ancient civilization of its own and a rival alien culture with imperial traditions and a rich store of political, military, and cultural experience there is indeed matter for surprise and reflection. It was not as if the new rulers had descended from some other world, as the Spaniards appeared in Mexico and Peru. The British had traded in India for a century and a half before taking up arms. They and other Europeans like the Portuguese and the Dutch were well known to Indian men-of-affairs who thought that they had taken their measure. The fact of the British success would therefore certainly seem to require some explanation. The theory that pleased nineteenth-century Europeans was the intrinsic superiority of the west over the east, to which the late century imperialists added the rider of the exceptional qualities of the Anglo-Saxon race. What could an Asian do against a Clive or a Hastings, a Lawrence or a Nicholson? Later experience of no less able Europeans

* Charles Metcalfe, 'King' of Delhi 1810–18, was thirty-three in 1818.

striving with very different results, if not the still small voice of reason, has sufficiently exposed the fallacy of this view. Nor is the old nationalist argument of British perfidy and wickedness any more convincing. The British of the time were no better than others and no doubt had their share of wickedness, but there had never been a case where mere badness produced such large results. And did not the Evangelicals hold that Indian civilization itself was wicked and corrupt? Some other factors were plainly at work.

Setting aside the arguments of intrinsic superiority and wickedness we come to the question of leadership. In imperialist eyes this was a facet of general superiority, heaven-born leaders being merely embodiments of the general principle. In the persons of men like Clive, Warren Hastings, Lord and Arthur Wellesley, Charles Metcalfe, and Mountstuart Elphinstone the British did in fact enjoy exceptional leadership. But the fact must also be faced that India had exceptional leaders too. Haidar Ali and Tipu Sultan, a line of Peshwas, Nana Fadnavis of Poona, Madhu Rao Sindia, Jaswant Rao Holkar, and Ranjit Singh were all men in the front rank of leadership with qualities, diplomatic or military, quite equal to those of their British confrères. In fact brilliant leadership in itself can be disruptive as well as creative, as in the case of Charles XII of Sweden. The effectiveness of leadership depends on the milieu of its exercise and it is here that we can see a British advantage. The British in eighteenth-century India, even the private-trading merchants turned rulers, were under some form of discipline and possessed some form of common outlook. Even Lord Pigot's arrest by the Madras Council in 1776 and the 'White mutiny' of 1766 were attempts to influence authority rather than overthrow it. The Indian leaders, on the other hand, were mostly men of fortune who depended upon the passive acquiescence of the peasantry and the active support of other adventurers. Their instruments were mercenaries and other men as ambitious as themselves. Thus the Company's agents in a crisis tended to draw together, while a prince's followers, in the same situation, tended to fly apart. Changing sides, setting up on one's own, was normal practice in eighteenth-century India.

This factor of discipline, I think, was significant in the general field of obedience to command, of cohesion and unity of purpose, as applied to civilians as well as to soldiers, even more than in the particular field of military discipline. It is true the European methods of war and discipline gave the Company a great initial advantage. It was the perception of this advantage which caused Indian princes in the mid century to scramble for European support. But European military discipline and fire-power did not remain European monopolies for long. So early as 1763 Mir Kasim had trained an army on European lines which gave a good account of itself against the Company's troops. Later Sindia's troops under de Boigne were probably as good as the Company's and later still the Sikh army certainly was. When the British defeated such armies it was for other reasons than superiority in discipline or weapons.

The item of general discipline leads on to the still less tangible but even more potent factor of spirit or *esprit de corps*. The age in Europe was one of mounting self-confidence and optimism. British opinion reflected this spirit and added an expansionism born of steadily expanding trade soon to be stimulated by the first stages of the Industrial Revolution. This confidence, optimism, and pride communicated itself to the Company's servants and the process speeded up with the increased intercourse with England which followed the conquest of Bengal. The new air of progress was exhilarating and gave to those who breathed in something of the supreme confidence which marked the Arabs in the early days of Islam or the communists in the early days of Soviet Russia. No defeat was more than a set-back, a rut in the golden road of manifest destiny. There was the conviction that the universe was on one's side. This state of mind gave the British leadership a tenacity of purpose and a resilience which could not be matched on the Indian side. It is a climate of opinion which commonly exists when apparently small forces achieve surprising victories over much larger ones.

Next comes the question of resources. A commercial company and a sub-continent would seem to be unequally matched, but in fact this was not so. The resources of India were divided and used against itself; the resources of the British were unified. The British themselves used Indian resources, not only of man-power, but also financial. India possessed a mainly subsistence economy with hand industries like cotton and silk as 'fringe' factors. Britain possessed a rapidly expanding commerce, with industries fed both by overseas raw materials such as cotton and by indigenous minerals such as iron and coal. It possessed a rapidly expanding market in Europe and America, and, with the first inventions of the first industrial revolution, the means of supplying that market with an unprecedented scale of produc-tion. The Indian foreign market, on the other hand, was stationary or if anything in recession owing to the troubles in Persia following the fall of the Safavid dynasty and mounting Dutch control in South-east Asia. Finally, sea-power gave Britain the ability to concentrate her resources in a way impossible for India as a whole. Thus the British were resilient in adversity and could quickly replace what was lost in one place from reserves elsewhere. For Indian powers defeat meant not only loss of prestige but a contraction of resources. Figures in cases like these are apt to be misleading owing to the number of disturb-ing factors involved but a single illustration may give some hint of the relative financial position. The revenue of Akbar's empire in 1600, covering an area equivalent to two thirds of British India (without Burma), was estimated to be £17·5 millions.* The revenue of Pitt's Great Britain about 1790 was around £16 millions.

It can in fact be asserted that while the Company's resources, with British state support, were concentrated, relatively well-organized, and expansive, those of India were divided, contract-ing rather than expanding, and irreplaceable after loss.

In judging this matter it is not enough to consider the positive advantages of the British; we also have to note the special dis-advantages on the Indian side. The foremost of these was divi-sion. This was not so much a chronic malady, as suggested by many British historians, as a periodic malaise caused by the nature of the Indian polity and the tensions produced by over-lapping races and rival cultures in a sub-continent which pro-

* Reckoning at the then rate of ten rupees to the pound.

vides few convenient physical compartments for the growth of integrated nationalities. Groups which developed into nations tended to grow into empires, ossify into aristocracies, and decay in dispersion. There was never an Indian concept of the balance-of-power of stable states within the orbit of Indian culture. Instead there was a continuing tradition of empire and overlordship from the *Chakravarti* raja with his horse sacrifice as token of supremacy in ancient times to the great Mughals of the seventeenth century. India expected a strong central power and would always submit to a leader who could make good his claim to supremacy. In the eighteenth century the Mughal leaders had fallen. The political constituents of India had no idea of forming a 'concert of India'. Instead, they either reached for empire themselves like the Marathas or sought to win as much as possible before a new supremacy arose like Oudh or the Nizam or prepared to attach themselves to the winning side like the Rajputs. There was no thought of unity and no thought of stability. Every promising leader thought of himself, as he had done while the Mughal empire was a-building, as a potential empire-builder, a Sher Shah or an Akbar. And every ruler, as of course, looked to any rising distant power for help against the nearer one. When the Akbar of the age visibly arrived they would as naturally tender their allegiance to him.

This brings us to a further factor which was an essential element of the then Indian scene. This was the absence of the phenomenon of nationalism, then as since so dominant in Europe as to be taken for granted in assessing the political field. In India the horizontal divisions of caste and the vertical divisions of religion were more important than those of race. Tribalism was important as with the Afghans but rarely deepened into anything like nationalism because of the two Indian factors of dispersion, owing to the lack of geographical barriers, and community separation, because of caste. The Rohillas of the upper Ganges valley never became a nation because religion and caste separated them from the local Hindu cultivators and landlords. Physical union across the psychic barriers only led to new social groups, often servile and usually disowned by both parental communities. The Rajputs, for all their common sentiment, remained an aristocracy divided by clan spirit because they could not unite physically or psychically with their immediate neighbours. Some castes, like the Nairs and Brahmins of Malabar, had race as well as religion as an element in their composition, but it was the caste feeling of separateness and superiority which prevented an organic union of sentiment. There was thus no Malabari nation in spite of centuries of living together on an isolated jungle-protected sea-coast and in spite of the stimulus of foreign interference. The only case of something like nationalism was that of the Marathas in the time of Sivaji and his immediate successors. The Marathas enjoyed the advantages of a geographically distinct (if sterile) homeland, a common language, and a love of independence. The spark which ignited the flame of incipient nationalism as distinct from tribalism or community spirit was Mughal interference promoting hatred of Islam. It was fanned by the genius of Sivaji in calling for the defence of the *desh* (homeland) and the cow (religion) and in federating the various communities on a functional basis. In the early years of the eighteenth century this incipient nationalism was developing and promising. But in the next fifty years it faded away. In the homeland the sentiment of unity withered because the communities failed to follow federation by fusion. The masses returned to their passive role under Maratha and Brahmin leadership, while Marathas and Brahmins jostled each other for power. Beyond Maharashtra nationalism turned to imperialism with military success, so that soon Maratha aristocracies were ruling and exploiting non-Maratha areas, and Maratha armies were mercenary like the rest, whose leaders contended for power at Poona. The Marathas were in this phase by the time of Warren Hastings. Their own nationalism had become a sentiment and memory to themselves, and their imperialism a nightmare to others. The Indian tradition of imperial unification and the absence of national feeling explain the lack of any sense of shame on the part of Indian rulers either to seek foreign help in defeating a local rival or to accept foreign overlordship when it was seen to be capable of enforcing it.

As a tailpiece to this discussion may be added the Indian side of the argument of superior British resources. In the eighteenth century Indian poverty was relative, not only to British prosperity, but to their own situation a century before. Under the great Mughals the surplus wealth of the country had in the main been concentrated in the central government. After allowing for the extravagance of display and building there remained sufficient resources in central hands to control the country and deal with foreign threats. Production and trade proceeded broadly unimpaired. In the eighteenth century all this changed. The resources of the centre were squandered in the succession struggles of 1707, 1712, 1713, 1719–20, 1752–53, as well as in wars with Marathas, Persians, and Afghans. The local resources denied the centre were in turn used for local wars by local chiefs. The Marathas anticipated the British in using local resources to subjugate areas, their instrument being *chauth* or a levy of one fourth of the revenue. This process had gone so far by the last years of the century that in the Punjab any adventurer who could collect some followers might seize a mud fort, terrorize the countryside, and in a few years build himself up as a recognized raja. The British sailor George Thomas who seized Hansi was one of these. Charles Metcalfe, in his list of Delhi local chiefs, described a number of them as 'the plunderers' of this or that. Revenue came from the countryside and in these conditions could only be collected by moving through it. So it came about that the movements of Indian armies were often determined by the need to collect revenue. Mercenaries demand pay; campaigns would be broken in order to collect revenue to stave off a mutiny for arrears. In these circumstances Indian generals often feared their own troops more than the enemy's.

If these were good reasons why the British should be successful in their contest for the control of India we have still to consider why they made the attempt. The essential answer is commerce and vested interests, but the details of the answer are very different from those one might expect from the previous history. The Company's trade had centred chiefly on cotton goods in the north and the Madras coast, with ancillaries like spices in the south, indigo in Gujarat, and saltpetre in Bengal. At the same time a private or 'country trade' developed between India and the Far East, in the private hands of the Company's merchants. The British government carried on the French wars of the eighteenth century to India in support of this trade, and then found that the Company had acquired overnight, through the action of Clive, a dominion in India on its own. Until the end of Warren Hastings's time the Company was faced with threats to its existence in India which gave it no chance for large decisions of policy. At the end of the century, however, the deteriorating situation in Indian India, with the consequent necessity of maintaining large forces at three separate centres, raised the question : would it be cheaper in the long run to control the whole of India with its consequent administrative costs than to continue with an armed and warring India, with anarchy spreading from the centre? The imperialist answer, represented by Lord Wellesley, was an unhesitating 'March'. He was helped by the current fear of French intervention in Napoleon's oriental phase. But the reasons why Pitt and Dundas supported him for several years and their successors later completed unification were essentially commercial. If there had been no money in it, they would certainly have withdrawn. The Company's trade in India was no longer profitable, for its profits, instead of being augmented by the revenues of Bengal, were in fact absorbed by the costs of administration. Its profits came from China, where the tea trade increased rapidly from the time of the passing of Pitt's Commutation Act in 1784. While China provided tea for the Company it was willing to take opium from India. This trade, carried on indirectly in China, for it was repeatedly banned by the Chinese government, eventually more than paid for the Company's tea investment, and was responsible for its continued commercial prosperity. Here was something which could not be given up, something which was made more profitable by political control. Without that control it would have declined and might have withered altogether. A cogent economic argument for the hegemony of India was the preservation of the China trade.

To this motive of preserving existing trade must be added the hope of more to come. The private merchants of London looked longingly at the size of India (as they later did at Tibet) and its population and were convinced that a great market lay waiting to be tapped. Only a monopolist and restrictive company stood in the way. These men belonged to the rising school of free traders, and they all supported the establishment of the Company's hegemony as a supplement to the breaking of the Company's monopoly. When admitted to India in 1813 their expectations were at first disappointed, but their hopes were strong and they would not be baulked.

A third influence was that of the vested interests. During the course of the Company's operations a variety of interests had grown up which found in India a profitable field of activity. A withdrawal would ruin their prospects, the *status quo* would leave them uncertain, but advance would improve them. There was the opium trade interest in India, but more important were the interests in Britain which could influence policy-making in London. Here was the powerful and independent shipping interest, upon whom the whole British position in India depended. Then there was the supply of stores for the administration, civil and military, which, owing to the absence of European equipment in India at that time, was on a very extensive scale. The cotton interest in England hoped for a larger market for its manufactured goods. And then there was the human vested interest of Indian service. Formerly men went to India to seek a fortune but more often found a grave. By 1800 increasing numbers sought a career in the Company's civil and military services. The mortality and isolation from Europe were growing less, companionship and social centres were increasing, the services were expanding and prospects improving of rewards for distinction and of ease in retirement. Clive and Warren Hastings were sent out as a last resort or as an escape from responsibility; in 1800 Charles Metcalfe was sent out by an established Anglo-oriental family because of the prospects. The friends and relations of all these, actual and prospective, formed a powerful group, and were beginning that process which caused Indian service to be later described as a system of outdoor relief for the middle classes. The argument for retaining the position in India was fundamentally economic (the anti-French argument was temporary to Napoleon). Once this was admitted the argument for advance as a long-term economy grew stronger with every year of central Indian anarchy. It was in securing the transition from argument to action that the private traders' hope of profits to come and the vested interests hopes of advantages to increase proved to be potent and effective.

10

THE NEW POLICY

WHEN the British completed their hegemony of India up to the Sutlej in 1818 they inherited a country very different from the India of the great Mughals and in large measure down to the year 1748. Babur was able to step into the shoes of the Delhi sultan without any other dislocation than the losses involved in battle. Though he complained of what he found in India he took over a going concern. The British found a country in ruins. Everywhere, in north and south, while elated by the breadth of their new dominion, they were depressed by the ruins of past glory and prosperity. Not only did they encounter dismantled fortresses and deserted palaces, but canals run dry, tanks or reservoirs broken, roads neglected, towns in decay, and whole regions depopulated. The first descriptions of the officers sent to restore administration, whether by Metcalfe in the north or Malcolm in the centre or Elphinstone in the west, are of the ravages and social breakdown caused by lengthy wars. India was exhausted and for the moment without inspiration. The wisest of the British realized that great stores of energy lay behind the apparently decayed façade of Indian religion and suspected the cultural depths which were later to be discovered. But the less experienced and perceptive had some excuse for thinking that they controlled a land containing an ancient civilization which was moribund and peopled by divided and hopeless races.

The Indian political system, based on Mughal supremacy recognizing a number of local autonomies like that of the Rajput princes, had collapsed. The chief engineers of that collapse, the Marathas, had attempted to replace the Mughals with a *raj* of their own. But this design was frustrated at Panipat in 1761 and the Maratha confederacy had dissolved, as the Mughal empire had done, in warring fragments. For a time Madhaji Sindia seemed likely to repair the disaster of Panipat, but with his death in 1794 the Maratha empire followed the Mughal into dissolution. A nascent western Indian nationalism had become a

Maratha imperialism, hated by Hindu Rajputs and Bengalis as much as by the Mughals and Muslims. The Marathas passed from the imperial stage of India unhonoured and unsung. In north India the political vacuum thus created was gradually filled by the Sikhs who found a leader of genius in Ranjit Singh. Before his time the Sikh state conformed to St Augustine's definition: 'What are states, but robber bands, and what are robber bands but little states?' Ranjit restored order but engrossed the revenue to maintain his army. Further south in the Delhi region the country was slowly recovering not only from the great anarchy of forty years, but also from the famine of 1782, which swept away half to two thirds of the population. In central India the decline of the Maratha military monarchies allowed virtual anarchy to prevail. The Nizam's dominions, racked by the movements of predatory armies, lay prostrate and recovery was hindered by the demands of the Nizam's ministers and *mansabdars*. Everywhere the links between the rulers and the people had been snapped. Revenue officers would go round with armed bands to collect what they could from the villagers. The villagers, on their part, fortified themselves behind mud walls or ensconced themselves in old enclosures, and in the early days of British rule would sometimes receive the Company's forces 'with such briskness as temporarily to stagger them'. The revenue officers, on their part, handed over as little as they could to their superiors. The rule of force was universal and politically there was no hope.

In British India, which before 1818 consisted mainly of Bengal, Bihar, and Orissa, a tract to the north of the Ganges running up to Delhi, and the coastal Carnatic in the south, we have a different but hardly more cheerful picture. Everywhere order was restored and people moved freely about. The revenue was collected punctually and robbers or *dacoits* were put down. The age of wholesale corruption and intimidation in Bengal had passed with the rule of Cornwallis. But the countryside lay lifeless and inert, passive and apathetic. People had reached a dead end and saw no signs of a fresh start. The revenue assessments at this period were commonly too high, which led to large displacements of *zamindars*. Too frequently the often unsatisfactory but familiar and perhaps understanding *zamindar* was replaced by the enterprising entrepreneur from Calcutta hungry for rents and unaware of humanity. The Permanent Settlement had made the peasants the tenants of the landlords, with very little protection from abuse. Rents could not be questioned even if eviction was not yet practicable owing to depopulation. Thus both upper and lower classes had suffered in position and in prospects. Further, the British monopoly of office under Cornwallis meant the loss of income, of status, and of prospects for large numbers of people. The Mughal rule was alien and often arbitrary, but something you could take part in; British rule was less arbitrary and more regular, but remote and olympian. The Bengal Muslim historian complained of British 'aloofness, absorption in their own concerns, and surrounding themselves with sycophants'. A man complaining of conditions in Oudh in 1824 exclaimed in reply to the suggestion that he would be better off under British rule, 'Of all miseries keep us from that' because 'the name and honour of our nation would perish'. Only in Calcutta were there some stirrings of new intellectual life and any sense of enlargement. And this was among the merchants enriched by their relations as bankers with the British and their share in the China trade.

The economic state of the country matched the political. Trade could only move with difficulty and caution in the presence of armies whose soldiers thought loot a legitimate substitute for arrears of pay and of *dacoits* for whom loot *was* pay. Only goods large and valuable enough to warrant strong guards could easily be moved. In consequence the inter-district and inter-town commerce which had flourished in Mughal times in spite of restrictions and tolls came to a standstill. Large tracts virtually returned to a subsistence type of economy because the means of exchange were lacking. Only in the great ports was there activity, where chests of opium, bales of cotton and cotton goods and consignments of saltpetre supplied the Indo-British export trade. The great Indian textile handicraft industry was also languishing, partly because disorder interfered with production but more because Lancashire machine goods had replaced the foreign demand and had begun to invade the Indian home market itself.

Bishop Heber's tour of Bengal contains many references to the distress of the weavers.

Socially and culturally the country was at a low ebb. Social diseases proliferated like sores on an unhealthy body and by unwary observers were taken to be typical of the country's life. The most obvious of this was *dacoity* or gang robbery whose prevalence, like that of banditry in China, is a kind of thermometer of governmental authority in India. From being endemic it had become epidemic and had flared up into a cancer in central India with the pitiless Pindaris. All travellers had to have escorts, and find protection at night; at Delhi at the coming of the British it was not safe to picnic in daylight in the environs of the city for fear of snipers lurking behind tombs. A feature of this malaise was the religious sanction claimed by many of these groups. Thus we have the Thugs, who combined robbery with ritual murder in honour of the goddess Kali. Their cult had long existed in a small way, but with the troubled times they grew until they were a terror all over central India and into the north. Suttee, or the burning of widows on the funeral pyres of their husbands as a religious rite long known to exist and be extensively practised in Hindu courts, increased notably among the upper classes of Bengal. Acts of religious fanaticism multiplied, like hook-swinging in honour of a god or casting oneself before the car of Jaganath of Puri. Strangest of all, perhaps, was the appearance of armed religious ascetics in a land where nonviolent ideas were widespread and associated with religious devotion. They went about in bands variously described as *nagas, bairagis, sannyasis,* and *gosains.* Some took service as mercenaries and their leaders became generals. The supreme case was that of the Sikhs who transmuted from religious quietism to militant gospelling to achieve statehood and something like nationhood.

The arts suffered in the political confusion and the economic decline. Their patrons were too busy buying arms and soldiers for their campaigns to pay their artists or give them intelligent directions. So architecture declined in size, vigour of conception and execution. Even where money was available, as in Lucknow, taste was lacking, so that we find there a mixture rather than a fusion of styles and imitation rather than creation. Painting in the Mughal and Rajput styles languished from the same lack of patronage and inspiration. Only the handicrafts, where buyers were available, maintained their skill.

The same blight spread over the intellectual life of the country. Sanskrit and Arabic were still studied in the *tols* and *madrasahs*, *swamis* still sought realization in meditation, each with his circle of disciples. But there was little sign of new thought or creative achievement. The keynote was withdrawal. For the people there were bizarre cults appealing to the emotions; for the intellectual detachment and non-involvement. In the India of the late eighteenth century there were only two creative achievements. One was the rise of Urdu, the graceful daughter of Persian and Hindi, to the status of a major language, and the other the work of Shah Wali-ullah and his school of theologians in Delhi to which some trace the early seeds of the Pakistan movement. It is typical of the times that while the influence of the one was unifying that of the other was divisive.

The British who surveyed the Indian scheme were both exhilarated and sobered by their achievement. They were exhilarated by the magnitude of their achievement, which they thought could compare with that of Rome. They were sobered by the thought of their responsibilities and the problems of developing the country. Though triumphant at the moment the more farseeing regarded India more as a temporarily quiescent volcano which might erupt again at any moment than a prostrate body. The hidden fire was religion, whose revival, they thought, would end the British dominion in the absence of foreign invasion, mutiny, or improvement.

There followed one of the great debates of nineteenth-century Britain, carried on not so much in Parliament as by publicists, minute-writers at their desks, and public men around dinner tables. What was to be done with India now that Britain controlled it? To re-establish law and order, to protect the frontier with the Sikhs and Sind, was simple and relatively easy. To organize the land revenue was more difficult but this could be done with increasing knowledge and experience. Trade could be encouraged, and the important step of opening India had already been taken in 1813. But what then? What was to be done for the people, for the promotion of whose welfare Parliament had committed itself in the late eighteenth century under the spur of Burke?

There were a number of answers to this question and it took from twelve to fifteen years for one of them to reach the status of a policy. It should be remembered that at the time the debate began (1818) Britain was still under the Tories, influenced by fear of the Jacobins and Napoleon, with an unreformed parliament and local government, and that the leaders of radical thought were not to come to the top for a dozen years. It was a time of stirring and intellectual ferment, but at the time the shape of things to come was anybody's guess.

The first answer was the conservative one whose most distinguished proponents were Warren Hastings and the orientalist H. H. Wilson. Essentially, it was to leave things as they were. The Company should govern in the Mughal and general Indian tradition, that is, providing a framework of security beneath which traditional society could continue its wonted course. Peace would promote trade and trade would be to Britain's advantage. The soul of the people was to be found in the religio-social institutions and we should interfere with these at our peril. We should content ourselves with the patronage of art, literature, and even religion, and avoid any provocation of established customs. This not only brought about the discouragement of missionary activity in the Company's territories but opposition to the suppression of such things as infanticide and suttee. This view, propagated by the older generation of the Company's servants found support in Britain among right-wing Tories. But it was challenged by two groups whose ideas and views were then fermenting in English society. The first was the Evangelicals. In many ways they were close to the Tories for they had an equal abhorrence of the French Enlightenment and Jacobinism. But their motives were different. To the secular Tory the French threat was to property; to the Evangelical the French horror was atheism. When the Evangelicals looked to India their reaction was quite different from that of the average Tory. They had a horror of idolatry and India was the land of idolatry *par excellence*. They had a thirst for souls and here were millions rushing to perdition without a chance of Christian salvation. They had a humanism which they believed to be part of the Gospel and had led them on crusades against slavery, and here were practices like suttee crying out for redress. They believed it their duty to preach the gospel whose light would dissolve the mists of superstition and cruelty enshrouding the Indian people. They had influential members in society, such as Wilberforce, the confidant of Pitt, Charles Grant, a chairman of the Directors, and his son a cabinet minister. Their programme was, bring the Christian west to the East, and India will reform herself as a flower turns to the sun.

The other pressure group was that of the Radicals and Utilitarians. Their free trade views had already, in 1813, broken the Company's trade monopoly and secured the free entry of private merchants, as Wilberforce had secured the free entry of missionaries. But they wished to go far beyond economics. They believed passionately in the superiority of the western world, and in its indefinite progress with the release of the principle of reason as the mainspring of development. All other civilizations were static or in decay; moreover they lacked the secret which might enable them to catch up. Could western enlightenment and reason be withheld from India where they would certainly cause all who came in contact with them to abandon their superstitions and abuses? The Radicals were humanists too and, with a faith in reason as strong as the Evangelical confidence in the Gospel, they joined with them in denouncing customs which seemed to offend against humanity. The Utilitarians, too, had influential members, the most important being James Mill, whose *History of India* (1817) won him a key position in the Company's policy making at the India House.

There was another group who should also be mentioned. It was the younger generation of Company's servants who had shared in its rise to supremacy and now held key posts in India itself. They were often influenced by liberal ideas but they were also aware of the forces still existing below the surface of Indian society. They pleaded for gradual change with due regard to Indian susceptibilities, and their views may be said to have been broadly accepted by conservatives of a later generation. Such men were Mountstuart Elphinstone, who cherished the Maratha *sirdars* while he was introducing western education into Bombay; Charles Metcalfe, who tried to put liberal principles into practice when he ruled the Delhi Territory, and John Malcolm who coined a slogan for the group with the phrase 'Let us, therefore, calmly proceed in a course of gradual improvement'.

It was the Radicals and Evangelicals, helped by the victory of the reformers from 1830, who carried the day. The decision was a momentous one for it both determined the nature of Indian development and so the nature of the new Indian state in 1947, and provided a pattern of European relations with Asia in the twentieth century without which intimacy and friendship might have turned into aloofness and hostility to the immeasurable loss of both parties. While Holland was content with the economic exploitation of Indonesia and France was later to present westernism in south-east Asia in so drastic a form that it won no acceptance, Britain took the line of offering the west to the east without compelling its acceptance. Whatever one may say of the mistakes and crudities which accompanied the policy, the fact remains that the decision was a momentous one, affecting not only Britain and India but Asia and perhaps the world as well.

Lord William Bentinck, Governor-General from 1828–35, was the pilot mainly responsible for trimming the sails of the British-Indian state to the wind of change. The change of direction in that wind can be gauged from these facts. In 1793, during the discussion on the renewal of the Company's Charter for twenty years, the determined effort of Wilberforce to secure government support for Christian missionary activity was defeated in the Commons. Philanthropy was not part of government. Lord Wellesley's concern about suttee or widow burning at the turn of the century was disregarded and a decision repeatedly postponed. In 1813 the Company's trading monopoly was abolished. The country was opened to missionary activity but without government support and £10,000 was set aside annually for the promotion of learning among the people of India. It needed a further puff of wind to implement this clause by the creation of a

Committee of Public Instruction, which at once began to argue about the relative merits of western and eastern learning. By 1828 the wind was blowing more strongly for we find a Tory President of the Board of Control writing to Bentinck 'We have a great moral duty to perform in India'. It was this change of sentiment on India which enabled Bentinck to survive the hostility of Wellington's Tory government during his first two years in India and to achieve so much thereafter. It happened that a radical was in charge of India at a time of radical change in England.

Bentinck owed his appointment partly to his desire to wipe out the memory of his recall from the Madras governorship in 1807, partly to his connexions (his father had been a Whig Prime Minister), partly to the Company's need of a strong hand to enforce economies, partly to the unwillingness of others to go, and not at all to his opinions. Once there, with the wind of change behind him, his opinions, those of a Benthamite radical, became of prime importance. He was a convinced westerner and humanist, with little sympathy for Indian culture or institutions. His liberalism, however, made him impatient of racialism, and tolerant if unsympathetic to Indian customs. But first he had to satisfy the Company's injunction to economize. Faced with one of the twenty-year Parliamentary inquests on their administration of India, the Directors were anxious to show at least a clean financial sheet. But India was in fact burdened with heavy debts as the result of the recent Burman war. Bentinck had therefore first to engage in a rigorous economy drive. In this he succeeded, converting a deficit of a million pounds a year into a surplus of one and a half millions. But it was at the cost of a most distasteful clash with the Company's military officers (Bentinck was himself a full general), whose allowances he reduced on the direct orders of the Directors. He became the 'clipping Dutchman', and long after the army had forgotten him service historians could find little good to say of him. With this out of the way Bentinck proceeded on a great northern tour and set in motion a new land revenue policy based on detailed surveys made on the spot. This, in the hands of men like R. M. Bird and James Thomason, became the basis of north-Indian land administration during the British period. He reformed the judicial system creating two new grades of Indian judges. Justified to the Directors on the ground of economy, it was the first real breakaway from the Cornwallis system of European monopoly of higher office.

So far Bentinck, though a reformer, was running along the accepted lines of government. A reforming Mughal, we might say, but still a Mughal. It was his other measures which may fairly be said to have introduced the west to the east and to have set in motion that process which has produced the India of today. Before his time there were tendencies; afterwards a movement which could not be stopped. He first attacked in the name of universal moral law (which for him was the western moral law) social evils which could claim some support from orthodox opinion. In 1828 he suppressed suttee or the burning of widows on the funeral pyres of their husbands. In the Bengal presidency in the previous fifteen years recorded burnings only had varied from 500 to 850 annually. In orthodox theory this practice was a voluntary action on the part of the Hindu widow anxious to rejoin her god-husband through the purifying flames. She was *sati* or devoted. In practice it was often induced by relatives ambitious for the prestige of a *sati* in the family, greedy of her property, or wanting one less mouth to feed. For over twenty years successive governor-generals hesitated to move, but when Bentinck acted there was surprisingly little opposition. Many Hindus were glad to see the incubus removed for them and a small Bengali group led by Ram Mohan Roy actually supported him. His next move was the suppression of thuggee, or the practice in Central India of ritual murder and robbery in the name of the goddess Kali. Even the orthodox needed little persuasion to accept this action, though both this and the action on suttee represented the imposition of western values on Indian society. Here, however, positive interference stopped. Indian customs ethically 'indifferent' from the western point of view were left untouched.

Bentinck's next measures were more subtle and in the long run perhaps more far-reaching. They amounted to planting western ideas and institutions on Indian soil and leaving them to grow as they would. The method is reminiscent of the way in which the trial by jury system was placed side by side with the old trial by ordeal in medieval England and left to the judgement of local opinion over the years. The first field of activity was that of education. Up to 1813 the Company had followed the traditional pattern of governmental patronage to Indian learning, though on a much more modest scale than that of the Mughals. There was Warren Hastings's college of Arabic and Persian studies in Calcutta and Jonathan Duncan's Sanskrit college in Benares. In 1813 the Charter Act sanctioned the annual sum of £10,000 towards 'the revival and improvement of literature and the encouragement of the learned Natives of India and for the introduction and promotion of a knowledge of the sciences among the inhabitants of the British Territories in India'.* From this clause the modern Indian educational system has sprung. It was not until 1823 that a Committee of Public Instruction was formed to give effect to this provision. It immediately perceived the ambiguity between the two halves of the clause, the one appearing to favour oriental and the other occidental learning, and plunged into a lively controversy as to the correct interpretation. At first the orientalists prevailed and something was done to promote the printing of classics and the translation of modern works into Sanskrit. This was the situation which Bentinck found on his arrival and of which he took advantage. In 1829 he wrote of 'the British language, the key to all improvements', and in 1834 'general education is my panacea for the regeneration of India'. He found support in India House from James Mill, with his convinced westernism and passion for 'useful knowledge', and later from the reforming Whig ministry with its radical tendencies. In Calcutta he found a forward-looking group of intellectuals led by Ram Mohan Roy who had helped to found a college for western learning and advocated its introduction. In 1834 he received a powerful English reinforcement in the arrival of the new Law member, Thomas Babington Macaulay. The result was the decision to launch English education and western knowledge into India, a decision unique in colonial annals in Asia to that time. The resolution of 7 March

* Stat. 53 Geo. III, Cl. 155 sect. 43.

1835 declared 'that the great objects of the British government ought to be the promotion of European literature and science' and that available funds should 'be henceforth employed in imparting to the Native population knowledge of English literature and science through the medium of the English language'.

From this time the government began to set up schools and colleges imparting western knowledge in the English language. To this was added another measure of the greatest importance. English replaced Persian (the court language of the Mughals) as the official state language and the medium of the higher courts of law, local languages replacing Persian in the lower courts. By one stroke the learning of English was given a great stimulus for practical purposes, its cultivation involving contact with the western ideas and values of which it was the vehicle. At the same time the local languages were brought down from poetry to prose, and were given a function and a status which has led to their modern development.

Western science was specifically introduced in the form of western medicine, of which the Calcutta Medical College was the first institution. Science also received attention in both schools and colleges. Western technology spread through engineering works like roads, canals, and later railways, and the Indians who were trained to build and administer them. The process was hastened by the increase in the number of Indians entering the administration as a result of Bentinck's policy of Indianization. Thus, as the administration became more western in outlook, it also began to become more Indian in personnel.

Macaulay as law member started the codification of Indian public law from the main basis of Cornwallis's revision of the Mughal–Islamic criminal law. The work was not completed until 1861 but it was of the utmost importance. For it introduced English procedures and the assumptions behind them into all the Indian courts. This was the department of public life in which Indians first attained high position and where their subtle minds had fullest play. Here the interaction of western and eastern ideas and minds was widespread, penetrating, and sustained.

To sum up, we may say that Bentinck's measures, made possible by a conjunction of political forces and ideological tendencies close to the time of his appointment, amounted to a presentation of the west to the east. Of course it was an English version of the west and the presentation was from one small *élite* to another. It was easy to go out into the countryside and say that traditional life went on just as before; it was easy to laugh at some of the early cultural hybrids; it might seem smart to declare that when the two cultures met each borrowed the worst of the other. These things were said for many years, but the fact remains that these measures began a creative contact between the two countries which was to transform India within a century and fulfil Elphinstone's dream in less than twenty years more.

11

THE COMPLETION OF DOMINION

THE events of 1818 transformed the Company's dominion in India to the dominion of India. It was henceforth accurate to speak of Britain's Indian empire. But around its periphery there still remained some regions which were geographically no part of India. The frontier ran with the coast from Bengal to Kathiawar, except for French Pondicherry and Portuguese Goa. To the north-west it ran through the Thar desert and along the Sutlej nearly to the Himalayan range. The great hills were the northern boundary except for the Gurkha state of Nepal until the frontier lost itself in the tangled hills of Assam and the north-east. Beyond this line to the north-west lay the Punjab, Kashmir, Sind, and the Afghan kingdom, and to the east Burma or the kingdom of Ava. All these, except northern Burma and the Afghans, were absorbed by 1852; and, since some of these regions have proved to be of great significance to the sub-continent's later history, the circumstances of the acquisitions deserve some attention.

On the surface one might conclude that a record of two large kingdoms conquered, another two thirds overrun, and a fourth attacked and occupied for a time, in the course of thirty-five years, argues naked imperialism. The motives were in fact various, and it is worth looking at them for a moment before recording the actual events. A primary motive was of course security. In this case there was little to fear from neighbouring states, but behind them in the north-west lay the bugbear of Russian influence. Since the defeat of Napoleon Russia was regarded as the strongest power in Europe. She was encroaching on both Turkey and Persia; while Bentinck was carrying the west to India in the thirties, Palmerston was making it his business to check Russian ambitions in the Near East. A threat from India to her influence in the Middle East was a useful diplomatic counterweight. The need to check the Russian drive to the Mediterranean was urgent and the potential threat to India had some substance. But security in the minds of people both expansive and nervous can weave strange fantasies and easily induce its victims to ignore reality and outrun discretion in an excess of caution.

Another potent motive was that of trade. The merchants and manufacturers of England, now freed from the East India Company's monopoly, soon found that the expected market in India could not be fully tapped because of the poverty of the people and the lack of communications. They tended to look longingly beyond the frontiers for the missing markets of India. Must not Tibetans require warm clothing of which Yorkshire was in plentiful supply; would not Burman products be cheaper but for the obstacles created by the effete monarchy of Ava; and would not the Punjab, with its virile population and its potential of irrigation in its great rivers, be much better off under the British? Many of these expectations were as unfounded as the early hopes of the Indian market, but their cherishers possessed influence in Britain and formed a continuously active pressure group on Indian policy.

Then came the moral superiority arguments. The religious bodies and specially the Evangelicals formed another important pressure group on Indian policy. Their success in securing the toleration of missionary activity in India (in 1813) was followed by the suppression of suttee and thuggee. Their campaign against idols bore fruit in the withdrawal of governmental patronage of certain Hindu temples and festivals. To them the surrounding regions were ones of darkness. Slavery, the great target of religious endeavour in Africa and the West Indies, flourished in the north-west; suttee continued in the Punjab; and in Burma the nameless cruelties reported from Ava had become a legend. The pressure exercised by these groups was not as great as that of the merchants; in this connexion they were important as providing a public ready to justify 'forward' moves on currently respectable grounds.

Lastly we may note the developing superiority complex of the nation as a whole. Distilled from the optimistic rationalism of the French philosophers came the European belief that its civilization was superior to all others, with a lead that was growing daily greater. The principle of reason had given it the secret of progress which was manifested in the material sphere by the advance of science, in the moral by the growth of humanism, and in the religious by the spread of Christianity. Other civilizations were static, Europe was leaving behind the Chinese with their cycle of Cathay and the immobile Brahmin dreaming of the Absolute, just as she had emerged from her own dark ages. The Victorian seriously believed that he was five times as good as other people because he travelled five times as fast. This sentiment of all-round and increasing superiority was one which pervaded all classes of the opinion-forming public. This feeling expressed itself in the slogan 'the inestimable benefits of civilization', in its turn transmuted into the phrase 'the blessings of British rule'. Thus annexation, if sufficient reason along these lines could be found for it, was now generally regarded as a 'good thing', whereas fifty years earlier, as expressed in Pitt's India Act of 1784, it was generally regarded as a 'bad thing'.

The Burman annexations were broadly due to the security motive and mismanagement. The aggressive Burman dynasty established in the north in 1752, after overrunning the south, defeating the Siamese, and occupying Assam, turned to Bengal. The Burmans believed Ava to be the centre of the world and demanded the cession of Chittagong and East Bengal as a matter of routine. An invasion was attempted and thus war became inevitable. The invasion repulsed, the customary riposte 'to prevent repetition' was planned. European trading relations with Burma in the previous two centuries had been few and fleeting owing to the unstable nature of the various Burman régimes, but there was teak to be had from the forests and this provided a motive for an imposed settlement. A badly mismanaged campaign, which nearly cost Lord Amherst his governor-generalship, ended in 1826 with the Treaty of Yandaboo. Burma yielded a series of recent conquests with Assam, Manipur, and the long coastal strips of Arakan and Tenasserim. During the next twenty-six years there were attempts to have relations with the wayward court of Ava (two successive kings became insane and had to be put under restraint) and to do business at Rangoon under an unpredictable governor. In 1852 a commercial dispute flared up through lack of understanding on both sides. Dalhousie, the Indian governor-general, was genuinely reluctant to embark on a campaign, because he thought it would be unprofitable. But once involved he organized a model campaign which cost on the British side 377 lives and less than a million pounds and ended with the annexation of lower Burma or Pegu. Dalhousie considered upper Burma, the real seat of the Burman race, likely to be very expensive to subdue and unprofitable to maintain. The final annexation was therefore delayed until 1886 in the time of Lord Dufferin. The motive on this occasion was that of security. It was a reply to the build-up of French influence in Indo-China, which was itself part of the policy of 'compensation' for the loss of Alsace-Lorraine to Germany. The French concluded a public treaty and appointed a consul; later correspondence promising a supply of arms was intercepted. The grievances of the Bombay-Burma Trading Corporation against the unstable Ava court also had their relevance; it would seem that it was the liquid of imagined insecurity which finally caused the cup of commercial grievance to overflow. Burman Burma thus became part of the Indian empire in 1886 to demonstrate during the next fifty years to generations of administrators the soundness of Dalhousie's reluctance to move north.

In the north-west a much greater problem faced the British policy-makers. Beyond the Sutlej lay the Punjab kingdom of the Sikhs with their one-eyed leader of genius Ranjit Singh and a formidable army. Beyond again lay the Afghan kingdom, at first distracted by civil wars, but later in the capable hands of Dost Muhammad Khan, while along the lower Indus into Sind lay the chaotic realm of the Sind Amirs, a splinter first of the Mughal empire and then of the Afghan kingdom. Behind again lay the Persian empire, elegant and decrepit, across which was now spreading the long shadow of Russia. The parallel advance of Russia towards Constantinople, which reached its peak in the Treaty of Unkiar Skelessi in 1833, provoked a diplomatic reaction directed by Palmerston and thus linked British European and Asian policies. It was in these circumstances that the Persian threat to Herat under Russian influence in 1837 was thought to involve a threat to the British position in India. The decision to replace the ruler of Kabul by the ex-king Shah Shuja was part of the policy of forestalling the advance of Russia by embarrassing her position in central Asia. It led through the coercion of the Amirs of Sind to the restoration of Shah Shuja and the discovery that he could only be maintained by an army of occupation. Two years later a national revolt led to the débâcle of this army and the arrival of a survivor Dr Brydon alone at Jalalabad. After a formal re-occupation the Afghans were abandoned to their own devices. But an aftermath was the seizure of Sind in 1843. The Amirs were primitive, obscurantist, suspicious, and arrogant by turns. They must sooner or later have given way to some more progressive régime. But they had been faithful if not willing allies; their only public crime was that they controlled the Indus, a fancied artery to the Panjab, and the fertile region of lower Sind. A sharp campaign in 1843 added Sind to the Indian empire and started a famous Outram–Napier public controversy. Its essence was, can the 'blessings of civilization' justify war and annexation of backward regions in defiance of international usage and the principle of self-determination? The issue was clouded by the unattractive nature of the Amirs and their rule and prejudged by the prevailing British sentiment of the time. The motives for the seizure were mixed, as such things always are. They included the idea of security against the north-west and the Sikh Punjab, the hope of profit from the control of the Indus and lower Sind with a dash of desire to restore the British name in India after the Afghan fiasco by some dramatic stroke. Little sympathy need be expended on the obscurantist Amirs or credit given to the British managers of this episode, Lord Ellenborough the Governor-General, and Sir Charles Napier.

The annexation of the Punjab deserves more attention, since its consequences are still with us today. From the time of Alexander the Punjab had been the home of vigorous and turbulent tribes. Its fertility had encouraged settlements and its openness north-west and south-east constant ingress and egress. Only as the country filled up did the inhabitants become more static and even then there was constant change and the piling of one group upon another. In consequence a territorial feeling of nationality, though often present, was always subordinate to a community feeling of separateness. Over the centuries the tribal communities sorted themselves out into Hindu and Muslim groupings. The majority Muslims, from the eleventh century onwards, were partly of Turkish and Afghan or Pathan stock, but also partly of Hindu descent, specially Rajput and Jat. The backbone of the Hindus were Rajputs and Jats with pastoral Gujars and Ahirs and a sprinkling of Brahmins and merchants in the towns. Everywhere the population was mixed, Muslims being more numerous in the north-west and Hindus in the south-east. Only in Kashmir was there a general change-over to Islam and even there the Brahmins survived as a small minority. The cardinal problem of the Punjab has been to evolve a community or national consciousness from such deeply divided ethnic and religious groupings.

Under the Mughals a new movement arose which at first promised something of the kind. It began as part of a general religious stirring during the fourteenth and fifteenth centuries which was in part a revival of 'heart' religion within Hinduism and in part, to use a current term, a 'dialogue' between Hinduism and Islam. In the Punjab Baba Nanak preached an ecstatic monotheism which was to unite the followers of the two religions in quietist devotion. His teachings, expressed in his own and like-minded saints' poems, were embodied in the *Adi Granth* or *Granth Sahib*. By the time of his death in 1539 Nanak had become the first *Guru* or spiritual head of a new sect. Nine other gurus followed until 1708, their followers calling themselves disciples or Sikhs. They acquired a headquarters at the Golden Temple in Amritsar; their temples were called *gurudwaras* or abodes of the gurus. During the seventeenth century the sect underwent a radical transformation which turned an unworldly sect into a militant community. The *gurus* went into Mughal politics and soon found themselves in opposition. Religious passions were aroused, culminating in the crusade of the last Guru Gobind against Aurangzeb. The Sikhs were welded into a militant brotherhood with customs which distinguished them from both Hindus and Muslims. They abandoned caste and encouraged a sense of belonging by such habits as wearing unshorn hair (hence the characteristic beard and turban), the initiation ceremony, and the concept of holy war (borrowed from the Muslims). The Mughals drove them to the hills for a generation, but on their collapse the Sikhs emerged as marauding bands whose leaders soon became the founders of little states. Among these appeared at the end of the century a youth of political genius in the person of Ranjit Singh. By 1820 he had welded the disparate elements of the Punjab into a powerful state. But it was not just a state of the traditional Indian pattern with a dignified durbar, a disorderly army, and intriguing landholders. Its distinctive feature was a highly trained army on western lines, partly officered by Europeans, and backed by a powerful artillery. Ranjit held all the strings of power so that no *sirdar* plotted assassination, because each had more to hope from the ruler alive than from his peers in the mêlée which would follow his death. No one dared to touch him even when he lay a helpless paralytic for months before his death. The Sikh kingdom, for all its apparent solidarity, was a brittle one, for it was essentially a minority dictatorship in a divided and turbulent country. Ranjit employed both Hindus and Muslims freely but they were subordinate to the ruling group; they knew it and were only accommodating themselves to circumstances until the next turn in fortune's wheel. There was, moreover, no capable successor to Ranjit in sight. A Sikh nation had been created within the Punjab; with the help of Ranjit it had dominated the Punjab; but no Punjab nation had been born. Punjabi unity was in fact further off than ever.

These facts were revealed on the death of Ranjit in 1839. Two rulers and a whole posse of leading chiefs died violently in the next six years. The army became the tumultuous arbiter of politics until in late 1845 it was moved into British India by a distracted Regent and chief minister as a way of escape. The first Sikh war was bloody but brief. It ended in the setting up of a 'sponsored state' under the direction of Sir Henry Lawrence. The experiment did not survive his departure on leave in 1848. Within weeks a revolt began which soon engulfed the Sikh chiefs who thought, with some reason, that they had been cheated by their generals in the first war. The second Sikh war of 1848–49

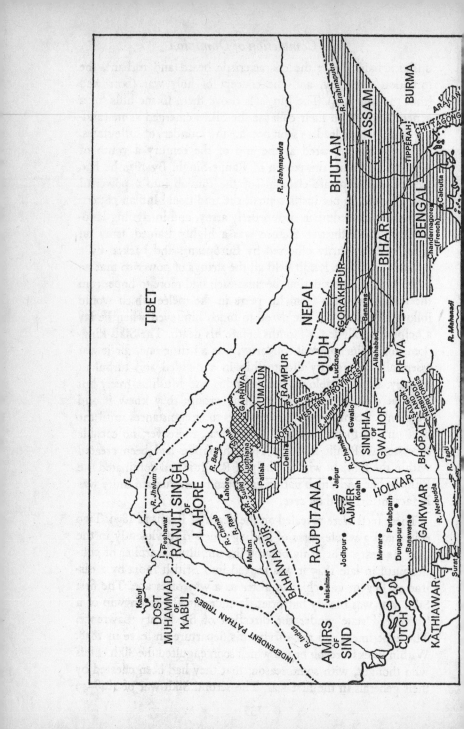

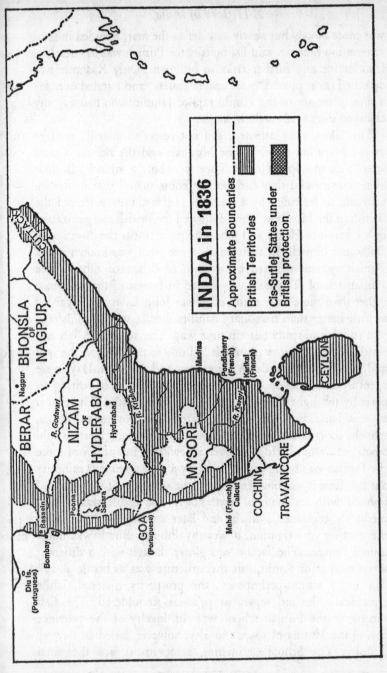

INDIA in 1836

Approximate Boundaries

British Territories

Cis-Sutlej States under British protection

CUTTACK

BERAR

Nagpur BHONSLA OF NAGPUR

R. Godavari

NIZAM OF HYDERABAD

Hyderabad

R. Krishna

Madras

Pondicherry (French)

Karikal (French)

R. Kaveri

MYSORE

COCHIN

TRAVANCORE

Mahé (French)

Calicut

Poona

Satara

GOA (Portuguese)

Bassein

Bombay

Diu Is. (Portuguese)

CEYLON

was more bloody but nearly as brief as the first; it ended in total annexation because, said Dalhousie, the Punjab was too near the frontier for any further risks to be taken. Only Kashmir was detached (as it proved, most unfortunately) and handed over for a sum of money to the Hindu raja of Jammu who had adroitly changed sides at the right moment.

The Sikhs, thus defeated, did not resort to guerilla warfare as the Marathas did with the Mughals and the Burmans were later to do in upper Burma. They were only a minority in their own country and they had not yet come to feel that it was intolerable to be ruled by a stranger. In fact they preferred the British to the Muslims. There followed the British reorganization in the hands of Henry and John Lawrence under the direction of Dalhousie himself. In their hands arose what was known as the Punjab system operated by a band of dedicated officers, the Punjab school. The land was settled in favour of the cultivator rather than the chiefs, many of whom John Lawrence regarded as little better than hereditary bandits. Justice was administered in a rough-and-ready but effective way. The administration was elastic and untiring, with much latitude to the man on the spot and the heavy demands on his energy and devotion. Days were spent in the saddle under a burning sun and nights in writing reports by the light of candles stuck into beer bottles. The gospel of this band was justice and material improvement. Roads, schools, court-houses were the order of the day; engineers would croon over a new bridge as over a new-born infant. Once more the Punjab was being put in order by a new dominant minority but this time it was one armed with the resources of the west and imbued with its material mythology. The result was an immediately contented Punjab, and later a prosperous and, with the coming of irrigation, a wealthy Punjab. But it was not a united Punjab. The façade was glossy though with a different sheen to that of Ranjit, but the structure was as brittle as his. The unity was superimposed, the prosperity material, while underneath the old separatist passions smouldered. The first success of the Punjab school was the loyalty of the province during the Mutiny of 1857, a loyalty, however, based on its very disunity. The School's crowning achievement was the canal colonies and the prosperity they brought, its nemesis the Amritsar massacre which revealed the failure of rulers and ruled to understand each other and the 1947 massacres which proclaimed the failure to develop any real Punjabi feeling.

This period of expansion is properly rounded off by the Mutiny of 1857-58. It has been variously regarded as a military mutiny only, as a deep-laid conspiracy set off too soon, as a popular movement of protest against innovation of various kinds, and as the first modern Indian war of independence. There were elements of all these factors to be found in the upheaval, but it is best understood by viewing it against the social and ideological background of nineteenth-century India. We have noted that an exhausted country in 1818 was quite ready to accept another foreign régime which might be regarded as a continuation or revival of Mughal rule, provided that the socio-religious fabric of society, both Hindu and Muslim, was left untouched. In general the Mughals had done this and had been able to extend their authority both in range and depth without arousing any popular reaction until they struck the nascent nationalism of the Marathas. This nationalism had burnt itself out in the furnace of predatory imperialism; it would be long before the smouldering embers could glow again with patriotic fervour. But this imposition of neutral rule over a traditional society was in fact, for all their professions, just what the British did not do. The start of the British Indian state under Warren Hastings was along these lines, but we have seen how this policy was transformed in the time of Bentinck. Western civilization, through the medium of western education and learning, of Christian missionary propaganda, of western material techniques and instruments, and above all the English language, was to be introduced. There was no destruction of the old, but an introduction of the new alongside. The new received government countenance, which in Indian eyes meant patronage, so that the government came to be associated no longer with the idea of neutral authority (like improved Mughals) but with the idea of innovation. As this impression spread, so the attitude of the traditional classes changed, for Indians are amongst the most conservative people in the world. The government gave no help to missionaries, but they were thought to countenance them and blamed for allowing them. Innovations like the telegraph were thought to be evil, and must therefore be in some way directed against the social order. Western education sowed doubts in the minds of Indian youth about Hindu orthodoxy, doubts which threatened to spread to sacred Benares itself. To these ideological disquiets were added more concrete grievances. There were the social disturbances caused by the great land settlements of northern India which displaced many landholders who could not show valid titles for their holdings. There was the confiscations of the Inam commission which resumed many rent-free holdings often originally given for religious or learned merit. The successors of the grantees were usually neither religious nor learned, but this did not prevent them and their neighbours from regarding their loss as a blow to the traditional order. In a vague and generalized way religion, then the most powerful factor in Indian life, was felt to be in danger. The resentments of the dispossessed and the fears of the orthodox were more potent than the gratitude of the beneficiaries or the hopes of the tiny new westernized class.

Thus Indian society by 1850 had entered a period of stress. Tension was inevitable if the new world of the west was to mingle with the old. In favourable circumstances the process might have been kept under control until the tension eased with the growth of understanding and of new classes committed to the new. But at this moment the tensions were brought to a focus by the activity of the new Governor-General, the Marquess of Dalhousie (1848–56). Perhaps the ablest and most energetic of the whole series in the nineteenth century he wore himself out with his exertions to die in 1860 at the age of forty-eight. Dalhousie was a convinced westernizer and it so happened that events played into his hands. Internally, he pushed forward public works more vigorously than ever before. Qualified by his experience with Gladstone at the Board of Trade in dealing with the English railway boom of the forties he planned and began the execution of the Indian railway system. He introduced the telegraph and developed roads. He directed the Lawrences in the organization of the Punjab. He pushed forward western education and planned (with Sir Charles Wood) the first three Indian universities. These were solid achievements but they were all westernizing ones and they tended to increase the existing general unease. They were capped by his most spectacular measures, the annexation of Indian states. Dalhousie considered British rule so superior to Indian that the more territory directly administered by the British the better would it be for the Indian people. So he evolved a doctrine of lapse by which the states of Hindu princes without direct heirs could be taken over despite the Hindu custom of adoption. He also appealed to chronic misgovernment as a valid ground for annexation. On these grounds in the course of eight years he annexed eight states including two Maratha states and the great Muslim state of Oudh. He also abolished two titular sovereignties and gave notice to the pensionary Mughal emperor at Delhi that his title would lapse at his death. There is no doubt that these measures alarmed the whole upper class. The annexation of Oudh for misgovernment was perhaps the most damaging of all though in its way the most justified, because it was generally regarded as a breach of faith. Thus when Dalhousie left India in 1856 the apparent public tranquillity concealed an explosive mixture which some incident might bring to a flashpoint.

That incident was provided by the military authorities with the army as its carrier. The Indian army contained a large Brahmin element which was particularly susceptible to the unease above described. It had shouldered the burden of successive campaigns during the last twenty years and believed itself to be indispensable to the British. It disliked, on religious grounds, the increasing tendency to employ it in distant regions beyond India and specially overseas. Then came the greased cartridges for the new Enfield rifles, smeared with cows' and pigs' fat, unclean to both Hindus and Muslims. The mistake was genuine, the cartridges were withdrawn, explanations were offered, but the flashpoint had been reached. The conviction ran like wildfire that there was a plot against the old cultures; the Mutiny followed.

The Mutiny proper began with the rising at Meerut on 10 May 1857 and the seizure of Delhi the next day; it virtually ended with the fall of Gwalior on 20 June 1858. In spite of four months' previous military unrest and successive incidents the authorities were caught by surprise with forces denuded for the recent Crimean war. For a time they had their backs to the wall. The arrival of reinforcements settled the issue which had never, in the long term not obvious to the combatants at the time, been in doubt. The highlights were the siege of Delhi and its recovery in late September, the operations round Kanpur and Lucknow including their famous sieges, and the central Indian campaign in 1858 of Tantia Topi and the Rani of Jhansi. Cardinal factors in the successful early British stand were the loyalty of the Punjab, due largely to Sikh dislike of Muslims and distrust of the revived Mughal régime in Delhi, and the passivity of the Deccan and South India. The war was fought with great ferocity on both sides, and reprisals were savage. The reason for this must be sought in the fact that the tensions on both sides were extreme. The Indian soldier was divided between strong feelings of loyalty and equally strong fears for his caste or religion, all that gave life meaning in fact. To him at that moment while mutiny meant probable death obedience meant probable degradation. The keenness of inner conflict was reflected in the extremity of outward action. The British on their side seemed hopelessly outnumbered and saw themselves and their families suddenly threatened with destruction. Their world of easy authority had dissolved in a moment, their most trusted subordinates had risen in revolt, they could no longer distinguish between friend and foe; their former self-confidence was profoundly shaken. Many of the atrocities on the British side were an index of this shaken morale. The later reprisals were inexcusable but must be understood as the acts of men distraught by the loss of their families as well as their comrades, and by many months of campaigning in conditions of terrible strain. Neither of these factors helps to explain the behaviour of the Calcutta Europeans, which must be put down to the mass hysteria which occasionally overtakes Europeans congregated in big eastern cities. The lasting effect of these horrors was in fact less than might have been expected. The sense of shock and insecurity long lingered, it is true, in British minds in the north. But the Indian people as a whole regarded the event as another of those *gardis* or calamities which periodically afflict their country. Soldiers were not expected to behave well in the heat of campaigns, while the plundering of cities and pillaging of innocent townsmen had often been suffered from other conquerors. The British were not thought to be worse than others; what was discovered was that, when roused, they were no better.

The revolt, originally military, evoked a number of other responses in India during its fourteen months' course. Delhi with its aged emperor formed a rallying point for Muslim revivalist sentiment which spread to parts of the western provinces. Nana Sahib became a focus for Maratha revivalism, agrarian grievances brought out many landholders in Bihar, and finally mismanagement brought out all the Oudh landlords. The peasants were notably passive, following their lords if they rose and otherwise cultivating their fields. These facts make it impossible to maintain that the revolt was purely military. Nor can any serious evidence be found for the idea of a clever conspiracy making use of military and local grievances. What, then, was the mutiny's real significance in the development of modern India? The actual mutiny had definite religious motives behind it. The revolts, so far as they had definite direction, looked backwards to the defunct Mughal and Maratha régimes which in their day had bitterly clashed. The agrarian risings reflected grievances stemming from government action. Nowhere can be found any sign of forward-looking action towards a united India. All the new westernized class were on the British side. Yet the whole mutiny-cum-revolt was highly significant and fraught with great consequences. Looking deeper into the situation as a whole I think it can be described as a last convulsive movement of protest against the coming of the west on the part of traditional India. The state of the army and the greased cartridges incident provided the occasion for violence which otherwise might never have occurred; thereafter the shape of the affair was determined by traditional memories, hopes, and fears. The form of the revolt was fragmentary, its climate nostalgic.

The mutiny had important results on both sides. The British received a severe shock to the self-confidence which for a generation had replaced their previous caution. They made important changes in policy and administration (which will be noted in the next chapter) in relation to the army and finance, the Indian states, the northern landlords, westernizing reform, and consultation with Indian opinion. By and large there was a change of attitude in two directions. It was realized that the government should be in closer touch with, and more sensitive to, Indian opinion, particularly the established classes who could control the general mass of the people, and there was a new caution in implementing the westernizing policy. Public works rather than public morals or western values was the guiding star of the postmutiny reformer. The effect of the mutiny on Indian opinion is far more difficult to gauge because one can only judge from a general trend of opinion as expressed by the small articulate section of the public. But in general terms the effect would seem to have been profound. As the bitterness cleared away it gradually became clear that the country as a whole had turned away from the guardian prophets of past glories. It liked the impinging west no better but realized that it now had to be lived with and absorbed into Indian life, as many foreign intrusions before. As a corollary it lost confidence in the traditional leaders, rajahs, chiefs, *zamindars*, and began to turn, without openly admitting it, to the new westernized class. The chiefs remained as decorative survivals enjoying much outward respect, but hopes for the future were more and more fastened on the new English-knowing upstarts. The evidence of this silent and fundamental shift in opinion is to be found in the sudden upsurge of English education in the course of the next generation. The pace had formerly been made by the government and missionaries; now it was to be set from the Indian side.

12

THE IMPERIAL HEYDAY

THE Mutiny, as has been noticed, came as a profound shock to the British. But it was a shock to their complacency rather than to their self-confidence. The manner of its outbreak and the shape which it took convinced them that it was specific mistakes on their part rather than inherent weakness in their rule which had caused the outbreak. The lack of good leadership (until it was too late), the inability of the rebels to combine for long, the backward-looking nature of the tentatively established régimes, convinced them that there was no serious danger of a united revolt on a secular issue, and no such thing as yet as nationalism in the European sense. India was still enmeshed in her socio-religious systems, and if these were respected there seemed no reason why the British *raj* should not last indefinitely. The western faith in progress was still strong. If the west was progressing materially, technically, and morally, whereas Hinduism and Islam were assumed to be static, it followed that the *raj* might expect to became steadily stronger rather than weaker.

But the mistakes had been serious and they had to be rectified. This attitude led to an extensive reorganization and re-orientation which gave British India its character during the next sixty years. The most obvious target of reform was the army, the most important part of which, the Bengal army, had virtually ceased to exist. Here, though the policy of caution or closing the empty stable door was dominant, another feature of the settlement, that of closer understanding between British and Indian, can also be perceived. The army took on the form which survived till independence, and whose traditions live on in the present Indian and Pakistani armies. The separation of the three armies of Bengal, Bombay, and Madras was retained because each group had its own tradition and their distinctness had prevented the spread of the mutiny virus from the Bengal to the other armies. But the Bengal army was completely recast. The Company's European troops, 16,000 strong, were paid off or absorbed into the British army. The rest of the army was reformed into community regiments, two battalions of which were always brigaded with a British battalion. The personnel of the army was modified. The Brahmin element from Uttar Pradesh, the core of the original mutiny, was heavily reduced and its place taken by Gurkhas, Sikhs, and Punjabis (Jats and Rajputs). This was so successful that the northern element was later increased with infusions of Pathans and Punjabis at the expense of men from the south. The ratio of European to Indian troops in the Bengal army was raised to parity, and nearly one to two for the army as a whole (65,000 to 140,000). Lastly the formidable artillery of the old army was abolished except for a few mountain batteries. Officers continued to be European but more of these were appointed and they lived in far closer touch with their men than before. The new principle of knowledge and understanding worked so successfully in practice that the army became a close brotherhood proverbial for cameraderie and *esprit de corps* which withstood all political pressures and carried it through to the new era.

The financial reorganization was also drastic, but was the expression not so much of repentance for the past as a determination to seize the occasion of a financial crisis and general upheaval to bring the financial structure up-to-date. Successive financiers were imported from Britain. Their task was to liquidate an annual deficit of seven million pounds and adjust Indian finances to the transition from a self-contained rural economy into the orbit of world economic forces. Apart from economies the new measures included an income-tax for five years, a uniform revenue tariff of ten per cent, a convertible paper currency, and the introduction of annual budgets and statements of accounts. Apart from improvements in techniques, these changes meant that India no longer needed to rely mainly on the inelastic revenue from land tax, but could tap new resources from the increasing external and internal trade by means of a revenue tariff and income tax. After an interlude of free trade doctrine, this system provided the basis for the expanding revenue of the twentieth century.

We now come to the main outlines of the settlement. More important than its details (though these cannot wholly be skipped) was the endeavour to learn from what were thought to be the mistakes of the past and a change of attitude towards the various classes in the country. The effect most emphasized in the various post-mortems, and underlined by the most searching Indian analysis of the upheaval,* was the lack of liaison between European officers and Indians of all classes. The criticism of Mirza Ghulum Husain three quarters of a century earlier, that the British 'were aloof and absorbed in their own concerns', was now accepted. Even if you are too superior to associate with those you govern, ran the argument, you should know what is going on. The lack of liaison was most glaring in the army but it was felt to have been prevalent on the civil side as well. Ignorance of the feelings aroused by Dalhousie's annexations of Indian states and treatment of the pensionary emperor, of the effect of the land assessments in the minds of discontented dispossessed land-holders, of the reaction of orthodox sentiment to western inno-vations, was thought to be partly responsible for the later revolts of some chiefs and landholders, and for Muslim participation. On the other hand it was noticed that the princes in general stood firm, to be described by a grateful Canning as 'breakwaters in a storm', and that so did the bulk of the landholders. The peasants, however, in whose favour the great northern land settlements had in general been made, had remained apathetic. The limit of their horizon was still the village boundary and they would not stir to defend a distant and alien benefactor from the often oppressive but familiar landholder at their doors. A third impression which the upheaval left behind was disenchantment with the Indian response to the advent of the west. In the thirties it had been assumed that it was only necessary to place the better western institution or innovation beside the traditional eastern custom for Indians to welcome the former. Superstition would give way to reason and ignorance to the new knowledge. But it was now sadly admitted that this was not so. The citadels of religious tradition and custom were stronger than had been thought.

Out of these reflections there arose three resolves. There must be closer touch with Indian opinion. Misunderstanding was too expensive in its results to be made an excuse for over-confidence

* By Sayyid Ahmad Khan, *The Causes of the Indian Revolt*, 1873.

or superiority. The classes with a stake in the country must be treated with more consideration and actively enlisted on the British side. And great caution must be exercised in dealing with established customs or institutions in any way connected with religion. We will trace the practical consequences of each attitude in turn.

The first casualty on the ignorance count was the East India Company itself. It was, indeed, but a shadow of its former self, and, but for the inherent British conservatism and tenderness for vested interests, would probably have been abolished at the last Charter renewal Act in 1853. It had lost all its trade and was now nothing more than a managing agency for the administration of India subject to the British government's direction in matters of policy. But it was held to have failed to gauge Indian opinion, to be inert and backward-looking. The occasion of the Mutiny was thus a convenient one to end an administrative anomaly which had become an anachronism. The Company was also a convenient scapegoat to divert attention from sins of omission. So, in spite of John Stuart Mill's pleas for a corporation which had preserved Indian administration from the whirlpool of British politics and did not now even have the patronage of its own services, its governing powers were abolished. The Crown stood forth, in name as well as in fact, as the ruler of India. Queen Victoria took her relationship to her new subjects very seriously and contrived, by some esoteric magic of her own, to convey her concern to them. At any rate the new régime was more personal, something which Indians liked. In the next thirty years, helped by the Queen's initial proclamation, there grew an extraordinary attachment and even reverence for the Queen's person which littered Indian cities with her statues and certainly strengthened Anglo-Indian ties. Without apparent effort Victoria had captured the mystique of Akbar.

The Board of Control disappeared in favour of a Secretary of State and the Court of Directors melted into the minister's India Council. The change was not as great as it looked on paper, but on the whole it was for the better, in its overtones more than in its main themes. A certain small-mindedness which had lingered with mercantile directors disappeared. Experience on the spot replaced business interest in the India Council; though this on occasion could be backward-looking it at any rate added experience to the British direction. An important loss was the twenty-year inquests at charter renewals, but in compensation was the fact that Indian administration as well as policy could now come under daily Parliamentary scrutiny. The Indian interest in the Commons was small but it could be effective.

In India the Governor-General retained his title but added the honorific of Viceroy. He gained thereby in prestige as the personal representative of the monarch. But more important was the remodelling of the Legislative Council. Here the principle of Indian consultation came in. The existing council, set up in 1853, had representatives of the three presidencies but they were British officials, not Indians. It was an interesting body for it had modelled its procedure on Parliament and had proved a sore trial to Lord Canning. The new council contained up to twelve members additional to the Executive Council and half were to be non-official. In practice these were aristocratic Indians, princes, landed gentry, or states administrators. Its powers were limited to considering matters laid before it. Such a body may be regarded as the proverbial mouse emerging from the travail of the mutiny mountain. But it had a significance, for it marked the beginning of Indian participation in government at the top. After years of dwarfdom, the mouse was to grow into an elephant.

The second resolve was to conciliate and reward the princes and landed classes. The loyalty of the Rajput, Maratha, and Sikh chiefs, in spite of Dalhousie's annexations, and of the Nizam (in spite of the virtual loss of Berar four years before) had been of the utmost value in preventing the spread of the revolt. Yet they were entirely outside the British-Indian system. The attempt was now made to integrate as well as reward them. Their territories were guaranteed and some received material recognition for special service. But the most significant change was the psychological. They were now regarded as members of an Order, not just survivals and anachronisms. They were an integral part of the Indian empire and had a personal relationship to the monarch. Men like Lords Mayo and Lytton saw them as props of imperialism from whose class a self-governing and pro-British India might ultimately arise. They were to be taught modern administration. They were to be encouraged to become enlightened despots on the eighteenth-century model with nineteenth-century standards. Lord Lytton even proposed an Indian peerage for them. This whole procedure was a far-reaching and imaginative reversal of previous policy. Had it been pursued vigorously and consistently it might have had far-reaching effects and transformed India as known today. But neither of these things was done and the policy eventually fizzled out in a series of half-measures. At least, however, it gave a new lease of life to the states and an immediate stability to the British *raj*.

The same attitude was reflected in the revised land policy of the government. The tactless treatment of the Oudh *taluqdars* had at one time confronted the British with a whole province in revolt when it was found that, after all Sleeman and others had written about them with truth, the peasants would still follow them as their traditional overlords. It was noted that it was dispossessed landholders in Bihar who turned the mutiny there into something like an agrarian revolt. Further, even where there were settlements with village communities and landlords, as around Delhi, the villagers remained inert. All this prompted what has recently been termed the aristocratic reaction in land policy.* The extension of the Permanent Settlement of Bengal, of great advantage to the landholders, was seriously considered. Short of this their estates were safeguarded, they themselves were cherished with such devices as honorary magistracies,† the tendency to come between them and their tenants was checked, and they were treated as important props to the administration. The authorities tried to picture them as improving British resident landlords, which in fact they were not, and herein lay the fallacy in the whole of this change of front. The obscurantist and inert attitudes of the United Provinces landlords in the 1920s after sixty years of official 'nursing' showed that the landlords had changed from their previous character even less than the

* On this subject the recent work of three young scholars, Dr T. Metcalf, Dr G. Hambly, and Dr G. Reeves, is of great value.
† The Indian version of J.P.s.

princes had done. An attempt was even made to revise the Punjab settlement in favour of dispossessed landlords. But at this point (1864) John Lawrence, the life-long 'cherisher of the poor', returned to India as Viceroy. One of the most significant episodes of his misunderstood Viceroyalty was his battle against the aristocratic reaction, entrenched in Bengal and now advancing to the north. As a result the movement was checked and ended in a British compromise – landlords in the east, small holdings in the north with the safeguarding of tenant-rights as the shuttlecock of official discussions and legislative action.

The third change of attitude affected the policy of westernization. The confidence of Bentinck and the radicals, that reason must triumph, and of Dalhousie, that all good things came from the west and the more of them the better, had received a rude shock. The Mutiny was considered in one aspect as a resurgence of the old order against western innovations. It was now thought that the upper classes must be conciliated, because the humbler would follow them. In the long run this deduction was fallacious but it nevertheless expressed the prevailing feeling. The upper classes (reckoned by caste, by money, or by birth) were the most conservative in a conservative country. All interference was therefore eschewed from this time on; it was fortunate that suttee had been suppressed thirty years before. Such measures as Dalhousie's Widows Remarriage Act and the allowing of converts to inherit property were no longer thought of. After the promulgation of the Indian Penal Code in 1861, which involved little practical change, there was no social legislation until the Age of Consent (Sarda) Act of 1929 which, however, the government did not seriously attempt to enforce. Behind this attitude lay not only a realization that India had not responded as quickly as had been hoped to the play of western influences. There was a certain irritation at encrusted Indian conservatism, which, thought the rulers, did not know a good thing when it saw it. But deeper than this there was widespread pessimism as to the rate of possible change. It is no use trying to force change, was the new attitude. One must sit back and wait patiently for it to come. This new attitude, however, involved a dilemma. Britain was now too deeply committeed to the western enterprise to with-

draw completely. Dalhousie, the great westernizer, had achieved
at least this in his eight years of rule. The answer was found in
the vigorous pursuits of material projects while avoiding overt
interference in the social system. John Lawrence in the Punjab
had done both : suttee and infanticide went down as bridges
and roads went up. Canning and his successors dropped the
former to intensify the latter. The government thus assumed an
'enabling' role in this matter. Their public works provided the
means for the growth of western influence, whether in commerce, industry, irrigation, education, or science; the Indian
people were left to make what they liked of it. This accounts for
the 'patchy' nature of Indian development in the next fifty years.
Industry developed slowly because enablement, by means of
railways, was not followed by promotion. Inter-communication
developed fast because Indians took to the new transport enablement, and so did western education because they decided to exploit the new college system. Outstanding among these public
works were roads and railways. The railway system planned in
1853 was virtually complete by 1900, giving India the best
system in Asia. Though some of the lines were strategical in
motive and unremunerative in practice the system as a whole
encouraged commerce and made the development of modern
industry possible. A second major public work was the development of irrigation. The process had begun by 1820 with the
repair of Mughal canals in the north and old 'tanks' or irrigation
lakes in the south. It was pushed forward by Dalhousie and
reached its apogee in the Punjab and Sind. By 1947 one fifth of
the cultivable area was under irrigation and so immune from
monsoon vagaries. The Sukkur barrage in Sind, now a mainstay
of Pakistan agriculture, was the last great public work completed
by the British in India. Canals were part of the campaign against
famine, which was finally brought under control in the eighties
with the development of the great Famine Code. To canals
were added later hydroelectric projects, harbour works, and great
new bridges. The new attitude may be said to have taken shape
as the importation of the body of the west without its soul.

The new attitude involved certain corollaries. The belief that
India would remain backward-looking or self-centred for a long

time meant that British rule might be expected to continue almost indefinitely. Self-government, towards which the eager westernizer Dalhousie was considering the first tentative steps, was a thing of the distant future. The concept of prolonged trusteeship for a ward in court replaced that of deliberate westernization with an expectation of ultimate self-government. This view was expressed most eloquently by Lord Curzon on the eve of its overthrow at the turn of the century. Though not undisputed in Britain, it was the creed of officialdom in India and the working rule of its government. The assumption that India was almost changeless and that safety was to be sought in conciliating the upper class had another important consequence. It led to an underrating, in fact to a neglect, of the new rising westernized middle class. This English-knowing group of clerks, professional men like lawyers and teachers, subordinate officials, and a few leisured men, had staunchly supported the government in the Mutiny crisis. Their existence was indeed involved in its fortunes. But they were not thought important enough to be noticed or rewarded. They were government hacks or hangers-on of the west; what help could they be in governing the millions of the traditionally-minded? Accordingly the government looked to the leaders of the old class for signs of progress. They looked in vain, for the main object of this class was to keep things as they were. Nevertheless they continued to look and so failed to notice what was going on at their own office desks, in the lawyers' clubs, and in schools and colleges all over the country. The fissure between the British and the new India began at this point.

The period from Canning's proclamation of the end of the revolt in 1858 to the Partition of Bengal in 1905 can be called the heyday of British rule in India. The British not only felt themselves to be superior but they found their superiority acknowledged both by the old traditionalists and by the new westernized classes. For the former it was the superiority of power, for the latter the magic of the new knowledge. This feeling was well expressed by Sir W. Hunter in his *India of the Queen* (1887), an acute observer apt in catching prevailing currents of opinion. From Lord Canning there proceeded a stately procession of Viceroys down to Lord Curzon whose collective image was passed on to the British public by Kipling as wise, benevolent, and inscrutable rulers, the dispensers of justice and friends of the poor, saying little in public while in private countering with humanity and craft the machinations of foreign powers and the schemes of the unrighteous. The stately procession moved on, hiding behind its pageantry many controversies and much activity. There was John Lawrence with his battle for tenant rights against the aristocratic reaction. There was Lord Mayo, an Irishman who wooed the princes, bemused the Afghans, and was murdered by a convict. Then came the banker Northbrook with the exterior of a Dombey and the will of an autocrat, governing with rigour the most colourful of lands with the most colourless of letters. His successor was the brilliant Lytton (1876-80) who shocked Simla society by smoking cigarettes between courses at dinner and the British cabinet by his wilfulness towards the Afghans. At the same time he set in motion the great famine control scheme which saved India from famine starvation down to 1943. By contrast his successor Ripon (1880-84) was a Gladstone without his mentor's eloquence or drive. The polished Dufferin, who did nothing in particular and did it very well, the aristocrat Lord Lansdowne, and the Scottish working-peer Elgin make up the list to 1899. Through all these years railways were being built, canals dug, famine combated, and the land system improved. Western education was developing and modern industry was establishing itself. In the former case a grant-in-aid system enabled Indians to run their own private colleges which were affiliated to a central university. Higher education therefore went ahead while the literacy of the people lagged behind. In the latter, industries sprang up through both Indian and British enterprise, taking advantage of the new conditions of world trade and the new facilities for transport provided by railways and the Suez canal. The government share was the 'enabling' action of railway construction. It was this period which saw the rise of the plantation industries of jute and cotton, the coal industry, and the iron industry which later developed into the famous Tata steel mills. The plantation industries were mainly British-managed and owned. Cotton was almost entirely in the hands of Indians and Parsees in Bombay and western

India; it got under way with the opening of the Empress mill in Nagpur in 1887 by J. N. Tata. The jute industry, mainly British-owned and Scots-managed, was started in Calcutta when Russian jute was cut off during the Crimean war. The coalfields in Bengal and Behar were in British hands but they came to feed the iron and steel industry which was the achievement of the Parsee Tata family.

Maintaining the stage across which the Viceroys walked were the I.C.S.s, the administrative maids-of-all-work. They numbered about a thousand, administered all the districts and manned the secretariats, rising to the Governor-General's council and the governorships of the newer provinces. It was a strenuous service but also the best rewarded in the world at that time in power, prestige, and money. It threw up many able and some remarkable figures and collectively was one of the ablest groups of men to be found anywhere. It was almost entirely British. Since 1853 it had been recruited by competition and took the cream of the more adventurous talent from the universities. But it still, with its associated army, political, educational, and technical services, retained close family connexions. These services ran India with a high degree of both efficiency and devotion. At the same time they were as a whole dedicated to maintaining things as they were. Their disbelief in Indian capacity was pronounced, distrust of Indian claims profound, and opposition to Indian encroachment in the higher services determined. The service was at once the strength and weakness of the British *raj* in India, for while it served the needs of a static society to admiration it was temperamentally unsuited to adapt itself to the demands of a changing society and larger world.

To this stately symphony of imperial themes and measured material harmonies must be added a discordant ideological note. The liberal upsurge in Britain associated with Gladstone between 1868 and 1886 found its way to India with Lord Ripon (1880–84). Ideas of self-government were for a time once more in the air. Gladstone announced that it was 'our weakness and our calamity' that 'we have not been able to give to India the benefits and blessings of free institutions'. On his electoral victory in 1880 he sent Lord Ripon to start to put these sentiments into practice. In four years Ripon introduced a system of local self-government for both town and country, and pushed forward education until he ran against the solid European non-official and general official resistance with his proposal that Indian sessions judges should be allowed to try Europeans in the Ilbert bill. The racial storm thus roused subdued Ripon to a compromise but when he retired he received an Indian ovation accorded to no other viceroy before or after. Had he been a stronger man, or politics in Britain taken a different turn, partnership instead of resistance to the new nationalism might have been the keynote of Indo-British relations from then, with very different results for later relationships.

There remains to notice Indian foreign policy during the half-century after the Mutiny. From 1830 India had been exercised by the possible advance of Russia towards India and it was this fear, along with considerations of European policy, which prompted the first Afghan war in 1839. This adventure and the disaster of 1841 revealed both the strength of Afghan resistance to inter-ference and the weakness of Russia in this distant field. The annexation of the Punjab in 1849 added the turbulent tribesmen of the mountains to the problems of Indian statecraft. The two first factors and the latter complication produced the policy described as 'masterly inactivity'. It was thought that Afghans were the best defenders of their own independence, that the Rus-sians were still far off, and that the tribes should be kept within bounds rather than directly controlled. This policy lasted until the seventies, when the steady advance of Russia in central Asia again aroused alarm. The coincidence of this movement with the Balkan crisis of 1875-78 induced Disraeli and Salisbury again to seek safety in Asia by using the Afghans as a buttress against Russia. Their agent, Lord Lytton, had dreams of marching into Turkistan, and plunged into the second Afghan war (1878-80). Once again it was shown that the Afghans were easier to defeat in open battle than to subdue and that the Russians would not stand by such distant protégés when it came to the trial. The gifted chief Abdur Rahman restored the *status quo* which con-tinued, with one short interlude, for the rest of the British period.

Upper Burma was annexed by Dufferin in 1886 as a counter

to French moves and an expedition sent to Lhasa in 1904 by Curzon as a reply to imagined Russian activity. Both moves were ill-judged, the Tibetan being discreditable as well. In fact during this period India was as externally secure as at any time in her history. Persia and China were too weak to be a threat and Russia too distant and preoccupied. The British fleet effectively excluded the French, while in south-east Asia the Dutch, supported in Europe by Britain, were in effect British agents. Up to 1900 the Indian external sky in general seemed clear.

13

THE NATIONAL MOVEMENT: CULTURAL AND POLITICAL

BENEATH the burnished cover of the British administration the mind of India was actually in ferment. Western ideas and ways of life had not been accepted or rejected but they were under serious examination all over the sub-continent. For the first time in many centuries – from the time, in fact, of the first large-scale contact with Islam – India was seriously considering an alternative philosophy. India had seen the collapse of the Mughals, the struggle of Afghan and Rohilla, and the rise of the British, unmoved. She regarded the empire of merchants as just another foreign oddity and their military skills as just a new expertise. But the import of western ideas and their spread through western education, foreign officials, and administrative methods was a different matter. Christianity as a system was already known and discounted. It was not dogma but pervasive universal ideas appealing to the basis of Hindu philosophy itself which alarmed them. From this concern with the new ideological invasion which could not be evaded arose the phenomenon which we call Indian nationalism. A better title for the whole movement would perhaps be the Indian transformation. For it was by no means nationalism in the commonly accepted western sense, a common aspiration for self-government based on a common language, territory, or racial strain. Rather it was a mingling of old ideas with new which produced both a political movement against the foreigners and a transformation of traditional society. The concept of an Indian nation of equal citizens was itself novel with important consequences for the social structure itself.

In looking for the roots of Indian nationalism we can begin with an emotion and a tradition. The emotion was dislike of the foreigner which in India for many ages has gone along with a tolerance of his presence. The tradition was that of Hinduism deeply rooted and the basis of what has been called the fundamental unity of India. The Arab philosopher Albiruni noted in the eleventh century that the Hindus believed 'that there was no country like theirs, no kings like theirs, no religion like theirs, no science like theirs'. The foreigner was impure in a stronger sense than the barbarian to the Greek or the Gentile to the Jew. Foreign rule was thus impure, whether it was Muslim, Turkish, or Christian. But for all its aversion to the strange and the external the Hindu system did not easily lend itself to united action. The system of castes was inward looking and divisive, of cults competing and often conflicting. It naturally expressed itself in a medley of religious movements, social castes, and political kingdoms so that united action against the foreigners was rare and difficult. At the advent of the British there was the further complication of the presence of the Muslims. As a religio-social system Islam was inimical to Hinduism, and, though hostility had been softened by time and compromise, the basic antagonism remained.

But xenophobia and pride in tradition was not a sufficient foundation for a new movement. The end of such yearnings was the Mutiny fiasco. They provided influences in such a movement but could not create it. There was one other factor within India which played a part. This may be called tribalism or regionalism and is associated with the Marathas of western India. Alone among the Indian peoples in recent times the Marathas developed a community spirit which transcended the horizontal barriers of caste. Brahmin, soldier, cultivator, and outcaste Prabhu felt a common allegiance to Maharashtra. They regarded the war against the Mughals as a struggle for independence as well as a defence of religion. Alone in India, when their princes were defeated in the field, they took to the hills and to horse in guerilla warfare. This could not be the basis for an all-India nationalism for the feeling was anti-Muslim and too exclusively Maratha. But it set an example and was also an important influence on the movement which was to arise.

This was the background to the modern national movement. India was not herself going to produce secular nationalism; it would require some sort of stimulus from outside. But what sort of stimulus? India had it seemed developed a socio-religious chrysalis which sheltered it from the emotional pains of foreign conquest and from most of the strains of rival religious attack. When the adoption of European military methods failed to prevent the British supremacy India accepted it as she had accepted the Mughals. When British merchants exploited Bengal, Indian financiers adjusted by attaching themselves to the exploiters. Why did they not treat western civilization as something to be lived with like Islam, but not to be absorbed? Why did the chrysalis break, or at least crack, under the impact of the west? I think the answer is that the western influence came, not as the challenge of a closed religious system, but in the form of universal ideas in a secular setting, which could be accepted and even acted upon to some extent, without open treason to social and religious tradition. The early western incursion of the Portuguese in the sixteenth century presented the west in the form of Renaissance and Counter-Reformation catholicism. It presented a choice of 'either', 'or', and this choice was one which Hindu society knew well how to deal with. Western influence came into Bengal with the establishment and extension of British rule from Warren Hastings's time on. Though Indian customs were respected and a few like Hastings himself and Sir W. Jones studied the Indian cultural heritage, it became fashionable to learn English for career purposes and the nimble Bengali mind was soon absorbing the ideas within it. In 1816 the Hindu College was founded where English was taught and its literature studied. The career motive beside this move can be seen in the fact that the leader of Calcutta orthodoxy was a prominent promoter.

But the new ideas soon started people asking questions. What was the reason for the extraordinary success of the apparently godless English? If the attitudes of western thought were applied to current Hinduism was there no need for reform? If physical force was no remedy for this foreign rule, could their ideas be borrowed and used against them? Should rights replace cannons as weapons and speeches volleys of musketry?

This tension was sharpened by the increasingly critical tone of the Europeans. Evangelical criticism of idolatry could be born but their campaigns against suttee and infanticide stirred uneasy consciences. Radical emphasis on reason in the attacks on superstition was embarrassing because the whole of Hindu philosophy claimed to be based on this concept. So was the talk of human rights, contrasting, as it did, with the situation of many classes. Dilemmas like these, which might have passed over the head of an indifferent aristocrat, intent on his hunting and musical entertainments, or the self-absorbed merchant or cultivator, had to be faced in Calcutta. These were the reasons that the first stirrings of change in Hindu society began in the early nineteenth century and why they began in Calcutta.

These reflections produced an attitude which may be summarized in these queries. How can we get even with this new monster from the west without being false to our own tradition and is there, perhaps, something in the west which might be of value in reforming our own society? So began that process of adaptation to the new intrusion which Hinduism has staged many times before. India was fortunate in finding at this moment a man who crystallized in his life and thought this whole situation and provided lines of development for the future. He was Ram Mohan Roy, a Brahmin who took service with the British, made a fortune in Calcutta, worked as assistant of the Collector of Rangpur, and then spent his life advocating and promoting reform in all directions. Born about 1772 he ended his career as the ambassador of the pensionary Mughal emperor to Britain and died in Bristol on 19 September 1833.* He mastered Greek and Latin as well as Sanskrit, Arabic, and Persian; his activities included the printing of the first Indian newspaper, the founding of a religious sect, the advocacy of the abolition of suttee, the promotion of civil and political rights, and a journey to England. Ram Mohan Roy took his stand on the principles of reason and the rights of the individual. These, he said, were basic to both Hindu and western thought and formed a basis upon which they could mutually borrow. Reason and human right, he considered, underlay the philosophic *Upanishads* and on this basis Indians could claim the same rights as Europeans. By the same token Hindus could and should reform their own society by removing the accretions of ages. On these grounds, with copious scriptural quotation, he attacked the institution of suttee and the

* A pilgrimage now annually visits his tomb in the Arno Vale cemetery on each anniverary.

abuses of caste, advocated the raising of the status of women and the abolition of idolatry. Since the west was not essentially inimical to Hindu ideas, Hindus could borrow freely from it. He therefore advocated the cultivation of the English language, the study of English literature and specially sciences, and the replacement of Persian by English as the official language.

These ideas were of course limited at first to a very small circle and they lacked at first a social class to act as their carriers. This need was provided by the administrative measures of the British. English in fact replaced Persian as the language of government business and the higher courts. At a stroke therefore its knowledge became necessary for all who had relations with government, whether in or out of service. Western knowledge became the content of government-sponsored education to whom ambitious youths now turned, from the same date. Thus a widespread knowledge of English and the western knowledge to which it was the key was secured at the same time. Around governmental activity arose a new middle class drawing into its elements the old professional groups, but unifying them with a common relationship to public life and a common intellectual equipment. This class consisted of government, subordinate executive, and legal officers down to the point where only a local language was required, the ministerial staffs of the secretariats in the chief cities; teachers, lawyers, and western-trained doctors, an emerging class of technicians, some groups of merchants in the cities (like the Parsees in Bombay) and of landholders, like the *zamindars* of Bengal. The old middle class was compartmentalized, separated by differences of language, interest, and mental background. Some of these like the Muslim *maulanas* and Sanskrit teaching pundits, the practitioners of the Hindu and Muslim systems of medicine, were left behind to linger on in isolation, but many joined the new class. The Hindu physicians of Bengal, for example, took to western medicine in large numbers and are prominent practitioners today. This new class was nourished by the English press which grew up to serve it.

From this point we may divide the movement of renaissance broadly into two streams, the religious and the secular. We may start in the religious stream with the most radical current of all.

There was a group in Calcutta who, influenced by the rationalism of Hume and Paine, regarded the whole structure of
Hinduism as superstitious and archaic. They found a gifted exponent in the young Anglo-Indian Derozio whose meteoric
career ended in an early death after expulsion from his lectureship in the Hindu college. The solution of total rejection of the
old was matched by the solution of total acceptance of the new.
Another Calcutta group, influenced by the Scottish Presbyterian
Alexander Duff, regarded the adoption of Christianity as the
natural corollary of a general acceptance of the west. For a time a
stream of high caste converts provided the future leaders of the
north Indian Christian community and one of them, Michael
Sudhan Datta, attained a high place in the Bengali literary renaissance. From 1840 these movements died away but we may here
note the place of Christian missions both Catholic and Protestant
in the Indian transformation of the nineteenth century. The isolated individuals of the eighteenth century were followed by the
Baptist William Carey in 1792, who, settling in Danish Seram-
pore, launched a large scale translation of the gospels into Indian
languages. From 1813, when British India was opened to missionaries, a trickle grew into a flood by the mid century. English
Protestants were joined by Americans and Germans, while
Catholic activity revived, specially in the south. Their activities
were evangelistic and pastoral, educational, leading up to a network of colleges, and philanthropic, in particular medical. We
have noted that Christian propaganda, often insensitive and
wounding, was one of the irritants to the orthodox before the
Mutiny. But what other results did this activity have? The Duff
episode was the only instance of direct impact on the Hindu
mind on any scale. But Christian (and with it general western)
influence was significant in two ways. The schools and colleges
imparted both Christian ethics and western ideas which perceptibly influenced the mind of the new middle class. The
medical work with its circle of hospitals deeply appealed to the
conscience of India. The toll of converts was not large from
either of these methods but the effect on the mind and heart of
India was very great. Here, said the thoughtful, was true religion
at work. Hindu reform movements came to imitate their

methods. The whole episode prepared the way for the break-through in Hinduism itself from passive realization to the active philanthropy associated with the name of Mahatma Gandhi.

The last result of mission activity was the gradual formation of a Christian community of about seven million souls. Drawn mainly from the lower castes this body was at first little regarded. The western influences it received were in a religious mould and could not therefore be easily passed on to a resistant Hinduism. But the body has grown steadily in weight as well as numbers and is now recognized as one of the regular constituents of Indian society.

The first of the Indian religious movements was that of Ram Mohan Roy himself. He considered that reason as expressed in the Upanishads * was the basis of Hindu religion and that all social institutions or customs should be judged from that standpoint. From this premise he drew two conclusions, that Hindu society needed radical reform and that Hinduism could welcome external influences which were not contrary to the spirit of reason. He also considered that the recognition of human rights was consistent with basic Hindu thought. He expressed this idea in his Brahmo Samaj or Divine Society, founded in 1828. He substituted theism for classical monism and denounced suttee, infanticide, idolatry, and polygamy. From the west he borrowed the Christian ethic, expounded in his book the *Precepts of Jesus,* and a belief in modern science. The group was joined by the grandfather of Rabindranath Tagore, whose son became its second head. It spread its branches over India and while its numbers remained small and its intellectualism denied it a large popular appeal, it became an important influence in the new class and indirectly all over India.

With the *Arya Samaj* founded by the Gujarati Brahmin Swami Dayananda in 1875 we pass to a return to the past on more orthodox and more drastic lines. Dayananda went back to the Vedas, the original scriptures of Hinduism. These, he said, contained all knowledge and from this fundamentalist basis he examined the later accretions of Hindu society. Most of them he rejected to produce a simple and dynamic creed which proved

* Philosophical treaties constituting the *Vedanta* or 'after the Vedas'.

specially attractive to the people of the Punjab. He rejected caste along with idolatry, polygamy, child marriage, and the seclusion of widows. Ritual centred on the simple fire ceremony of the early Aryans and worship became congregational. This movement has been an important force in the transformation of India, but a certain aggressiveness confined its main appeal to the Punjab, while its fundamentalism led it into intolerance towards both Muslims and Christians. The first of these phobias had grave effects on communal relations in the north during the twentieth century.

A further movement was that of Ramkrishna (1834–86) who lived for many years largely in trance at the Vaishnavite temple of Dakshineshwar in Bengal. At first sight he seemed to be a typical medieval Hindu saint in the tradition of Chaitanya, but he inspired his vedantist follower Swami Vivekananda to found the Ramkrishna Mission. With saffron-robed monks in the place of white missionaries this body carried on educational, medical, and spiritual work all over India. Its message is the essential oneness of all paths to reality and the expression of spirit in fruitful action. Finally there were a series of individual teachers like Sri Arabindo Ghose of Pondicherry and more recently Ramana Maharshi of Ernakulam who taught without founding sects.

None of these bodies triggered off a mass movement though the Arya Samaj approached it. The Brahmos were too eclectic, the Aryas too regionally temperamental and the Ramkrishna disciples too absorbed in the individual. Hinduism was not going to meet the west by means of a massive organized religious reform movement. But the transformation of society was nevertheless proceeding at a slower pace and a more subdued tempo. It is to the developing outlook in the new middle class that we must now turn. Individuals among them joined the different sects but the majority, like majorities elsewhere, lived mainly secular lives with religion providing a background and social framework into which they had somehow to contrive to fit. Fortified by these leaders to regard borrowings from the west as legitimate while assured that their ancestral religion contained the essence of wisdom, they were occupied in the task of selection and absorption. In the course of fifty years from 1830 their numbers not only grew but their outlook subtly changed. Without abandoning caste or traditional ritual they added western ideas and superficial customs. It might be described as caste in the home, equal rights in the street, the *dhoti* at ease, the western suit on duty. The mixture was illogical and seemed often absurd but it worked because it was based on the belief that ultimately the two systems could be reconciled. Why then despise the occasional incongruities of the trial-and-error process? Changes in personal and social values went on by an unseen and immeasurable process. Social customs remained at first un-affected because of their rigidity. But there were no such barriers in the realms of personal sentiment or political ideas. These last were readily embraced and soon became the working creed of the new class as a whole. As rationalism undermined personal belief in the old gods, as distinct from social acceptance, the new class felt a chill vacuum at the vital point of religious experience. This was filled by the new sentiment of political nationalism. Mother India had become a necessity and so she was created. Freedom was an interesting idea but patriotism was a warm emotion. In this way Indian nationalism was superimposed upon Bengali and Marathi regionalism by the new class.

The ideas which were imbibed from the rulers' literature and attitudes were nationalism, civil liberties, and constitutional self-government. No one could be in contact with Englishmen at that time for long or read Shakespeare (prescribed reading in the colleges) without catching the infection of nationalism. In addition, the new class was prone to it, as it were, because of the emotional void created by the increasing scepticism towards the traditional cults. The tone towards civil liberties was set by Ram Mohan Roy himself who held a public dinner in celebration of the French revolution of 1830 and championed civil rights with the government of his day. Political liberalism was then in the air, abounding in the literature read by the new class and im-plicit in the behaviour of the Englishmen with whom they came into contact. A corollary of such views was personal equality and mutual respect; and it was here that a cleavage between the new Indians and the new rulers began. In the past the arrogance of the Mughal magnate and the pride of the Brahmin had been accepted as part of the natural order of things. The pride of the new rulers was at first accepted on the same basis. But such attitudes did not agree with the new notions of equality and democratic rights. The new class began to feel inferior not as clients to patrons but as Indians to Europeans. This developed into the later charges of racialism. In the meantime the new class sought means to support their self-respect. They found it in the works of Europeans glorifying the history and cultural achievements of the Indian past. Sanskritists like Sir William Jones and Max Muller revived their confidence in themselves. Tod's *Annals of Rajasthan*, celebrating the deeds of Rajput chivalry, which has only seen three English editions in a hundred and thirty years, became a bestseller in pirate editions in nineteenth-century India. Thus the new intelligentsia sustained its ego.

As in other matters the Mutiny of 1857 proved to be a turning-point for the new class. They supported the new régime to a man, and received no recognition. But the old aristocratic classes above them were finally discredited as possible saviours of Indian society. Henceforth the new men were the hope of the future and were looked upon with a new respect by the traditional Indian for all (to him) their queer ways and foreign lispings. One symptom of this is what is now described as the educational explosion from about 1870 onwards. Before 1857 it was the government which was founding colleges and pushing education; after 1870 it was the public which was setting up private colleges with the help of grants-in-aid and agitating for new universities. A second symptom was the emergence of political agitation in a concrete form. The first Indian suggestions about Indian government were made by the Bengal landlords association in the Charter discussions of 1853. In 1876 the Indian Association was founded by Surendranath Banerjea, a young member of the middle class who had been ejected from the I.C.S. upon what appeared to be insufficient grounds. This body focussed criticism on Lytton's apparently aggressive Afghan policy, legislation against the Indian press, the lowering of the civil service examination age, thus making it more difficult for Indians to compete in London, and the abolition of the revenue tariff, thus giving Lancashire cotton goods an advantage over Indian. With the coming of Lord Ripon in 1880 and his liberal measures the new class was immensely encouraged. But it still had an organization only in Bengal. An occasion was needed to precipitate still further middle-class sentiment into political form. The occasion was provided by Lord Ripon himself with the Ilbert bill; its political precipitation was the Indian National Congress.

14

CONGRESS, CURZON, AND REFORM

THE Ilbert bill proposal arose naturally out of the circumstances of the previous few years. What was unexpected was the explosion of feeling on both sides which it occasioned. This was because the growth of the middle class had been so gradual and so widely spread as to be hardly noticeable to the average observer. But in the previous twenty-five years it had spread a thin covering over the whole of India. In number, as Lord Dufferin remarked a few years later, it was still a microscopic minority. But the minority now possessed a language, ideas, and attitudes in common; it had a common mind and speech, as no other middle class in India had had before, and it could take an all-India view. And it is always minorities, though Lord Dufferin forgot to add this, provided they are dynamic, that change the shape of nations.

The cohesion of this class had been promoted by the joint stimuli of encouragement and irritation. The encouragement came partly from the government's liberal measures such as the introduction of examinations for I.C.S. entry, Queen Victoria's proclamation and the beginnings of municipal self-government under Mayo. It came also from the work of Oriental scholars, who presented ancient India as a great civilization with a profound philosophy. This helped to produce a positive reaction to the other group of stimuli. The contempt of Europeans both racially and culturally was widespread and very wounding to people taught to believe in human and civil rights. The virtual exclusion of Indians from all high office was increasingly resented. The government's use of Indian troops for imperial purposes, manipulation of tariffs, and handling of the press, were all thought to be attacks on the dignity of the new conception of Mother India. Lord Ripon's government intensified both these trends. His liquidation of the Afghan adventure was welcomed as a renunciation of imperialism; his local government reforms were hailed as a rich promise for the future. Then came the Ilbert bill. In essence this was a simple measure putting Indian judges on the same footing as European in dealing with all cases

in the Bengal Presidency. It was occasioned by the fact that
Indians were now rising in the ranks of the judicial service. But
it involved the possible trial of Europeans by an Indian judge
without a jury. As this fact dawned on the Calcutta European
commercial community it exploded in wrath. A raging campaign was worked up, culminating in a threat to kidnap the
Viceroy. Lord Ripon then found that the civil service was largely
in sympathy with the opposition. A Clive, a Dalhousie, or an
Irwin would have driven through but Ripon agreed to a compromise which satisfied neither side. The flag of racialism had
been hoisted by the Europeans and an example of violent political agitation set. In the fluid state of the new middle class, with
its nascent nationalism, this seemed a crucial issue. There followed the first meeting of the Indian National Congress at
Bombay in December 1885.

At the start the Congress was a modest body, having only
seventy delegates at its first session. But from the first it formed
a focus for the new classes' political opinions. By 1900 it had
spread all over India and was regarded by the forward-looking
members of the new class as the natural mouthpiece of their
aspirations. Its support came mainly from the new professionals
with a sprinkling of businessmen in Bombay and of landlords in
Bengal. There was much sympathy for it amongst Indian
officials, some of whom joined it on retirement. At first it was
supported by a number of Englishmen, of whom one, the retired
civilian A. O. Hume, was a sponsor of its foundation and three
of whom were elected to the annual presidency by 1900. The
Viceroy Dufferin even gave it guarded initial approval. Its
early proceedings began with declarations of loyalty and gratitude for the blessings of British rule. But this harmony did not
long persist. Such a body could only survive with suggestions,
criticisms and positive proposals. The British bureaucracy, the
bulk of whom were administering the Indian countryside on
paternalist lines, was too rigid to adapt itself to this new development. The officials were in general devoted to the peasants and
served them well. They liked the old order and were on friendly
terms with them. But these new men seemed to them to be
neither Indian nor western; they were not easy-going like the

old aristocrats or respectful like peasants. They criticized, they carped, they claimed rights. To the average official in provincial city or country town this savoured of sedition and congressmen were frowned on accordingly. It was these officials that the average congressmen mainly met, so that the fissure of opinion between government and Congress was soon accompanied by a fissure of feeling. Thus by 1900 the Congress had grown into a position of constitutional opposition to the government.

As the Congress spread its roots through the new class diverging tendencies began to reveal themselves. It happened that the leaders of the two main tendencies were both members of the same section of Chitpavan Brahmins in western India who had once provided the heart of the Maratha resistance to the British. Gopal Krishna Gokhale, and Bal Gangadhar Tilak were alike in ability and devotion to their country, but opposites in everything else. Gokhale was an admirer of the west, persuasive, conciliatory, and constructive; Tilak was an admirer of the Indian past, rugged in personality, sardonic and provocative in expression, a stickler for rights, a relentless and bonnie fighter. Gokhale with his polished speeches, his parliamentary manner, his facts, and his formidable logic, was the westward-looking Indian's pride; Tilak, with his terse and forceful Marathi writings and speeches, the nostalgic Maratha's delight. The contrast was reminiscent of Gladstone and Disraeli and the play between them in its way as dramatic. The two men in fact stood for different tendencies, which under different guises outlasted the British period. Gokhale took Gladstonian liberalism as his political creed. He looked forward to a self-governing India on western lines, justified in its turn by large social reforms. Though no revolutionary in any sense he realized that if western concepts were to prevail in politics they must find expression in society also. He was thus essentially friendly to the British; his divergence consisted in asking for more than they were then prepared to give. Tilak, on the other hand, looked back nostalgically to the days of Maratha and Hindu glory. He was orthodox and accustomed to postpone social reform until 'after freedom is won'. Western knowledge and institutions were for him only a means towards an end, the end of independence. He differed also on means. He sought to exploit orthodox Hindu sentiment and Maratha patriotism in the service of the new nationalism. To this end he revived the Sivaji cult, promoted the Ganpati festival, and aroused orthodox feelings over the government measures against the outbreak of plague in Bombay in 1897. He insisted on rights as his rival asked for concessions, made demands to the other's requests. He believed that nothing would come of moderation, that the British could be squeezed but not cajoled. Gokhale's attitude appealed to the judgement of the cautious bourgeois, while Tilak's made the blood tingle with promptings to direct action. The dilemma of the time was that, as Gokhale believed and Tilak was to discover, the government was too strong for open defiance.

The two groups came to be known as Moderates and Extremists. There was no immediate break because there were many issues upon which they agreed. By 1900 the Government-Congress position was broadly as follows. There was first the matter of representation. All congressmen were dissatisfied with the Indian Councils Act of 1892, which was the government's tepid response to their appearance. After six years of discussion the legislative councils at the centre and in the provinces were somewhat enlarged, and the principle of election was introduced under the euphemism of 'recommendation for nomination'. The Imperial Council could only discuss bills submitted but a budget discussion was allowed which gave Gokhale the opportunity for his annual masterly surveys of government policy in general. This incident well illustrates the difference in approach and in sense of urgency between the government and the most moderate of congressmen, and helps to explain the sense of irritation and even exasperation which often accompanied government concessions. It was easy for men of the Tilak school to believe that all government talk of progress was a sham. And behind the detailed controversy was the urge of increasing numbers of qualified men to take part in public life.

A second issue was the 'Indianization' of the higher services. It was increasingly felt to be unfair that the admission of Indians to the civil service should be so difficult. The government insisted that the examination should be in London and when

Indians began to compete in some numbers lowered the age limit to nineteen.* Virtually only boys educated in England could then compete and this limited the field to a microscopic and denationalized minority. This attitude fostered the suspicion that the government in fact wished to evade the principles of Queen Victoria's proclamation and that of no racial bar to office which went back to 1833. These issues affected the whole middle class at its most sensitive spot, its hopes and ambitions and sense of self-respect. The sense of self-respect was further wounded by the behaviour of the unofficial Europeans in general and sometimes by the officials as well. The admirer of Shakespeare and British institutions would too often find himself ejected with violence from railway carriages or treated with contumely in public places. Even more galling to a sensitive people perhaps than the violence of ill-bred whites was the aloofness and hauteur of many officials who could turn correctness into a form of contempt.

Beyond these issues were certain very practical questions. The business community increasingly felt that Indian interests were being subordinated to those of Britain. In Bombay it was believed, with some justice, that the government was injuring the nascent cotton industry in the interest of Lancashire. The ground for this opinion was the abolition of all tariff duties in 1879, a measure which indirectly benefited Lancashire, and the imposition in 1895 of an excise of five per cent on Indian cotton goods to countervail a similar tariff on Lancashire goods imposed in the interest of revenue. This was generally regarded as naked discrimination in favour of foreign goods. There were other matters also, such as the expense of rail construction, the alleged 'drain' of money to Britain without adequate return, the failure to encourage industry. In sum it amounted to a general belief, amounting to a passionate conviction in some quarters, that Britain had fastened a colonial economy on India which had impoverished the country and was reluctant to relax its grip. Thus the middle class and the government were gradually moving further apart. We should beware, however, at this stage,

---

* In 1878. The age limit was raised to 21–3 from 1892–1905 and to 22–4 from 1906, *Cambridge History of India,* Vol. VI, pp. 365–6.

of attaching too much weight to the Congress as a whole. Indian nationalism was still a movement rather than a force, an aspiration rather than a general dynamic. It was still confined to the westernized middle class, with the masses as yet mere lookers-on.

Then came Curzon. A romantic and brilliant aristocrat touched with late Victorian imperialism he stepped from promising junior governmental office to the Indian government at the age of forty. He was dazzled by the East like Napoleon and intended India to make his name and provide a stepping-stone to the premiership. But India beguiled him, as it had done Wellesley and Dalhousie before, and very nearly ended his career. For the present, however, all was activity, pomp, and brave words about the destinies of empires and the duties of rulers to their people. Curzon saw Britain in India as both trustee of her past and tutor to her future. She must labour hoping only for reward in the distant future; the Indian ward must qualify in westernism before entering into his inheritance. Imbued with this spirit Curzon undertook a complete overhaul of the administration. He first dealt with the frontier. The 'forward' policy of fully administering territory up to the Durand Line * had set the northern frontier tribes ablaze. He remodelled the whole frontier policy, withdrawing troops to bases where they acted as mobile reserves, using tribal levies to police tribal territory and improving communications. This was capped by the detachment of the north-west districts from the Panjab to form a new province supervised directly by the Government of India. Curzon was successful in his dealings with Afghanistan and staged, with home support, an impressive display of power in the Persian Gulf in order to warn off imperial Germany. He was less happy in his dealings with Tibet where he saw the spectre of Russian imperialism stalking in the northern wastes as his predecessors had seen it across the Afghan hills. This led to the march of the Younghusband expedition to Lhasa in 1904 and the early disavowal of most of its proceedings. It was the swan-song of British Indian imperialism.

In India itself he both glorified and hectored the princes. On

* Drawn in 1893. Roughly half-way in the tribal belt between India proper and Afghanistan.

balance, praise for the order and concrete acts like the formation of the Imperial Service Corps were more effective than the reproofs. The Princes gained confidence and gave an outburst of loyalty in 1914. Curzon overhauled the whole bureaucratic machine, beginning with a war on verbose minutes and bureaucratic delays. He made a close study of land questions, carrying the process of lightening the cultivator's assessment and of lengthening the settlement period a step further. He set up a department of agriculture and a research institute at Pusa.* He pushed ahead with public works, adding 6,000 miles to the 27,000 miles of existing line and increasing the irrigated area by 6½ million acres. In the cultural field he was equally active, providing a monument to British India in the Victoria Memorial at Calcutta, founding the Imperial Library, and above all creating an archaeological department to preserve existing monuments and antiquities and discover others.

So far he carried a rather breathless Indian public with him. The apogee of his reign was the stately Delhi durbar of 1903 to mark the accession of Edward VII, over which he presided. From then on all was controversy. Curzon's vanity and romanticism led him to accept a second term of office. This was filled with a controversy with Lord Kitchener, the Commander-in-Chief, over the administrative control of the army. The same weak cabinet which reappointed Curzon and allowed him to march to Lhasa produced a compromise which Curzon regarded as a defeat and caused him to retire in bitterness of soul. But it was his Indian controversies which affected the future of the country. In 1904 he passed his Universities Act after an inquiry into the state of higher education. The Act created the Calcutta post-graduate faculty and introduced a residential system. It also sought to control more effectively the numerous private colleges which had sprung up during the educational explosion under the grant-in-aid system and to stiffen the controlling university bodies by increasing their nominated, which meant their official influenced element. Here lay the rub. Higher education was something close to the heart of the new middle class; it had given them their opportunities and they largely controlled it.

* Since the Bihar earthquake (1934) in New Delhi.

They interpreted Curzon's measures as a declaration of war, describing it as bureaucratic interference and a calculated attack on the new nationalism.

Lastly came the Bengal partition. Bengal was an overgrown province of seventy-eight millions, comprising east * and west Bengal, Bihar, and Orissa. Its division had long been discussed and Curzon's contribution was to take an administratively tidy decision where others had talked. He created a new province of East Bengal and Assam with thirty-one million people and its capital at Dacca. But it happened that East Bengal was mainly Muslim in population while west Bengal was Hindu; moreover in the reduced Bengal of forty-seven millions, Bengalis were a minority amongst Biharis and Oriyas. The Bengali political class was deeply stirred, and not only the political class but the whole countryside as well. It was passionately believed that Curzon had deliberately divided the Bengal people because of their political activity and raised the backward Muslims of East Bengal as a counterpoise. In fact Curzon was as obtuse politically as he was clear headed and energetic in administration. It had never occurred to him to appoint an Indian to the commission which preceded his Universities Act, though Bengal was bristling with educationalists, nor did he consult Indian opinion about the partition. The agitation came as a complete surprise to him and he dismissed it as the vapourings of politicians without followers. Led by Surendranath Bannerjea and exasperated by official olympianism the opposition grew into a raging popular movement which culminated in a boycott of British goods and ceremonial burning of Lancashire cotton. The leaders followed the pattern set by the Europeans over the Ilbert bill and were astonished at the response they received. They were supported by Gokhale in council and Tilak in the west who proposed a no-tax campaign. More ominously the pent-up emotion in Bengal engendered a group of terrorists who thought the attainment of freedom a religious duty and of assassination as a sacred offering to the goddess Kali.

Bengal was partitioned and Curzon returned to Britain but India was never the same again. The whole middle class, and,

* Now East Pakistan.

in Bengal, the people as well, had been deeply stirred. Broadly the result was the capture of this class by a revivified Congress. The nationalism which had been the opinion and aspiration of the more active members of the class became their settled conviction and instinctive attitude. The pains of partition were the birth-pangs of Indian bourgeois nationalism. But there were other results as well. It had been shown that the despised bourgeois might on occasion get a popular backing. It had been shown that the old aristocratic leaders could not now restrain any more than they could lead the people. It had been shown that action could follow speech. The Congress had begun to possess political power as well as power of persuasion. But the omens were not all against the British bureaucratic authority. The feeling that the British government had set its face against the Indian renascence had not only inspired a splinter terrorist group in Bengal who were responsible for a series of outrages during the next few years. It had greatly increased anti-government feeling and correspondingly increased the following of Tilak. This feeling produced a split in the Congress itself at its Surat meeting in 1907 which resulted in Tilak's eclipse.* The whole country was stirred, restless, and perplexed.

Within weeks of Curzon's return to Britain occurred the Liberal landslide at the election of 1906. The new government were friendly to Indian aspirations and were expected to reverse Curzon's most controversial measures. In fact they allowed them to stand. The new secretary of state was John Morley, the biographer of Gladstone, a literary radical whose political hour had come when he had grown with age vain in his own opinions, dictatorial in manner, and timid in action. In Calcutta faced him Curzon's successor Minto, an imperial handyman newly translated from Canada, neither masterful nor brilliant, but cool, detached, full of knowledge of the world and of human nature. The two seemed an ill-assorted pair, but they worked unexpectedly well together. Minto's stolidity was a foil to Morley's fireworks and his cool-headedness an antidote for Morley's hesi-

* Two years later he was imprisoned for six years for incitement to violence. While in Mandalay gaol he wrote his famous commentary on the *Gita*.

tations. Though hesitant of immediate action the new government took the Indian situation very seriously. Without accepting any long-term political objective it determined that an attempt must be made to win back the goodwill of the political classes. On this basis exchanges were made between Morley and Minto and Gokhale was brought into consultation. The idea of a consultative assembly on the durbar principle was soon abandoned and discussion concentrated on proposals for bringing Indians into closer association with the administration and enlarging the powers and numbers of the existing legislative councils. These measures seem small today but in their context of Conservative suspicion and bureaucratic opposition they required courage. The split in Congress with the growth of extremism and the appearance of terrorism imparted a certain urgency but also provided conservative arguments for delay. When Indian membership of the Viceroy's executive council was first suggested, the first reaction of its members, wrote Professor Dodwell, was as if a pistol had been pointed at their heads.

The result of these discussions was the Indian Councils Act of 1909, usually known as the Morley–Minto reforms. Indians had already been appointed to the Viceroy's council and the Council of India in London; the way was now open for Indian membership of the provincial executive councils as well. The Imperial Legislative Council was enlarged from twenty-five to sixty members of whom twenty-seven were elected. The Viceroy still presided and there was no official majority, but supplementary questions and general resolutions in addition to questions and the annual budget discussion were now allowed. The provincial councils had similar changes. There were two innovations: direct election for non-official seats and separate or communal representation for Muslims. This was the result of the formation of the Muslim League in 1906 as a counter to growing Hindu influence; the plea being that with a property franchise poverty would prevent Muslims from having an influence in general constituencies in proportion to their numbers.* Taken as a whole, the act was a clear step towards repre-

* The Muslim question in general is dealt with in *The Rise of Pakistan*, ch. 18.

sentative and responsible government. Further development could only lead in that direction. But Morley vehemently denied any such intention, partly, perhaps, through sheer shortsightedness and partly to allay the fears of the British opposition.

By and large these measures gave satisfaction to the moderate Congressmen. Gokhale well knew how to use the new council facilities and turned the Imperial Council into a sounding-board of moderate nationalism. His first general resolution, for example, was a demand for universal elementary education.* This guarded satisfaction was increased by the actions of the new Viceroy, Lord Hardinge, who succeeded Minto in 1910. Hardinge was a diplomat of long experience and also a Liberal of courage and conviction. Beneath a formal and rather frigid exterior he concealed a talent for handling people and an unusual understanding of the Indian mind. He kept contact with Gokhale and was not afraid to consult unofficial opinion. The accession of George V gave occasion for the great Delhi Durbar of 1911 presided over by the new King and Queen in person. This was made the occasion for the reversal of the Bengal partition and the removal of the capital to Delhi. The two Bengals were reunited as a governor's province (a consolation to the Bengali sense of status for the loss of the capital), Assam reverted to a Chief Commisionership, while a new province of Bihar and Orissa was created with its capital at historic Patna on the Ganges. The transfer of the capital, considered periodically from the time of Lord William Bentinck, was one of the best-kept secrets of modern times. It enraged Lord Curzon and the Calcutta Europeans and grieved the Bengalis, but it pleased Indian sentiment as a whole. The view that Britain was moving into the heart of India could be re-read to portend the taking over of the new régime by India.

For the present all was glitter, bustle, and hopefulness. The Viceroy survived a bomb attack on his state entry into Delhi to secure Gokhale's appointment to the Islington Commission which was to recommend a larger Indian share in appointments to the services. He sent Gokhale to South Africa to plead the cause of Indians led by the young Gandhi in the new Union and

* This early Congress aim has not yet been achieved.

he followed this up by publicly stating 'the sympathy of India, deep and burning, and not only for Indians, but of all lovers of India like myself, for their resistance to invidious and unjust laws'. The Congress-government honeymoon had lasted five years when the First World War engulfed Europe with incalculable consequences for India. Extremism and terrorism had not disappeared but the one had diminished and the other ceased to be a danger. In general the new public felt that they again had links with the government and that the British meant at least a modicum of what they said about partnership and progress.

15

THE FIRST WORLD WAR AND THE
GREAT LEAP FORWARD

THE First World War formed a watershed in modern Indian development. It provoked a revolution in the Indian consciousness which in turn found expression in the ascendancy of Mahatma Gandhi. Before 1914 the Government of India on the whole held the initiative; after 1918 it was grasped by Congress. This mental revolution was not, of course, entirely novel. There had been signs of new stirrings and new attitudes in the past twenty years, but they were tentative and subordinate to the main theme of European superiority. Until 1914 it had seemed that self-government on western lines would come with stately strokes at intervals measured by the imperial government and that the new Indian rulers, when they arrived, would indeed be the brown-Englishmen of Macaulay's dream. Tilak had challenged this conception, and had been defeated both by government and his own countrymen. Tilak was in Mandalay gaol and no Indian hand had been held out to him.

The stirrings before 1914 had been associated with the new national movements of Asia. There was the case of Japan. Her frank westernization pleased the right-wing nationalists, but gave little comfort to Tilak's friends. Her defeat of Russia in 1904-5 electrified all parties, for here was the first successful defiance of the west by an eastern power in centuries. There followed the Persian, the Turkish, and the Chinese revolutions, but these were not successful enough to do more than raise hopes. In 1914 the modern Indian still viewed the world largely through British spectacles. For him there were two world powers, Britain and Russia. The other great European powers and the United States were rather hazily comprehended through the mist of British sea-power. They were not relevant to India – except perhaps Germany, and she mainly for trading purposes.

The World War transformed this attitude. Within three months Prime Minister Asquith was saying 'henceforth Indian questions would have to be approached from a new angle of vision', though with characteristic procrastination Cabinet action was delayed for nearly three more years. Indian opinion soon realized that Britain was only one among several approximately equal powers and that even her control of the sea was not unchallenged. She was removed from the Victorian pedestal she had occupied so long. The prestige of Europe in general suffered a drastic shock from which it never recovered. Here were the western mentors of the east engaged in a fratricidal struggle and accusing each other of atrocities which they had taught Indians to believe were confined in modern times to their own country: Pindaris and lootywallahs. Could the west be so civilized after all; was it superior in any respect but command of the means of destruction? To this loss of awe of British power and respect for western civilization were added two events which upset all previously held notions of the world. The Russian revolution in 1917 meant, for India, the collapse of the great reactionary world power. Thereafter Russian appeals on behalf of oppressed nationalities weighed more with Indian opinion than the communism of Lenin and Trotsky. With the Tsardom crashed the whole pre-war Indian idea of world politics. The second event was the entry of the United States into the war in 1917 and President Wilson's world ascendancy during 1918. His now forgotten Fourteen Points contained the declaration on self-determination and this, Indian opinion noted, had been accepted by the British willy-nilly. The Americans talked about rights, it was further observed, while the British talked about concessions and safeguards. The whole Indian mental outlook became more radical and a sense of expectancy, of a new dawn breaking, filled the air. What before 1914 would have been regarded as a gracious concession was now looked upon as little short of an insult. The Gokhale gasp of 'so much' gave place to the Tilak snort of 'so little!'

In Europe, of course, mental revolutions also occurred under the stress of war. But this did not apply to the British bureaucracy in India. The younger members of the I.C.S. were foolishly allowed to serve with the forces so that they could not follow these changes in Indian attitudes and came back to a world quite strange to them. The older officials were overstrained by the prolonged period of extra duty in difficult conditions; they had few reserves left to face the crisis of post-war India or understand the rapid changes which were occurring. If we match a tired and depleted bureaucracy with the new dynamism of the emerging Indian middle class we get a clue to the post-war friction between government and people.

The outbreak of the war saw an outburst of loyalty to the British. The princes responded to their recent treatment by vying with each other in offers of services. The middle class in general was enthusiastic. Here were the dividends of the previous decade's policy. But the government failed to take any advantage of them. Offers of help were blandly ignored and as the war lengthened the mood changed. Indian troops were sent to France, Egypt, and Iraq, and distinguished themselves in each field, but the government's answer to all proposals for change was 'after the war'. Its answer in England was the same, of course, but Britain was fighting for her life, while India, proud though she was of her martial achievements, was herself essentially a ringside spectator. The Indian war effort was considerable but it was an enterprise rather than a national struggle. Indians could not therefore be expected to postpone all consequences to a nebulous future and it was only reasonable to expect some recognition of the efforts made. The delays and disdain, the talk about loyalty and the repeated call for sacrifice therefore became gradually irritating to the point of exasperation. In the early stages all opposition to the government ceased and there was a general support for war measures. 1,200,000 men, of whom 800,000 were combatants, were recruited, a hundred million pounds were given outright to Britain and between twenty and thirty million pounds contributed annually towards war expenses. India undertook her own defence so that for a time there were only 15,000 British troops in the country.

Time soon brought with it the miseries as well as the grandeur of war. After the thrill of the landing of an Indian army in France came the winter in the trenches for which Indian troops were quite unprepared, the long watch on the Suez canal, the advance and then defeat, and scandals of mismanagement in Iraq. Village India saw Europe in its sordid wartime clothes and was not impressed with what it saw. In India itself there was some economic activity but the opportunity of industrial expansion was largely missed. Only in 1916 was a commission appointed (on pressure from London) which recommended the first steps towards planned development. It was the prelude to the arrival of the concept of Indian economic autonomy, but the benefit was not felt till after the war. The German submarine war against Britain led to demands for wheat which sent up prices and caused shortages. The continued demand for manpower gave such urgency to the efforts of recruiting agents that in the Punjab it verged on compulsion. Muslim loyalties were strained by the war against Turkey whose sultan was still to millions of them a revered figure as Khalifa (caliph) or the head of the Islamic brotherhood. Finally came the great influenza epidemic which swept away five million people. At the same time were occurring the changes already mentioned in Russia and America.

It was in these circumstances that the mood of the political classes changed from loyalty and anxiety to help into one of restless irritation and expectation of change. The imperial giant who was to hand out democracy as the reward of loyal support turned out to be not such a giant after all. He remained aloof and apparently interested only in calling for sacrifice. More and more began to think in the terms of Tilak who had returned from his prison in Mandalay just before the war. As the feeling mounted Gokhale, worn out by his efforts, died at the age of forty-nine, in December 1915. In 1916 both Mrs Besant, the theosophist founder of Benares University and Tilak, started Home Rule Leagues to press their views. At the end of the year Tilak captured the Congress and electrified India by concluding the Lucknow Pact with the Muslims. The essence of this was Muslim support for the Congress demand for self-government in return for the recognition of separate Muslim constituencies.*

---

* 'Separate electorates' were one of the bones of contention between Hindus and Muslims. Muslims contended that with a property franchise a joint electorate would mean the swamping of Muslims by Hindus in the great majority of cases because of Muslim poverty. They therefore demanded separate constituencies containing only Muslim voters.

Tilak had lost none of his tactical skill and now showed that he could think on an all-India scale. At this juncture the government stirred and began to consider a declaration of post-war policy. It was made to the House of Commons on 20 August 1917, by the new Secretary of State for India, Edwin Montagu, and contained these words:

The policy of H.M. government, with which the Government of India are in complete accord, is that of the increasing association of Indians in every branch of the administration, and the gradual development of self-governing institutions, with a view to the progressive realization of responsible government in India as an integral part of the Empire.

A declaration of policy had been delayed for three years, but when it came it proved to be radical. For it envisaged internal self-government of the kind then enjoyed by the dominions of Canada, Australia, South Africa, and New Zealand. Moreover it was a bi-partisan document, for its author was a prominent Conservative, Lord Curzon himself revised it, its enunciator was a Liberal, and the cabinet which approved it a Coalition one. It set the pattern of political development for the next thirty years and made possible, in spite of all that passed during that period, the emergence of India into friendly independence. It promised far more than any Indian would have hoped for before 1914; the fact that it seemed too little to so many was an index of the immense change in the climate of opinion brought about by the war years. It will now be convenient to follow the constitutional side of the question through. The new Secretary of State followed up the declaration by a cold weather tour (1917–18) which convinced him of the woodenness of many officials and of the reality and expectations of Indian political opinion. With the new Viceroy, Lord Chelmsford, he produced the Montagu–Chelmsford report in April 1918. It was an imaginative attempt to implement the declaration, its special features being the devolution of authority to the provinces, thus paving the way for federalism, the abolition of official majorities in the legislatures, reforms by stages, the introduction of ministerial responsibility in the provinces, and the system of dyarchy. It was these two which caught the imagination and aroused controversy. Many of the older generation of officials were deeply shocked and some retired prematurely rather than face the prospect of serving under Indian ministers. But the opposition in Parliament was confined to the extreme right wing and lacked organization. The bill became law in December 1919 and, with the usual interval for preparations on the Indian side, the reforms were inaugurated by the Duke of Connaught in March 1921.

The first principle of the new constitution was that of the realization of self-government by stages. The goal was always assumed to be parliamentary self-government because all enactments hitherto, Lord Morley's disclaimers notwithstanding, had pointed in this direction. But self-government did not yet mean independence. It was the reading of independence into dominion status at the Imperial Conference of 1926 which raised the issue in India and made the phrase 'Dominion status' a burning issue. The principle of progress by stages was secured by the retention of parliamentary authority for any change and a provision for an inquiry into the working of the Act after ten years. This provision itself contained a suggestion of further change at that time. The second important principle was devolution in the financial and legislative spheres. The concentration of control at the centre had proved increasingly irksome as the country developed, but opinion was not yet ready for a full-fledged federal system. The former divided heads of revenue were replaced by the allotment of different items to provinces and centre respectively,* thus endowing the provinces with a certain degree of financial flexibility. This flexibility proved to be limited because the expanding items went to the centre, but a system of grants from the centre helped to rectify this difficulty. The same practice was introduced for legislation. The local legislatures thus had more freedom, though, since their powers came by devolution from the centre and not as of right as in a federation, the overall control of the centre was retained.

* To the centre – customs, income tax, posts, salt, and railways. To the provinces – land tax, excise, irrigation, and stamps.

These changes not only prepared the way for the later introduction of federalism, but also made possible the new executive arrangements for which the reforms became famous. In the centre there was little change, only an extension of the principle of consultation. The Executive Council now had six members besides the Viceroy and the Commander-in-Chief and three of these were Indian. Prominent Indian public men were appointed to these three seats such as Sir Tej Bahadur Sapru, the distinguished Liberal or moderate, and Sir Fazl-i-Husain, the Punjabi Muslim leader. The Council now became a kind of Moderates' political heaven. In the provinces, however, the position was very different. Here 'dyarchy' or double government, the invention of the imperial theoretician Lionel Curtis, was introduced. The provincial executives were divided between the Governor's Executive Council, responsible only to him, and popular ministers responsible to the new legislative councils with popular majorities. An administrative division was made to match the executive one, subjects of administration controlled by the ministers being termed 'Transferred' and those retained in the governor's hands being called 'Reserved'. The reserved subjects covered land revenue and laws, justice and police, irrigation and labour matters. Broadly, they were the law and order and revenue departments. The transferred subjects were local self-government, education, public health, public works, agriculture, and co-operative societies. These were called 'nation-building' departments, the intention being to give the new ministers the opportunity of directing national development. Ministers were to develop, councillors were to conserve, and the governors were to harmonize the efforts of the two groups. Changes in the legislative councils were made to match the new executive arrangements. At the centre the official majority was abolished. There were one hundred and six elected and forty nominated (twenty-five officials) members in the new Legislative Assembly. An upper house, called the Council of State with sixty-one members was added. It had an unoffical majority and was intended to represent the larger landed interests. The provincial councils were largely increased,* not less than seventy per cent of their mem-

* Bengal had 139 members, Madras 127 and Bombay 111.

bers being non-official. All the provinces were equipped with full governors and executive councils.*

The new councils required electors for their elective members. Here the old limited franchise was cast aside and resort had to a nation-wide property qualification in addition to some special qualifications such as a university degree or membership of a chamber of commerce. The property qualification depended broadly on the payment of income or house tax in the towns and land tax in the country. The limits of payment varied, the aim being to bring roughly the same classes throughout the country into the new franchise. The result was to provide over five million voters for the provincial councils, about a million for the Legislative Council and 17,000 for the Council of State. These numbers were small compared with a total adult population of about a hundred and fifty million. But a start had been made from select constituencies to general ones, from the limited to the mass vote. Here was another milestone in Indian political development. The curiosity of dyarchy in the provinces was matched by the division of the constituencies into 'general' and 'special' and the sub-division of the general constituencies into 'general' and 'reserved'. The special constituencies represented special interests like universities, landholders, industry, and commerce and had no special future. But the division in the general constituencies was of fundamental importance. All shared the same general qualifications but some voters were placed in the reserved constituencies for special reasons. This applied specially to the Muslims whose grant of six seats in 1909 was now widely extended both at the centre and in the provinces, but Sikhs also received them in the Punjab, and Indian Christians, Anglo-Indians, and Europeans elsewhere. Communal representation, regarded as an exception to the rule in 1909, was now described as a regrettable necessity. It was to become an essential feature of Indian politics.

When the Montford reforms are viewed as a whole, it is clear that they marked a great departure. India had moved from the

* Full provincial status was given to the United Provinces, the Punjab, Bihar, Orissa in 1921, to Burma in 1923 and to the Frontier Province in 1932.

consultative to the first signs of the responsible principle, from select bureaucratic control to the first hint of mass politics. India was now a political as well as a legal entity in a way it had not been before. Moreover, the new arrangements were clearly transitional; they looked forward towards the extension of democratic rights, towards full self-government on the responsible parliamentary model. There could certainly be no going back, the only conceivable change would be to go forward. And the provision for the ten years' inquest brought the possibility of change into the fairly near future. Indian politics were committed to development along western lines, and India herself conceived as an international entity. Between the views of the many who said that too much or too little had been given, or that the reforms were a disaster or a farce, the fact remains that India had been set on a new path and that a beginning had been made with the transfer of power.

But the fate of the constitution was not decided by lawyers or parliamentarians. Before the constitution came into force feelings had been so deeply stirred that the India of 1921 was almost unrecognizable from that of 1914. The Home Rule agitation of 1916 and the Lucknow Pact between Hindus and Muslims at the end of the year was a warning that the political classes were stirring. Boons would not stop bombs in future; concessions must be replaced by recognition of rights. It was just this situation that the Government's declaration and the Montford proposals were designed to meet, and I think that, other things being equal, they would in fact have done so. But other things were not equal; the stirrings went far deeper than the politicians or their followers, and proceeded from causes beyond the control of either government or Congress. Disillusioned by the prolonged western belligerency, irritated by war shortages, restrictions, and soaring prices, dazzled by the Russian revolution and American talk of democratic rights and self-determination, India as a whole was restless, expectant, and hyper-sensitive. The large Muslim population was in addition alarmed by the steady collapse of Turkey, which preceded that of Germany by some months, and rumours of its partition. If Hindus were aroused by their discontents and their hopes, Muslims were stirred by their fears.

During 1917 and 1918 the political classes were occupied by the government's political moves. But the masses were getting steadily more restless. The precipitation of these feelings into an anti-government movement came about, as so often, by the government's attempt to prevent it. The terrorist movement which followed the Bengal partition agitation had never quite died down, and war strains led to some recrudescence. To advise on the situation the government appointed a committee presided over by Mr Justice Rowlatt, and then embodied its recommendations into two bills. The war ended before they came before the Legislative Council but the government persisted with them because the end of the war would also cause the lapse of the Defence of India Act. The two bills allowed judges to try political cases without juries and gave to provincial governments, in addition to the centre, the power of internment without trial. In the jumpy state of public opinion this was too much. The many months being taken to draft a bill embodying the Montford proposals was hotly compared to the few weeks needed for the Rowlatt bills. When the two bills came before the Council every non-official Indian voted against them, but they became law with the aid of the official majority. As a footnote on the actual need for the bills it may here be noted that their powers were never actually invoked.

The new indignation now found a new leader. He was Mohandas Karamchand Gandhi, a lawyer of forty-nine recently returned from South Africa and known as the leader of a successful passive resistance movement against the South African government and as a disciple of the late Gokhale. He had been familiarizing himself with Indian conditions and had tried one or two passive resistance experiments. But he had also helped in recruiting. He differed from Gokhale in believing in non-violence and being less friendly to the British, and from Tilak in thinking that politics and ethics were indissolubly connected. Few thought of him as a national leader to this time; all eyes were on Tilak and most would have said that he was too mild, too moral, and too impractical. But now he came forward in just that way and found that the mood of the country was with him. The Rowlatt bills, he said, raised moral issues of trust and self-respect and should be met with a moral response. So instead of public meetings he proposed a *hartal*, a traditional Indian method of protest by cessation of all activity for a day. In theory the soul is too shocked by some abuse to be able to attend to practical affairs for a time. It had in it something of the nature of a religious act, though there may not have been many signs of this in practice. *Hartals* were staged in the big cities and in the excited state of feeling it is not surprising that they also led to riots. The flash-point came in the Punjab, the hardest pressed by wartime strains, the greatest sufferer in manpower, and the most energetic part of India. Riots in Amritsar led to the apprehension of revolt. On 13 April 1919 General Dyer broke up a prohibited meeting in a closed space called Jallianwala Bagh by firing on them without warning. The crowd numbered between ten and twenty thousands; the known official casualties were 379 killed and over 1,200 wounded. This was followed up by martial, punitive measures and humiliating orders. Order was restored and the Governor thought he had saved India from revolution. He had, in fact, written *finis* to the old imperial régime. The facts were slow in leaking out and it was not until October that a committee of inquiry * was appointed by the Coalition government in London. Racial bitterness was now added to the general discontent but Gandhi's influence prevented large-scale outbreaks of violence. He now found himself borne on a great wave of national emotion, while Tilak, more practical but less attuned to the new mood, was fading quietly from view. The Hunter committee, when it reported in April 1920, was found to have divided on racial lines. Even the European members, however, censured General Dyer and the administration of martial law. Dyer was retired but India was shocked by a vote in his favour in the House of Lords and the raising of a heavily subscribed fund in appreciation of his services. Gandhi, the former proponent of cooperation with the British, now swung round. This attitude, he said, was not only wrong but wicked. He proclaimed that 'cooperation in any shape or form with this satanic government is sinful'. In August he carried the Congress with him in launching a non-cooperation movement with the gov-

* The Hunter Committee 1920 (Cmd. 681).

ernment. This included resignation of government office, with-drawal from government schools and colleges, and boycott of the forthcoming elections to the councils. This was too much for the moderates who finally split off to become the Liberals, soon to be an army of generals without soldiers. The movement caught the imagination of the country and gained a unique all-India character from the general support of the Muslims. They were shocked by the just concluded Treaty of Sèvres which threatened Turkey with partition; under the lead of the Ali brothers they started a *khilafat* movement in support of Turkey and linked with Gandhi in non-cooperation. Not many officials resigned or returned their titles; schools and colleges were disrupted for a time but substitute 'national' institutions soon wilted. The elec-tions were held but only a third of the electors went to the polls. Thus the councils existed and were dominated by the Liberals, but they could be described as unrepresentative. The government machine did not break down but it was under visible strain and for a time excitement was intense. In such an atmosphere out-breaks of violence might be expected and they did not fail to occur. These roused the fears and so cooled the enthusiasm of many of the patriots. Early in 1921 Lord Reading, a jurist of great reputation with a cool head and long view, succeeded Lord Chelmsford. He divined the essential disunity of the anti-govern-ment movement and calmly waited for it to fall apart. In August 1921 the rising of the fanatical Moplahs of Malabar, with its toll of killings and forcible conversions, alarmed a large section of Hindu opinion. In the autumn there was further violence during the attempted boycott of the Prince of Wales; by the end of the year it was clear that the flood-tide of emotion had begun to ebb. There was talk of a no-tax campaign when the Chauri-Chaura outrage occurred. Gandhi then himself called off the campaign and soon after was arrested and sentenced to six years' im-prisonment without serious disturbance.* The storm had blown itself out and subsided nearly as quickly as it arose. But things could never be the same again. The 'colonial' mentality had been discarded; Indians now felt themselves politically adult, able to treat with the government on equal terms. The government

* He was released after two years early in 1924.

never sank back quite into its old olympianism. It had suffered a great shock and now recognized that public opinion existed and that the Congress was a force to be reckoned with. Of the extent of that force it was uncertain, and of its serious existence the British governing class was still unconvinced. Both were to be enlightened within the next ten years.

16

MAHATMA

THE arrest of Gandhi in 1922 left India like a patient after a bout of fever. The attack was over; the patient and the world would not lose touch with each other; an accommodation must be found between them. It was clear both that the government was not yet ripe for overthrow and that the Congress could not be disregarded. But there was a sense of emptiness, a questioning of what to do next. This sense was increased by the collapse of the *Khilafat* movement. The national resurgence of Turkey under Kemal Ataturk at first encouraged the Indian Muslims, delighting them with the defeat of Greece in late 1922 and the revision of the Treaty of Sèvres at the bayonet-point. But these feelings were turned to perplexity and gloom as Ataturk in turn dethroned the Sultan and then abolished the Caliphate altogether. The effect was to make them feel more alone in the world than before. Without friends outside their apprehensions of Hindu domination revived. By 1924 communal riots had replaced the Congress–League alliance.

Meanwhile the country watched the performance of the liberal ministries under the new constitution. At the centre there were a number of liberal gestures. The Rowlatt Acts and the Press Act of 1910 were repealed; the first industrial social measures, including workmen's compensation, were introduced; a beginning was made with the Indianization of the officers' cadre in the army, and the Lee Commission's proposals to equalize the Indian and British membership of the I.C.S. accepted. The cotton excise was finally abolished in 1925. Indian *amour propre* was soothed by her membership of the new League of Nations. The effect of these measures was largely offset by the doubling of the salt tax for revenue purposes, but in fact they were substantial and amounted to meeting in large measure the demands of the early nationalists. The most significant for the future was perhaps the enlarged Indian recruitment for the I.C.S. and the army. It was the several hundred Indian civilians recruited from this time who carried India over the immediate post-partition years without any major breakdown, and the Indian military officers, few though they were who dribbled in from this date, who did the same service for the army.

Congressmen could say that these were merely tactical moves by a frightened government. But the same could not be said of the new provincial ministries. There were many complaints of the way in which the new reforms worked. The most solid was the claim that owing to the nature of the financial award between the centre and the provinces there was insufficient money for provincial development, leading to the financial starvation of 'nation-building' transferred departments. Ministers complained of official obstruction, of gubernatorial apathy, and of association with the unpopular foreign executive. But the first legislative term of three years proved to be enough to show that where ministers were determined and had solid support in the councils they could get things done. If half their troubles came from the constitution, the other half came from the confused group politics in many provinces. In Madras the Justice party secured a clear majority and was able to carry a number of measures including a reform of temple endowments. In the Punjab an agrarian Hindu–Muslim–Sikh coalition was able to launch an education programme and pass measures to check urban economic exploitation; its leader Fazli-Husain became virtually irreplaceable. If this could be done within the new hybrid constitution what of the future? The ministers grew in status and the councils in prestige.

Congress leaders proclaimed that the reforms were a sham and the ministers' powers a farce. But observation began to gainsay them and many Congressmen began to look with curiosity and then with interest and eagerness at the proceedings of the new bodies they had boycotted. Council entry and acceptance of office became major issues. The temporary disappearance of Gandhi helped on the reaction which had already begun. Led by C. R. Das of Bengal and Motilal Nehru the Congress at Gaya in 1923 decided to contest the next elections, and formed the Swaraj Party for this purpose. It was true that the purpose was to wreck the reforms from within by making the formation of popular governments impossible, but this involved the recognition that they could not be wrecked from without. In the elections of 1924 the Swarajists were able to bring ministerial rule to an end in two out of nine provinces, and became the largest party in the central Assembly. They were able to make a number of negative gestures, but the sight of some ministries continuing to function produced feelings of envy in some Congress hearts; erosion continued in the form of splinter groups who revived Tilak's slogan of 'responsive cooperation'. In fact the very entry of Congress into the Councils increased their importance and so made it more difficult to overthrow them. The Swarajists found themselves in the dilemma that they could neither overthrow the government from without or within the councils, nor take office because the gulf of opinion between them and the government was still too deep. The longer they continued as cooperating non-cooperators the weaker they became. There was a steady trickle to the responsivist and communal camps among the older men and towards direct action among the younger. From this dilemma they were rescued by Gandhi to whom we must now turn.

Mahatma Gandhi (as he must now be called) * was born at Porbandar, a small state in Kathiawar, in 1869. His father was the hereditary *diwan* or prime minister and his family belonged to the *vaish* or merchant caste. This group in the Kathiawar peninsula was closely connected with the sect of the Jains, with whom *ahimsa* or non-violence was a cardinal principle. From the start, therefore, Gandhi was brought up against a background of affairs, though on a small scale, and of pacifism, though this was not a prominent feature of Hinduism as a whole. He was also dissociated from the priestly Brahmin hierarchy. His early life is described vividly and meticulously in his *Story of my Experiments with Truth*. He was married as a boy to a child-wife and sent as a youth to London where he qualified as a barrister-at-law. This venture caused a split in his caste on his return, many of the members considering that he had broken

---

* The title of Mahatma or great soul was accorded to him by Rabindranath Tagore on his return to India in 1915 and was soon taken up by the people.

caste by his journey overseas. The London period was the first turning-point in his life. He remained a vegetarian under difficulties and began his dietetic experiments. He came into touch with liberal and Christian ideas and the then novel teachings of Tolstoy. He had his first experiences of racialism and British aloofness. On return he practised law in India for a time and then proceeded to South Africa where the existence of an Indian community formed by the immigration of indentured labour provided openings for a young man willing to live abroad. Gandhi stayed in South Africa until he was nearly forty-six. It was the second formative period in his life. Here he developed his ideas from a mixture of Christian, Hindu, and humanitarian sources.* He raised a family and used them as specimens for his dietetic experiments, he assumed the leadership of the Indian community and used them as a laboratory for experiments in non-violence. He became convinced that western civilization was corrupt and violence a canker of society. He kept in touch with India through his friendship with Gokhale whom he regarded as his *guru* or teacher and whose Servants of India Society of political and social missionaries he planned to join on his return. He expressed his ideas in a little book written at white heat on board ship between Africa and India in 1909 called *Hind Swaraj*.

This was the man, slight, bespectacled, and deprecating in manner, apparently the reverse of a man of action, who stirred the Indian masses to the depths, who swept the rugged veteran Tilak into oblivion, and who controlled the national movement for nearly twenty-eight years. A further experience awaited him in the first few years after his return to India. The poverty of the masses, whether the *kisans* on the indigo estates of Bihar, or in his own Gujarat, burnt into his soul. A mass leader, he considered, must identify himself with those he aspired to lead; and he must not only lead but raise them. Motives of both compassion and policy led him in 1921 to discard his dapper European clothes, not for the *swami's* saffron robe, but for the peasant's homespun cotton *dhoti* and shawl. It was this gesture

* He was in close touch with members of the Society of Friends and one of his closest collaborators, H. S. Polak, was a Jew.

which finally won the hearts of the people and marked him in their eyes as a great soul.

Gandhi's mystique consisted of a union of original ideas (or an original pattern of known ideas) with a remarkable flair for tactics and an uncanny insight into the mass or peasant mind. He considered himself a Hindu but he was by no means an orthodox one. He took certain ideas, expanded them, and gradually wove them into a system which was ethical and spiritual as well as practical and political. He came to believe that his ideas formed a universal ethic, as applicable to Hitler and Stalin as to Hindus. He believed in the rights of man which led him at once into collision, not only with the British and South Africans, but with Hindu caste distinctions and their attitude to the 'Untouchables'. He removed his own sacred thread when he found that the fourth (Sudra) caste, was not allowed to wear it; and he christened the untouchables or outcasts *Harijans* or Sons of God. He welcomed them into his *ashram* and found various ways of emphasizing their equality with others. He put humanity before caste rule and on an occasion ordered the mercy killing of a stricken sacred calf. These things did not endear him to the orthodox and it was a Brahmin who eventually struck him down. On this basis of fearless communal self-criticism he equally fearlessly claimed equal political rights for his countrymen.

At the heart of his ideas lay the doctrine of *ahimsa* or non-violence. Violence was the expression of unreason and hate, the antithesis of love, and love was the essence of the spirit which permeates the universe. Therefore the opponent must be met by reason and entreaty; if he insisted on violence this must be borne cheerfully as a form of self-purification. Accepted suffering, in Gandhi's view, had healing and converting qualities. The opponent, unmoved by reason, would be won by cheerful suffering in a good cause. Along with *ahimsa* went severe self-discipline which included vows and fasts of purification and penance. Non-violence was the most spectacular side of Gandhi's thought, but its centre was the concept of *satya* or truth. *Ahimsa* was only one expression or outworking as it were of *satya* which was the pervasive spirit of man's life and the object of all his endeavours. It can perhaps be compared with the Platonic idea of justice as the art of right living. Truth was what man had to pursue with all his strength, self-discipline, his personal equipment, and non-violence or *ahimsa* his method of proceeding. Those who dedicated their lives to this pursuit were *satyagrahis* or truth-fighters. This was the name chosen for his specially trained followers or *élite*. Truth found expression in many ways. Within, it was the old Vedantic ideal of self-realization, which Gandhi dramatized as listening to the Inner Voice, as Socrates had his 'demon'; in politics it was freedom from foreign domination, the welding of a united nation; in Hindu society it was the breaking down of barriers raised by caste and age-old custom. In society at large it was living as close to nature as possible. Gandhi envisaged a peasant society of self-supporting workers, with simplicity as its ideal and purity as its hall-mark; the state would be a loose federation of village republics. He rejected the mechanics of the west along with its glitter and preached the necessity of hand spinning and weaving while cheerfully receiving the contributions of Indian industrialists.

Gandhi united various elements of Hinduism and other creeds in a highly original way. He dramatized his ideas by a constant stream of articles, speeches, and declarations, and above all by his own example. Gandhi, in the peasant's loin-cloth and shawl, sitting at the spinning wheel, writing notes on his weekly day of silence, sitting lost in contemplation or lying exhausted during a fast, were all ways of getting his image across to a largely illiterate population. They were not Brahminic, priestly ways, but ways which made an immediate appeal to the ordinary man. This brings us to another facet of Gandhi's genius, his power as a popular psychologist. He could not only dramatize himself; he could dramatize an issue with an unerring instinct. When others called meetings of protest against the Rowlatt bills, Gandhi called a *hartal* or religious strike. When he moved against the British government, it was not a tyranny against which one should fight, but a 'satanic' institution, with which no conscientious person could cooperate. When others walked out of the Assembly as a gesture of defiance, Gandhi walked sixty miles to the sea at Dandi to make illicit salt. In all that he did he not only brought the issue in question vividly before his constituents' minds, but contrived to make them feel morally superior to their physically stronger opponents. The load of supposed western superiority, moral as well as material, which had weighed so heavily on mid- and late-Victorian India was finally lifted and thrown back on the westerners themselves.

As a politician Gandhi's great work was to unite the masses with the classes in the national movement. He could persuade the masses to follow the classes because they believed him to be a good Hindu, a great soul; he could persuade the classes to accept his Hindu and, as many of them thought, his primitivist habits because it won them the masses. The industrialist put up with his hand-spinning, the politician with his loin-cloth, the epicure with his diet sheet, because they knew that these things won them the support they needed. They also knew that, when it came to dealing with the British, Gandhi could surpass them all, in argument, in tactics, and above all in making the British feel uncomfortable in their cherished field of moral rectitude. If Gokhale and Tilak and Bannerjea gave nationalism to the classes, the Mahatma gave a nation to the country.

Gandhi was released from prison early in 1924 after a serious operation. Almost his first public act was a three-week fast in the summer in the cause of communal unity and as a reparation for recent severe riots. This led to a conference on unity and once more he was in the centre of affairs. But for the present the Swaraj party, with its recent election successes, was in full cry, and the Mahatma's only open supporters were the small group of 'no-changers'. His keen mind, however, easily detected the inherent contradiction in the Swarajist position, by which it became increasingly clear that the nearer you reached your immediate goal (bringing dyarchy to a standstill) the further you were from your ultimate one, the control of the government. Feelings of frustration, internal discontent, and public defections were bound to increase. Gandhi retired cheerfully into the side-wings waiting for the political wind to change. For several years he made the ashram on the banks of the Sabarmati near Ahmedabad his headquarters, from which he directed his *khadi* (hand-spinning and weaving) and *swadeshi* campaigns and above all his Harijan work, for the raising of the outcastes. This campaign, though a challenge to high Brahmin orthodoxy, had a subtle appeal to the country in general of which Gandhi was well aware. It appealed to the new classes because it was democratic (human rights for all) and to the Hindu opinion in general because it proposed to incorporate the outcastes in the general body of Hinduism. Opinion slowly swung in the Mahatma's favour and the high Brahmins found themselves isolated. All the time he was pouring out in articles in his weekly paper * his ideas on non-violence, satyagraha, untouchability, ethics, and politics. These were read more avidly than any debates in the legislative assemblies. Gandhi was already the invisible ruler of the new India.

The awaited issue was obligingly supplied by the government itself. The Act of 1919 included a provision for a parliamentary review after ten years. The Baldwin government decided on the early appointment of an inquiry commission as a gesture of goodwill. But the commission which was appointed in November 1927 and headed by Sir John Simon, had an all-British membership.† In the then state of feeling in the country indignation was as general as it was inevitable. Was the fate of India to be decided by foreigners over the heads of Indians? It was too much to be borne. Efforts were made to temper the shock by associating local committees with the commission's proceedings. But the Congress was able to organize a successful boycott and organize hostile demonstrations whenever the commission appeared. The political temperature began to rise and the extremists to reappear. The 1928 Congress meeting declared for complete independence or *purna swaraj*. An all-parties conference produced in the Nehru report a scheme of self-government which assumed responsible government and dominion status – then newly defined as independence within the Commonwealth.‡ The demand now was for a round-table conference to arrange the details of

* Then *Young India*. From 1932 the *Harijan*.

† The others members were Mr C. R. (later Earl) Attlee, Lords Burnham and Strathcona and Mt Royal, E. C. G. Cadogan, G. R. Lane-Fox and Vernon Hartshorn.

‡ The principal authors were Pt. Motilal Nehru and Sir Tej Bahadur Sapru.

dominion status. The young radicals led by the Jawarharlal Nehru and Subash Bose were already calling for a showdown with the government.

In these circumstances Gandhi rejoined the Congress ranks. The new Viceroy, Lord Irwin (later Lord Halifax), now took a bold initiative. He persuaded the Labour government and the Conservative leader Baldwin to agree to a declaration that dominion status was the goal of British policy and that a round-table conference should be called to consider the next step. Here was an overriding of the Simon Commission and many have been puzzled as to why so great an advance on the British side was met by direct action by the Congress. Gandhi's first instinct was to accept the offer and this would have been in accord with his general attitude. But, as I believe, he found at the ensuing Congress meeting at Lahore that left wing sentiment was now so strong that a compromise would split the Congress. Rather than see the young radicals tilt against the government and probably plunge the country into violence, he decided to keep the whole situation in control by leading a non-violent movement himself. So he insisted that the proposed conference should discuss not the next step towards, but the implementation of dominion status, and on this rather fine distinction led a united Congress against the government.

Gandhi's method was characteristic. He chose for attack the salt tax, paid indirectly by every peasant, gave notice to the government of his intention to make illicit salt, and publicized himself by a leisurely sixty-mile walk from Sabarmati to Dandi. In spite of initial government efforts to look the other way the Gandhian magic worked. Soon processions, arrests, *hartals*, and occasional riots were taking place all over India. In the course of the year some hundred thousand went to prison. A striking feature was the emergence of Hindu women, specially in western India, as speakers, marchers, picketers, and civil resisters. Another feature was the aloofness of the Muslims. In the summer the Viceroy scored a success by persuading non-Congressmen to attend the Round Table Conference in the autumn and this conference itself made history by accepting the federal principle in the new constitution. Both sides now realized that they could

not indefinitely afford to ignore each other and in the new year
Lord Irwin released Gandhi and began conversations. The two
men discovered unexpected areas of understanding and there
followed the Gandhi–Irwin truce. The Congress called off civil
disobedience and agreed to attend the next session of the conference while the government released all political prisoners except
those convicted of violence. The truce collapsed within the year
while Gandhi, as the sole representative of the Congress in
London, failed both to impress the ruling circles there, or to
compose conflicting communal claims for electoral seats in the
councils. At the end of the year the new Viceroy Lord Willing-
don, who disliked Gandhi, backed by the new Conservative
'National government', presented a stiff front to the Congress.
Civil disobedience recommenced and was met with severe repression. The sequel showed that during the year Congress had
fallen under the influence of the rising left wing. The people as
a whole were tired of conflict and the movement collapsed after
six months. It was formally called off in 1934. The truce, it
seemed, had been fruitless, but in fact things had radically
changed. Gandhi and Irwin had talked on a new footing and
with a new understanding. Each convinced himself of the other's
sincerity and Irwin convinced Gandhi of British intentions about
the grant of self-government. The great fear of going back behind 1917 was allayed; henceforth controversy would centre
on the rate of progress forwards.

During the thirties political interest lay in two directions. One
was the slow preparation of the Government of India Act of 1935
and its application to the country, and the other Gandhi's handling of the internal political situation. The first of these processes
lasted for nearly five years, from the opening of the first Round
Table Conference in 1930 to the Act's actual passing in 1935. It
was a great and complicated measure but only two years passed
between the Declaration of 1917 and the Act of 1919. The 1935
Act was delayed for at least two years by the determined resistance of the 'die-hard' group led by Sir W. (then Mr) Churchill
and Lord Lloyd. But for this time-lag the federal part of the Act
might have come into force before the Second World War and
the whole subsequent development in India have been changed.

Thus Sir W. Churchill can be counted as one of the architects of Nehru's India. Gandhi's own contribution to the succession of conferences, committees, and reports was his first fast to death against the British government's communal award in 1932. It was one of the most successful and least defensible actions of his life. His object was to have the Harijans officially included within the Hindu community; the means being extra seats for them in the legislatures. This he secured by the threat of death from the untouchable leader Ambedkar and thus prevented the possible emergence of a third force of over fifty millions of the scheduled castes, as they were officially called, into the arena of Indian politics.

After his release in 1934 Gandhi called off the already moribund mass civil disobedience. He contented himself with certain symbolic acts of individual disobedience and then settled down to build up the Congress again. There was no doubt of its strength; like a lever released from a spring it shot back to its previous position in the public mind. But Gandhi was confronted with a serious problem and his handling of it was one of his major feats of statesmanship. This was the emergence of a strong left-wing movement within Congress which called for direct action. The terrorist groups and the Communists, a growing group, were both repudiated by the Congress and remained small. But within Congress there was a surge of radical belligerent feeling which found spokesmen in the young figures of Subash Bose from Bengal and Jawarharlal Nehru from the Congress heartland of Uttar Pradesh. Disillusionment with the results of civil disobedience, resentment at the government's repression and scepticism about its professed intentions were reinforced by the tensions of the world-wide economic depression. Extremism was in the air; legalism was at a discount and impatience a virtue. The old guard of Congressmen looked upon this trend with undisguised disapproval, but Gandhi feared a disruption on these lines more than anything else. An impetuous anti-government movement by these leaders would mean violence, severe repression, a reaction in the country and break-up of the party, and a political setback for a generation. His method was to play these young leaders as a skilled fisherman plays with a fish at the end of a long line. His policy was to disarm by promotion and protection from irate seniors. He chose Nehru as his successor rather than Bose partly because his following was larger in India as a whole and partly because of his hereditary Congress position, but mainly because he found he could attach him to himself. Bose looked at Gandhi with respect and disapproval; Nehru disagreed but reverenced. In the last resort Gandhi was sure of him and so it proved until 1947. Nehru became President of Congress in 1936 and served an unprecedented second term. Bose followed him in 1938 and also wanted his second innings. Here came the crisis. Bose defeated the moderate candidate Sittaramayya in the presidential election. Gandhi then intervened and by a series of moves as relentless as they were deft, isolated Bose, and forced his resignation. He lost the Bengal youth but won young India. He must have considered that Bose's Indian National Army of the Japanese war and the embarrassments it brought was a small price to pay for the consolidation of the party behind him in the years ahead.

17

THE 1935 ACT AND THE SECOND
WORLD WAR

(i) *The Act and After*

The 1935 Government of India Act proved to be a landmark
in the development of India. For all its 'ifs' and 'buts', its com-
plications and hesitations, it marked a point of no-return in
constitutional development, which the Montford reforms did not.
They had left the ultimate goal hazy and with their periodic
inquiry, the next step uncertain. Dominion status was now the
accepted goal, federalism the accepted framework, and parliamentary institutions the accepted form of government. Provision
was made for changing the constitution from within. In many
ways the Act was a blueprint for independence, a fact to which
the retention of its general shape and the lifting of whole sections
of the text into the Constitution of 1950 testifies.

In Britain the Act represented a new consensus on India in a
way the 1919 Act can hardly be said to have done. Then there
was general agreement that an experiment should be made in the
direction of self-government, but no agreement as to its ultimate
outcome or future policy to be followed. In the sixteen interven-
ing years there was, in fact, a revolution in British opinion about
India. The successful working of the Montford reforms in
several provinces, in spite of setbacks in others and the rapid
development of the country, had had their effect. But, above all,
the strength and discipline of the Civil disobedience movement
of 1930–31, and the skill of its direction, together with the new
attitude of the princes, had convinced the mass of Conservative
opinion that the national movement was not only a reality, but
a paramount reality. Terms must be made with it, and, that
being the case, a Conservative government should seek to guide
the movement along its own lines rather than put up futile barriers to be swept away one by one by an ever rising nationalist
flood. The Act thus represented not only a consensus of British
political opinion but also a considered attempt to provide a conservative form for ultimate Indian independence. Britain would

go into partnership with an independent India, but she would see to it, if she could, that the new India was one in which the conservative interests predominated. The Act is thus not only significant as a British political compromise, or as a step towards meeting Congress demands, but also as a deliberate plan for the conservative political evolution of India. These conservative political features are to be seen specially in the federal structure, in the treatment of the princes, and in various constitutional devices. If pursued to its logical conclusion this policy would have seen an India independent indeed in ten to twenty years' time, but so weighted on the side of existing vested interests that its shape would have been quite different from that which we know today.

The first feature of the Act was the federal principle, which replaced the devolution of the Montford reforms. This was a logical step in the development of a united India since it was a necessary recognition of local differences and the need for local freedom within the overall control of the Centre. It also made it possible to include princely India in the whole. The problem of 'residuary powers' was resolved by the preparation of three detailed legislative lists, central, provincial, and concurrent, the latter enabling the centre to assume extra powers in time of emergency. The newly autonomous provinces were given a more elastic source of revenue by the allotment to them of a portion of income tax proceeds. The inclusion of the authoritarian princes was a major step which would have coloured the whole character of the new federal India. Since they had direct treaty rights with the Crown their adhesion had to be voluntary and it was therefore arranged that the federal centre would only come into force when half of them, reckoned by population, had acceded. For the same reason the princes were allowed to nominate their representatives in both central legislative chambers. They were given one third of the seats in the lower and two fifths in the upper house. This proportion roughly corresponded to their population strength, but in terms of their general contribution to Indian life represented a heavy weightage. With their block vote the princes could, with Muslim or Scheduled caste or even conservative Hindu support, have barred any proposal. It seemed that this might be a master stroke of conservative planning, but it involved one important difficulty. This was the character of the princes which made the task of persuading them to act in their own interests so arduous as to be impossible by ordinary methods.

The second innovation was provincial autonomy, not only in relation to the centre, but to that of the British as well. Dyarchy was swept away in favour of provincial ministries responsible to the electors and restricted only by emergency powers which in fact were never used under ministry rule. The provincial franchise was still a property one but its scope was enlarged to include thirty million voters, one sixth of the adult population, instead of the previous six.* No one could deny that these ministries would be powerful political units. By contrast, dyarchy was introduced into the proposed central legislature, certain ministers being responsible to the Assembly. On this basis complete self-government could not have been long delayed. A Federal Court was set up in anticipation of the completion of the federal structure. The appointment of Sir Maurice Gwyer, a principal draughtsman of the act, as the first Federal Chief Justice, gave to India a wise counsellor, both during his term of office and for many years afterwards.

The other principal features of the Act were consequential or extensions of previous practice. The provinces were rearranged. Burma was lopped off to become ultimately independent, thus ending an anomaly brought about by a historical accident. Orissa was taken from Bihar to form a new province with portions of Madras and the Central Provinces. Sind was separated from Bombay. These, with the North-West Frontier Province, promoted in 1932, became full provinces, giving British India its final complement of eleven governors' provinces, four chief commissionerships, and the Agency of Baluchistan. 'Safeguards' were retained by the governors, giving them power to resume administration in the absence of a ministry, as well as by the Governor-General. They provided talking points for critics but were in fact found very useful by the successor gov-

* Women received the vote on the same terms as men, but the surviving property qualification restricted their numbers.

ernments and found both place and use in the new constitution.
Communal representation was already a feature of the Montford
constitution, and this was extended in a logical way. A burning
issue was the allotment of 'reserved' seats in the legislature and
we may note here that the principle of weightage in favour of
minorities, while it gave the Muslims more than their propor-
tionate share of seats in the United Provinces, deprived them of
the majority they would otherwise have had in the Punjab. This
was to have portentous consequences in 1947.

If the constitution of 1935 was on the whole a far-sighted
document which merited the title of prelude to independence, it
also had serious defects. First, as has been pointed out, it proposed a conservative framework for an independent India. The
vital feature of this framework was princely participation. Given
the character of the then existing princes, this risked either breakdown through their lack of understanding cooperation, or the
undue strengthening of reactionary forces in the India to be.
An independent India dominated by the princes might have
been decorative and peaceful, but hardly effective or forward-
looking. It was something like stopping the clock just before the
alarm for the new age was due to go off. Secondly, the constitution failed to prevent partition. The pressure which had produced it in India was mainly a Hindu one and it was felt by
Muslims to be devised mainly in Hindu interests. It was thought
that the federal principle, which conceded larger powers to the
provinces, would allay Muslim fears since they would control
some of the provinces. This was true of Sind and the Frontier,
but in Bengal their majority was so small as always to require a
coalition ministry, while in the vital Punjab, as has been noticed,
their numbers fell just short of control. The obstinate British
adherence to ideas of a one community state with its doctrine of
parliamentary sovereignty and rule by majorities was an ill-wind
which was to reap the whirlwind of the post-partition massacres.
The policy-makers refused to recognize that there were areas in
life and conduct which no Muslim would take from a Hindu or
Hindu from a Muslim. Regional federalism was not enough; it
needed to be supplemented by a cultural guild federalism so that
the major communities could feel that their inner cultural life

could not be tampered with by anyone else. The issue had been obscured in the past by British religious neutrality. Because the British leaders had successfully ignored the religious issue they treated it as if it did not exist. It was India which had to pay for this folly.

The act was passed in 1935 and there was the usual delay while registers were prepared and schedules worked out. In 1936 Lord Linlithgow, already groomed as Chairman of an Agricultural Commission, was sent to inaugurate the new régime. He had good will, industry, and executive ability, but lacked the imagination and clear vision of Lord Irwin. In February 1937 provincial elections were held. The elections to the old Legislative Assembly in 1929 had already shown that the Congress still dominated Hindu India and the new elections confirmed the fact. In five of the eleven provinces they secured clear majorities; in Bombay they got home with the help of 'fellow-travellers'; in the Frontier province their 'Red Shirt' Pathan allies took control; only in the small provinces of Assam and Muslim Sind had they no voice and in the two important provinces of Bengal and the Punjab they were excluded, in the one by a Muslim dominated coalition and in the other by a Hindu–Muslim agrarian alliance. At once the Congress was faced with the dilemma of taking office. This time the substance of power in the provincial sphere was so obvious that the warnings of Jawarharlal Nehru and S. C. Bose against British perfidy were disregarded, and after three months' haggling over governors' 'reserve powers' Congress ministries were formed.

The Congress 'raj' lasted for two and a quarter years and would have lasted longer if the outbreak of the Second World War had not introduced a major new issue. It was a hopeful period, for the new ministries proved cooperative and constructive; eventually old officials and new ministers parted with mutual regret and esteem. In the absence of a central government to capture Congress sought to control the country by means of its High Command, a body of all India leaders who issued directives to provincial ministries. Its power was very real for it unseated one ministry which tried to take an independent line.*

* That of Dr Khare in the Central Provinces (1938).

It was accused of dictatorship, but it was in fact only a make-shift pending the formation of a Congress government at the centre. Behind this façade of spinning wheels and Daimler cars, of Gandhi caps and plumed white helmets two issues were being fought out. In the Congress camp the challenge of the left wing under S. C. Bose was met and defeated in early 1939. On the government side negotiations with the princes for accession to the federation were being conducted. Emissaries passed to and fro and memoranda blossomed like spring flowers. But the enthusiasm of 1930, when the princes accepted the principle of federation, had evaporated, to give place to doubts and fears of the future and hopes of some further period of irresponsible rule. The princes took advantage of the voluntary stipulation for accession to spin matters out. The new Viceroy either did not realize that accession could only be obtained by some measure of coercion or was unwilling to apply it. So the war came before anything was accomplished and with it went the last chance of any place for the princes in the new India. They had become living fossils.

Another development must also be noted here, though it is more fully dealt with elsewhere. The Muslims had long been politically divided, even the Muslim League being split into a League and a Conference. With the approach of the new constitution this schism was healed under the lead of the formerly Congress-minded Bombay lawyer, Muhammad Ali Jinnah. Jinnah contested the elections on a national as well as a communal ticket and hoped for coalitions in the Hindu majority provinces like the United Provinces. He was only moderately successful and was bitterly disappointed when the Congress leaders brushed his claims aside and seemed determined to break up his nascent party. From this time he began to attack the Congress and all its works and to attract mass as well as the selective middle- and upper-class support he had formerly enjoyed. The effects of these efforts were not immediately apparent but they were to prove pregnant for future developments.

The inter-war period was one of rapid development in India. Observers living in the country during this period could feel, as it were, the quickening of the pulse of Indian life. Economic development away from the colonial dependence of the nineteenth century was rapid. The fiscal autonomy of India was recognized in 1921 as part of the new Montford régime. In itself it was only a phrase but it was given tangible form by the creation of the Tariff Board in 1923. A symbol of the new autonomy was the suspension of the already moribund cotton excise in 1924 and its abolition in 1925. The Tariff Board used its powers for the safeguarding of existing industries and the development of new ones. The steel industry, the creation of the Parsi Tata family in the early years of the century, was saved from disaster in the depression of the early thirties by judicious protection, and the cotton industry protected from unduly cheap Japanese competition. Protection enabled the sugar industry to obviate the need for sugar imports from Indonesia, and the infant cement industry to develop. By 1939 India was certainly not an industrialized country, but it had its own modern machine industries. She was in fact emerging from a colonial phase to her traditional economy of a rural economy strengthened by supplementary industries. Balancing this hopeful feature was the ominous fact of the rapid increase of population which made it doubtful whether the rise in productivity and of national income had in fact benefited the average man at all, or only the upper minority. Between 1921 and 1941 the population rose by 70 millions from 319 to 389 millions. The only certain thing that could be said of him was that he now had, if not more to eat and wear, more amenities in the shape of general security, transport, public health, and freedom from total famine.

In education progress was also marked. Some of the new governments of the Montford period, particularly that of the Punjab inspired by Sir Fazli Husain, made vigorous attempts to extend primary education. Pupils in schools of all kinds increased between the wars by 170 per cent to fourteen and a half million. But higher education developed faster. Quantitatively this can be measured by the increase of degree colleges from 231 to 385 between 1921 and 1939. But following the monumental Sadler Commission report the structure of the university system was modified. New universities were founded as teaching institutions on the model of the new English universities instead of as simple examining bodies. Teaching faculties were added to the older universities and there was a development in depth by means of post-graduate studies as well as in range. The foundation of Annamalai university showed that private citizens now had enough confidence in modern education to make large benefactions. Indian scholars like Sir Jagadis Bose and Dr C. V. Raman in science, Sir S. Radhakrishnan and Dr Gas Gupta in philosophy, Sir J. Sarkar in history, and Sir M. Iqbal the poet-philosopher, increasingly entered the world intellectual stage. In general, in spite of Mahatma Gandhi with his call to simple Vedic living the trend was a westernizing one. Western amenities, western machines, western thought including Marxism were gaining ground. But Hindu thought had a distinguished exponent in the mystic recluse Sri Arobindo, who from his retreat in French Pondicherry reinterpreted Vedantic thought in mellifluous English.

Social developments were no less striking. There was the Harijan movement of Mahatma Gandhi which perceptibly altered the attitude of caste Hindus to the lower castes in general. Gandhi was also, as it seems to me, responsible for the wide acceptance within Hindu society of the principle that man is his brother's keeper. The first impetus towards this came from missionary activity; the Ramkrishna mission's activities made the first Hindu impact upon society but it was Gandhi's efforts which secured for the principle general acceptance. A further feature of this period was the emergence of women into public life and activity. The earlier liberals had advocated women's rights without, save in one or two distinguished instances,* doing much about it in their own circles. In the twenties the trend towards education and public activity strengthened. Distinguished women like the poet-politician Sarojini Naidu, Begam Shah Nawaz, and later Mrs Pandit appeared. But the event which did more than any other single factor to speed the process was the Civil Disobedience movement of 1930–31. Feeling was then so strong that those already in public life joined Congress committees and took to organizing pickets for liquor and cloth shops,

* Pt. Vidyasagar and the Widows remarriage campaign; Dr Karve with his Women's University.

processions and demonstrations in addition to the usual Congress activities while many thousands came out of conditions of privacy and semi-seclusion to support the cause. Some of these were so ardent that at times, as in Delhi, they directed the whole Congress movement in an area until arrested. Many of them went to prison and as a whole they showed a discipline and devotion rivalling Gandhi's trained *satyagrahis*. The leap forward then achieved was pushed further by Gandhi's open encouragement in his *ashram* and elsewhere and by Nehru's support. His sister was a minister in the first Congress cabinet in the United Provinces. Sarojini Naidu was a prominent member of the Congress committee. While the women pushed forward conservative Congressmen acquiesced for the sake of the cause. During this period women established a foothold in public life which has broadened with the years that have passed. Independent India has seen three women as State governors, one as a State Premier, one as a central cabinet minister, and several as State ministers. Mr Nehru's deputy for foreign affairs was for many years a woman.

(ii) *The Second World War*

It appeared at first that the war would affect India little, but in the event it proved a forcing-house of development. For a year India stood back to watch the 'phony' war. Opinion was divided between democratic disapproval of Hitler and Nazism and nationalist suspicion of British and French imperialism. Left wing Congressmen who followed Nehru while critical of Germany were suspicious of Britain. The followers of Bose with his authoritarian leanings were inclined to wait with some expectancy. The country as a whole was far more detached in attitude than it had been in 1914. India, it was generally felt, was no longer a country aspiring for recognition but an adult country still deprived of the right to manage its own affairs. The war was therefore none of her business. The collapse of France and the isolation of Britain caused general concern. When it was seen that Britain would stand alone and the battle of Britain followed, concern turned to admiration. But when it was realized, as the months passed by, that Britain was still post-poning all steps towards Dominion status until 'after the war', the mood changed again to one of sourness and suspicion. This prevailed until the entry of Japan brought the war to India's doorstep and made it an intimate concern.

The government itself did little in the first year of the war. The war was to be a mechanized one, said the experts. The Indian army was not mechanized and therefore nothing could be done. But with the spread of the war to the Middle East this atti-tude changed. India became the centre of a supply centre for this region with a corresponding stimulus to her industries. With Japan's entry at the end of 1941 she soon became a base for hostilities as well as supply. The South East Asia Command was based in Delhi until it moved to Ceylon. The forces of the Burma–Assamese hills had to be supplied across the country from Bombay and at the same time food supplies had to be dis-tributed at right-angles to this line in the absence of available sea transport. The Bengal famine of 1943, precipitated by the cutting off of Burma rice in 1942, complicated matters with the necessity of sending supplies to Bengal as well as by its toll of unnecessary human suffering. India was thus deeply involved by 1942. But she still kept aloof from any commitment because of the political situation. Those who felt strongest on this issue supported S. C. Bose who fled the country and raised the Indian National Army from Indian prisoners in Japanese hands. He hoped to return as an Indian dictator. Many others joined in the Congress 'revolt' in 1942.

Though the Indian heart was not in the war, the Indian war effort and record is nevertheless impressive, and its effects on the country profound. The army itself had a distinguished fighting record. Its first assignment was in the Middle East under General Wavell. It shared in his spectacular defeat of the Italians, and later in the campaigns of Generals Auchinleck and Montgomery. It took part in the Iraq, Syrian, and Persian operations and in the first of these its intervention was decisive. The Fourth and Seventh divisions became household words and were among the best troops turned out by either side. With the Japanese war their attention was mainly diverted to the eastern marches of India itself. Indian troops shared in the long retreat from Malaya and 90,000 were trapped when Singapore fell in February 1942. They bore an honourable part in General Alexander's retreat from Burma, and then manned India's eastern border. From 1943 they became a part of General Slim's Fourteenth Army, itself a component of the South East Asia Command (S.E.A.C.), under Admiral Mountbatten. In early 1944 the Seventh Division's heroic stand at Kohima broke the force of the Japanese advance on Assam, and thereafter they shared in Slim's triumphant return to Burma. They were poised for an assault on Malaya when the war ended in 1945.

During these years the peacetime strength of the army was expanded from 175,000 to two million. Large-scale mechanization and motorization produced thousands of technicians. As was not the case in 1914, the men came from all over India. The stirring and stimulation was thus countrywide and so was the distribution of newly acquired skills. Both the navy and the air force were built up into efficient modern units and became important westernizing influences. Women's auxiliary forces also appeared, thus adding force to the gathering momentum of the women's movement.

The supply of these troops stimulated Indian industry. This went beyond the already flourishing textile industry to iron and steel and new industries altogether. Tata's steel works were further extended and new works opened by the Bengal Steel Corporation and the Kumardhuti Group. The cement industry expanded in a spectacular way and so did the mica industry. Deposits of bauxite were exploited to create a new aluminium industry.

Against all this must be set the tragedy of the Bengal famine. The loss of Burma rice led to an overall food loss of about five per cent, which, however, was felt chiefly by the rice-eating regions of Bengal and in the south. The shortage was not catastrophic but stocks had to be moved over a transport system already clogged by the mounting allied war efforts. Prices began to rise; the peasant sold his stock to pay off his debts and then found himself with nothing to eat; black markets appeared and the peasants began to flock to Calcutta. The Bengal government proved unable to meet the crisis while the Central government refused to intervene from federal scruple of overriding a provincial administration. Thus what should have been a controlled shortage became the first famine of starvation since the Famine Code was devised in 1883 with a mortality of up to two millions. On his arrival as Viceroy in October 1943 Lord Wavell's first act was to visit Calcutta, turn on the British army to the control of relief distribution, make food control a central concern, and impose rationing on all large cities. Never had the British army been so popular.

We must now return to the political scene. The Indian attitude to the war would have been far more positive if the political situation had been clearer. But in fact this became steadily more confused. There would seem to have been rivalry as to which side should make the most mistakes. On the outbreak of war the Viceroy began with two. As a dependency India was automatically legally involved in a declaration of war by Britain, but the Viceroy announced the fact so baldly without any show of consultation with the Assembly, as to give general offence. At the same time he suspended negotiations with the princes instead of intensifying them, thus throwing away the last opportunity of setting up a conservative federation. The Congress replied on its side in the same coin. Without considering the consequences, it ordered the provincial ministries to resign in October as a protest. By this gesture they took their hands off the levers of provincial power at a critical moment. Possession of them during the war would have made it difficult for the League to grow in power as it did, for the Viceroy would have leaned on the Congress instead of encouraging the League. And after the war this position would have been irresistible.

Politics now entered a deadlock from which they did not emerge until 1947. The British stuck to their tradition of no change during a war; whatever you want after the war provided you are good. They were oblivious to the difference in these circumstances between a Britain fighting for her life and an India a spectator at the ringside. They forgot the disastrous results of this policy in Ireland in the First World War and its nearly fatal effects in India. This attitude produced mounting suspicion in Congress minds, and undermined the general sympathy at first felt for the allied cause. The schism in the Congress mind between democratic sympathies and suspicions of the British produced a sourness of soul which made negotiations increasingly difficult. In this deadlock was the Muslim League's chance. The League rejected Congress claims to represent all India and steadily built itself up as the representative of the second Indian nation, the hundred millions as Jinnah liked to call them. Jinnah matched Congress negation to the British with Muslim negation to the Congress. On the resignation of the Congress ministries he ordered a Thanksgiving Day which was widely observed. Early in 1940 he took the decisive step of declaring Pakistan the goal of League policy.

The deadlock remained unchanged until the fall of France in 1940. There was then a flurry of genuine alarm for India and sympathy for Britain. 'We do not seek independence out of Britain's ruin,' said Gandhiji. The government reply to this was the August offer which conceded an Indian constituent assembly as well as Dominion status 'after the war'. But by now the first mood of alarm and admiration for the British stand had passed and the offer was rejected with scorn. The deadlock continued, punctuated by an 'individual' civil disobedience campaign launched by Gandhi in the autumn of 1940. Vinoba Bhave was the first *satyagrahi* to offer himself for arrest; by the spring of 1941 there were 14,000 detainees but the movement was carefully controlled by Gandhi so as not to embarrass the government unduly. The Viceroy enlarged his Council to fifteen, eleven being Indians, but otherwise carried on as before.

A new chapter began with the entry of Japan and America into the war in December 1941. On the one hand India was now intimately concerned with events; on the other the British government was now subject to American suggestions and pressures which were not long in being applied. Mahatma Gandhi's pacifism was thrown overboard by the Congress almost overnight and the British could no longer maintain the sacred formula of 'after the war'. Churchill's own position in England was weakened by the loss of Singapore and Burma; Sir Stafford Cripps, newly returned with the laurels of Moscow, was now

Leader of the House of Commons and seemed almost an heir-apparent in an increasingly radical-minded Britain. It was in these circumstances that the despatch of Sir Stafford Cripps on a mission with a radical offer was announced on 11 March 1942. The offer caused great excitement in India and for a time it seemed as though the deadlock would be broken. There was an after-the-war air in the proposals but also a new breath of precision and commitment. The promised constituent assembly elected by the provincial legislatures would draw up a dominion constitution for India immediately after the end of the war. The constitution would then be embodied in a treaty on the lines of those with Scotland in 1707 and the Irish Free State in 1922. The right of secession from the Commonwealth and of a province to contract out of the federal union were recognized. The party leaders were invited to join the Viceroy's council, which would be treated as a responsible cabinet as far as possible. It was on this point that the discussions broke down for the Congress leaders insisted that the new council must have immediately the full powers of a dominion cabinet. It is thought that the majority of Congress leaders favoured a deal but that Gandhi, absent at the beginning of the discussions, turned the scale. He is said to have remarked that the offer was like drawing a cheque on a failing bank. The discussions took place in the shadow of the Japanese conquest of Burma. If the British were ready to concede so much then, would not they concede complete control when the Japanese were ready to invade India in October after the monsoon? Why not therefore wait a little longer. The achievement of full control would enable Congress to settle the Pakistan issue, and this was a stake worth playing for.

Once the offer was rejected a mood of bitterness and frustration ensued in proportion to the eagerness and hope which the proposals had aroused. The Congress, including Nehru, rallied behind Gandhi, and only Rajagopalachari stuck to his guns and was ejected. The government on its side stiffened its attitude. After some months of musing Gandhi now declared that the British in India were a provocation to the Japanese. With his usual skill he invented the 'Quit India' slogan and demanded

British withdrawal on pain of new civil disobedience which might well coincide with a Japanese advance in the autumn. 'After all,' he said, 'this is open rebellion.' So also thought the government. When the Congress passed its resolution on 7 August the whole Working Committee was interned at Poona. There followed a short but sharp outbreak by left-wing elements of the Congress. For a time communications were disrupted in Bihar and the United Provinces. About a thousand lives were lost and 60,000 were arrested by the end of the year, and damage worth a million pounds inflicted. The government called this a Congress rebellion, while the Congress claimed it as a spontaneous reaction to the intolerable strain to which the government had subjected the people.

Apart from the crisis of a Gandhian fast in early 1944 the deadlock continued in militant form for the rest of the European war. But in fact it was never as bad as it looked because neither side fully believed in their attitudes. Both knew that they must eventually come to terms with each other. The British, in the event, repelled the Japanese and under Lord Wavell grew steadily stronger and more confident. The Congress were seen to have made two serious mistakes. By rejecting the Cripps offer they had both lost the opportunity of entrenching themselves in the seats of power and also the chance of smothering the Muslim League before it was too late. The price of these errors was Partition.

LITTLE reference has so far been made to the part played by
Muslims in the rise of modern India. Yet they formed a quarter
of the population and had dominated the Indian scene for centuries. It has seemed best, at the cost of some repetition elsewhere, to concentrate attention on them in a special chapter
in order to make the rise of the Pakistan movement more
intelligible.

Muslims, in the form of Arab traders, first appeared on the
Malabar coast during the seventh century A.D. not many years after
the death of the Prophet Muhammad in 632 A.D. For centuries
they had important trading interests and political influence in
this region, and it was against them that the Portuguese battled
in the early sixteenth century. Their influence was also religious;
a raja of Calicut is said to have become a Muslim and some
historians think that they were an important influence in the
development of Hindu religious thought during that period.*

Early in the eighth century an Arab army conquered Sind.
But it was not until the Turkish irruptions of the eleventh and
twelfth centuries that the Muslim impact on India assumed large
proportions. In the early years of the eleventh century the raids
of Mahmud of Ghazni, culminating in the sack of the great
temple of Somnath in 1024, created the tradition among northern
Hindus of Muslim intolerance and ferocity. They occupied most
of the Punjab but were held there for nearly two centuries before
the break through into northern India occurred in 1192. Thereafter, under the aegis of the Delhi sultanate, Islamic dominion
spread over all northern India and by 1320 had reached the far
south.

It is during the centuries immediately succeeding the capture
of Delhi in 1192 that the Muslim community was created. Its
first components were the merchants and travellers of the earlier

* See I. H. Qureshi, *History of the Muslim Community in the Indian
Subcontinent*, ch, 1, 1962. The physical representatives of these Arabs today
are the Moplah community.

contacts, but these were only a fraction of the later community. The next and more significant group were the Turkish invaders themselves with their followers. These formed a military aristocracy thinly spread over the country, controlling an army of occupation which held the main centres of population. They were steadily recruited by groups and individuals from over the passes both Turkish and Persian and by Arab adventurers. These sustained the aristocracy and provided talented leadership down to the eighteenth century. But in sum their numbers were quite small and could not account for the whole Muslim body. A major source was accession from the Hindu ranks. A trickle came from the Hindu upper classes, some of whom became Muslims from conviction and some in hope of reward. The minister Khan Jahan in the fourteenth century was one such. A further group were forcibly converted in times of tumult or stress. The practice undoubtedly occurred but its extent tended to be exaggerated by bigoted and boastful chroniclers. In sum, like the foregoing categories it amounted to a small percentage. By far the largest element within the Muslim community came from voluntary conversion. Its causes and means were various but the fact is certain. There were Buddhist peasants under Brahmin rule who preferred the relative freedom of Islam to low caste status. There were groups of outcastes or exterior castes, as the anthropologists call them, who moved to Islam for the same reason, while in places militant clans or groups went over in a body as a political tactic. The means of these conversions varied. Some groups probably went over as a result of a communal decision. A very potent factor, however, was the preaching of Muslim *sufis* or devotees. Unlike the *'ulema* or doctors of Muslim law, who followed the Muslim courts and expounded a legalistic theism, the *sufis* appealed to the heart and went among the people in simplicity and devotion. Their emphasis on fraternalism and inner devotion appealed to the many who were dissatisfied with their own condition for any reason. The *'ulema* issued *fatwas* or interpretations of the law; the *sufis* established spiritual centres which soon became places of pilgrimage and shrines of devotion like the Chishti shrines at Ajmir and Delhi.

It was in this way that one fourth of the Indian population became Muslim and these factors which explain the distribution of the population. Thus over the whole of India will be found a Muslim minority, mainly in the towns, descended from merchants, soldiers, and officials of bygone courts. But in certain areas the proportion was much greater. Sind, except for a merchant class, was Muslim. In the Punjab they numbered more than half the population. From there to Bengal they were to be found as a thin spread of ex-officials in town and country with here and there proletarian groups like the Momims or the Meos. In eastern Bengal the whole countryside became Muslim, perhaps because an animistic-Buddhist peasantry resented a recent Brahmin domination, and certainly because they preferred Islam to their existing condition.

A notable feature of the Muslim community was the smallness of its middle or ministerial class. Apart from medical doctors or *hakims* and Muslim lawyers or clergy anyone of ability tended to gravitate to high posts in government and army. They were served by competent Hindu subordinates of whom there was always a sufficient supply. The heyday of the Muslim community was the Mughal empire during the sixteenth and seventeenth centuries, when they formed the ruling race of India with only the Rajputs as partial partners. Then came the collapse in the eighteenth century. This was not merely the loss of imperial power to Persians and Afghans and Marathas. This was only the start of a general decline which went much further. Wherever the Marathas spread, the Muslims as a class lost office and the wealth which went with it. The British at first retained the Muslim officials but from the time of Cornwallis replaced them in their own favour. Their position in the law courts was steadily undermined as the British revised public law and introduced their own procedures in the courts. They were still the exponents of the official language of Persian. But this ceased to be of value when Bentinck made English the language of official governmental and legal business in 1835. In the same year came the introduction of English education which soon became a qualification for a subordinate official career. Most Muslims were too conservative to learn English, many considering it the highway to infidelity. But the Hindu literate classes were not; they had learnt Persian for a livelihood, in the past, so why not English, and they soon monopolized the subordinate services. Muslims thus found themselves not only shut out from office, but deprived of all hope of ever returning to it. The crowning disaster was the Mutiny of 1857, which, though commenced on caste grounds by Hindus, was blamed on the Muslim community as an anti-British revolt.

By 1860, therefore, the Muslim community in India lay apparently prostrate, with little but its imperial memories to sustain it. It had little inclination to amalgamate with the Hindus because its way of life and whole philosophy differed too radically. Idolatry, including cow worship, and caste were anathema to Muslims, however much they might borrow in detail from Hindu customs. So were such doctrines as *karma* or the law of consequences and reincarnation, fundamental in Hindu thought. It seemed, therefore, that Islam must either find renewal from within or wither away in hopelessness and daily compromises with surrounding conditions. And it was not only Hinduism which now confronted it. The Christian-secular influences from the west were pouring in to bring attacks on the ethical and rationalistic fronts. If Islam withstood absorption by Hinduism it might yet disintegrate under the impact of western scepticism and moral criticism.

In this predicament Indian Islam turned to inner renewal. In fact the process had already begun though few, specially in the west, were aware of the fact. In essence it was a response to the triple challenge of syncretistic Hinduism, loss of political dominion, and western rationalism and moralism. For the beginnings of the response we go back to the theologian Shah Wali-ullah of Delhi (1703–62) though some would go back still further to Sheikh Ahmad Sirhindi (1562–1624). Shah Wali-ullah sought to meet the Hindu intellectual challenge by maintaining that the mystical experience of divine union did not imply or involve absorption in the deity. Thus *sufi* practice, the Islamic religion of the heart, could be reconciled with the orthodox doctrine of God's sovereignty over his creation. The political collapse he countered by a call to return to the religion of the

Koran. Emperors having failed, the people must rely on God. He took the revolutionary step of translating the Koran into Persian for its better understanding. This 'primitivist' movement then branched out in two directions. One became militant as well as puritan and was dubbed 'Wahabi' from the Arabian movement which influenced its leader Sayyid Ahmad of Bareilly. He died in battle with the Sikhs in 1831 and his followers, based on Patna, gave the British government much concern for many years. The other branch was peaceful and reformist concentrating on the elimination of Hindu practices amongst Muslims. Under this heading came the movements of Sheikh Karamat Ali and Haji Shariat-ullah in eastern India. To them we may add the heterodox movement of Mirza Ghulam Ahmad (1838–1908) in the Panjab, called Ahmadiya after its founder or Qadiani after its headquarters. Its founder's claim to prophethood on a level with Muhammad himself made it heretical, but it has proved a most enterprising missionary body and has distinguished adherents.*

These movements of renewal were so far on the lower levels of Muslim society and did nothing to meet the pressing western challenge. The lead was given by Sayyid Ahmad Khan of Delhi (1817–98) whose work was as important for the Muslims as Ram Mohan Roy's had been for the Hindus. He came of a Mughal official family and entered the British judicial service. He remained staunch during the Mutiny and published a forceful analysis of its causes afterwards. His experience convinced him that Indian Islam must make terms with the west as well as remain distinct from Hinduism if it was not to remain permanently in a social and political backwater. He stressed the community of fundamental Islamic and Christian ideas with their common Judaic heritage and exposure to the Greek intellectual tradition. Reason, as well as revelation, he argued, was basic to both intellectual systems and this led him to stress the importance of studying its practical application in western science. His forceful personality gathered followers and his sterling character disarmed prejudice. He joined the Viceroy's Legislative Council in

* e.g. Sir Zafar-ullah Khan, Member of the Viceroy's Council, Foreign Minister of Pakistan 1947–55.

1878 and was the unquestioned leader of Indian Islam at his death in 1898. The basis of the Sayyid's position was that Islam could be reconciled with the thought of the western world; the practical implication that young Muslims should take up western education and resume their rightful place in the public life of their country. To this end he founded the Aligarh College in 1875, which became the acknowledged centre of what may be called Muslim modernism. From it went forth a stream of young Muslims into the government services and the professions and around it a group of thinkers worked out a persuasive apologetic designed to meet western criticism.

Scarcely was this movement well under way than it was presented with the political challenge of the formation of the Indian National Congress. The Sayyid determined to hold aloof and this may be regarded as the first overt step towards Pakistan. A democratic régime, said the Sayyid, means majority rule, and majority rule in India would mean Hindu rule. Therefore the British cannot be dispensed with and Muslims should concentrate on fitting themselves to take that place in the state which their numbers justified. This position lasted until the great rise of national feeling connected with the partition of Bengal presaged some extension of the Indian share in the administration by the new Liberal government. The thought of elections sounded the tocsin of alarm in Muslim minds and there then began that process by which each constitutional advance was accompanied by a Muslim demand for safeguards. These safeguards took the form of special or 'separate' constituencies for Muslims on the ground that the property qualification proposed would always place them in a minority on account of their poverty compared to the Hindus. In 1906 Lord Minto admitted to a deputation of notables their claim for separate electorates, and this was followed by the formation of the Muslim League in December 1906 * at Dacca. These were embodied in the Government of India Act of 1909.

The First World War caused an unexpected diversion of this process. The entry of Turkey into the war on the German side placed a strain on orthodox Muslim loyalty because of the

* The League's first conference was held in December 1907 at Karachi.

Turkish Sultan's character of Caliph which was recognized in India. The nationalist leader Tilak took advantage of this to swing the Muslim leaders into the Congress camp. The inducement was the recognition by Congress of separate Muslim electorates in the Lucknow Pact of December 1916. After the war Muslim alarm and indignation deepened with the harsh terms of the Treaty of Sèvres and this induced them to join with Gandhi in the first non-cooperation movement. For a time brotherliness reigned supreme and no notice was taken of the implication of the Montford reforms. Then came the collapse. Ataturk defeated the Greeks, deposed the Sultan, and abolished the Caliphate (1922–24). The Indian government championed the Muslim cause while the non-cooperation movement collapsed. The result was a revival of fears and suspicion expressed in an increasing incidence of communal riots. League leaders like Jinnah who stood for cooperation with the Congress on a joint national platform found their position becoming more difficult. The turning-point for these men may be said to have been reached with the Motilal Nehru committee's rejection of separate electorates in their proposed constitution of 1928.

Once more the community felt themselves to be isolated, and this time from both Hindus and British. In the case of the Hindus they saw around them the already distinct degree of power transferred by the Montford reforms, and they looked forward to a further substantial transfer in the coming act of 1935. Abstention from the Civil Disobedience movement of 1930–31 might embarrass the Congress temporarily but it would not reverse the steady process of power transfer any more than it would win them goodwill. With the British they had broken over the *khilafat* issue and they were not prepared to go back to the subordinate partnership concept which in the Sayyid's time had seemed to be the only practical policy. They felt themselves to be divided and leaderless and looked fearfully ahead. It was at this time that the poet Sir Muhammad Iqbal came forward in 1930 with a proposal for a separate Muslim homeland in the north-west. In his treasured poems and widely read philosophic writings he had already provided a young Islam with an ideology more vigorous and acceptable than the Sayyid's rather dated occidentalism and Anglicism.* Independence and self-reliance were his theme. Islam was a dynamic religion whose secret was the progress of the soul towards freedom through constant striving. The west was sunk in materialism and would perish from the evils of its own inventions. Here was a message at once invigorating and apparently intellectual, something in tune with the urge to action of the time. Expressed in glowing and melodious verse, it gave new heart to the Aligarh class of Muslim and prepared him for the campaign which was to follow. At the same time the visionary Chaudhuri Rahmat Ali with a small group in Cambridge coined the word Pakistan † and evolved the idea of three Muslim states in the Indian subcontinent. In this scheme there was no fuss about Hindu minorities, large or small, and most observers laughed it off as chimerical. But here was a political egg, which however minute, others could incubate to produce a nation.

As the shape of the 1935 Act grew firmer, it became clear that the transfer of power would be substantial and that the final transfer at the centre could not be very long delayed. The articulate Muslims now had a creed, an ideology, a sense of separateness, and a sense of urgency; what they lacked was a leader. This they now found in Muhammad Ali Jinnah, the elegant westernized lawyer from Bombay who had long sought to promote cooperation between Muslims and the Congress. He was now hopeless of swaying the Congress itself, but still hoped to work with it along parallel lines. In 1935 he took over the almost moribund Muslim League and set about reviving it in preparation for the elections of 1937. He announced his willingness to work in coalition with Congress ministries and believed that Congress leaders shared his views. In the actual elections the League fared only moderately. It was on the Muslim electoral map but by no means exclusively so. The Congress, with assured majorities in six provinces, declined coalitions, offering office to Leaguers only on a personal basis. This was a bitter

* See his *Secrets of the Self* (transl. R. H. Nicholson, 1920) and *Lectures on the Reconstruction of Religious Thought in Islam*, (1934).

† P for Punjab, A for Afghans (Pathans), K for Kashmir, S for Sind and stan, the Persian suffix meaning country.

blow to Jinnah. It also formed a Rubicon in his life, to which, once crossed, he never looked back. He never trusted Congress leaders again and determined that the only way to deal with them was to throw their tactics of obstruction back on themselves. But he had first to secure his hold both on the Muslim classes and masses. For the classes he preached the western doctrine of national independence, the untrustworthiness of Hindus, and the two nations theory. Indian Islam was a separate nation which could never accept Hindu rule. For the masses he hammered on the danger of Hinduization and Hindu 'provocations'. Tactless words and actions by Congressmen under the ministries of 1937–39 provided welcome material for this line of which he made the most dexterous use. The success of his Thanksgiving Day on the Congress resignations in 1939 showed how much success he had achieved in so short a time. From this point it was but a step to the proclamation of Pakistan as the League's goal in March 1940. The word was new-fangled but the idea was the political expression of a deep-seated sense of separateness and a determination to maintain it in a new age.

19

INDEPENDENCE AND CONSOLIDATION

(i) Independence

The end of the war in Europe found the government of India in an apparently strong position. Under the firm hand of Lord Wavell the administration seemed stable and assured. India was full of armed men. The army was steadily moving forward into Burma and was full of confidence. The Congress leaders were detained but the country was quiet and the left wing had made no further move since the 1942 disturbances. Some of the Congress members had reappeared in the Assembly and talk of compromise was in the air. The Muslim League officially boycotted the war effort, but it did little to prevent Muslims from taking part; in the result they were engaged in the war effort in large numbers. The food and the inflationary situations were now in hand and there was nothing like the widespread mass irritation which had existed at the end of the First World War.

But the Viceroy knew very well that this was only a superficial view of the situation. India always responds to firm leadership, and had accepted the Wavell government for the duration of the war. But the war had only postponed and not solved the issue of self-government. The moment the war ended the same issues would re-emerge and there would also come a rapid diminution of British power as war-time concentrations of troops dispersed. The Cripps offer had been rejected by the Congress and withdrawn by the British, but the issue behind it, the way to and the nature of self-government remained. If there were thus good reasons for speedy action in India, the same held good for Britain too. It was thought in May 1945 that the Japanese war would last for another year, during which Britain would remain strong in India. But the political prospect was uncertain, with a general election pending and the break-up of the Coalition imminent. All considerations pointed to prompt action. Wavell made the first move by attempting to form a national administration on the lines of the Cripps proposals. The Congress leaders were released and summoned to Simla with the Leaguers. The new government was to complete the Japanese war and then arrange for the promised constituent assembly. These discussions foundered on the rocks of the allotment of seats in the Executive Council and the Congress refusal to recognize the League as the sole representative of the Muslims. One fact which emerged was the increased confidence of Jinnah and the Leaguers. Over the past three years they had won almost every by-election for the Assembly and now had a solid block of twenty-five members.* The Congress on their side capped their errors in renouncing office in 1939 and 1942 by refusing to recognize the increased League strength which those errors had helped to foster.

At this juncture came two unexpected events. A Labour government was returned to power in Britain with a large majority in late July and the Japanese war came to a sudden end in August with the Hiroshima and Nagasaki atomic bombs. In these circumstances it was agreed to test the strength of the parties by means of provincial and central elections, not held since the beginning of the war. There followed an uneasy six months while the slow-moving electoral wheels revolved. The decision was correct, but in the new situation the time required could scarcely be spared. Tension steadily mounted to find a focus in the trial of the leaders of Bose's 'National Army' in the Red Fort in the autumn and the brief naval mutiny in February 1946. In the former case the Congress leaders exploited the situation but in the latter, which seems to have been a spontaneous outbreak of youthful extremist exuberance, they were embarrassed and did their best to disavow and discourage it. The mutineers complained that the leaders of the cause they were trying to help had betrayed them. The Congress leaders were now fearful lest anarchy supervene before they were able to grasp the reins of government.

The elections clarified at least two points. While the Congress was overwhelmingly the strongest party in Hindu India, the League had an almost equal hold over the Muslim electorate. The two-nations theory of Mr Jinnah had found political expression. While Congress could block any solution by the

* Out of 104 elected members.

British short of complete self-government, the League could block, if it wished, any solution acceptable to the Congress short of partition. There was a third change in power relationships which was of vital importance. During these months the British ability to impose a decision or even to maintain the *status quo* was rapidly dwindling. The old attitude of 'we will hold the ring until the two parties come to an agreement' was no longer viable because neither the physical force, nor the will to power, nor the moral conviction was there to sustain it. The British election had made it clear that the British public was not prepared for any further sacrifices to maintain the British supremacy in India. Power was now in the hands of people who believed in Indian independence and who were therefore the more ready to recognize the emerging realities of the situation. From now on the only question was how soon can power be handed over and in what way. A further effect of the new mood of Britain was an insistence on a rapid demobilization of the army. By the spring of 1946 most of the war military units had disappeared so that the government no longer had much physical force at its disposal. The umpire holding the ring with forces in reserve to quell disorder now became a peacemaker and negotiator with reason, mutual respect and fears for the future as the chief weapons in his armoury.

In the tense events which followed the fate of India largely turned on five figures. There was the Mahatma, enigmatic as ever, expansive and haggling by turns. His guiding light was the unity of India which both led him to oppose partition until after the last possible moment and led him on campaigns of reconciliation in riot-stricken areas marked by the greatest courage and compassion. Next came Jawarharlal Nehru, now a mature national leader and Gandhi's accepted successor. Mercurial, magnetic, brilliant, and still unpredictable at times, he still underestimated the strength of the League and its underlying mass support, but riper judgement now largely controlled his impulsiveness and a wider vision his impatience. The third was Muhammad Ali Jinnah at the height of his powers. The impassive face, the slow and measured voice with its exact articulation, the neat Bond Street tailored figure formed a mask behind which lay an iron will and nerve, a supreme tactical skill, a power to inspire loyalty and impose discipline, and the ability to stir the masses almost as great as Gandhi's own. The man who could not speak Urdu could move the Muslim multitude. The last two figures were British. The stocky figure of Wavell was that of a reflective soldier of great intellectual power and much goodwill, who often lost by his silences what he had gained by his initiatives. He was out of his element in the dialectical arguments of the current polemical politics but he retained general respect and won the admiration of Maulana Azad. The fifth figure, Mountbatten, was yet to come, and, when he came, was to prove Wavell's opposite in nearly every respect. Brilliant, assured, talkative, ingenious and bold, a master of hustle, he dazzled equally with his own personality and his royal connexions. Yet between the result of the reticent prudence of Wavell and the headlong activism of Mountbatten the choice was not automatic and discussion will long revolve round the query whether the speed of the final settlement did not involve disasters as great as the calamities it was designed to forestall.

The London cabinet now acted. A mission headed by Lord Pethick-Lawrence, and consisting besides of Sir Stafford Cripps and Mr A. V. (later Viscount) Alexander, arrived in Delhi in April 1946. Their aim was to preserve a united India while satisfying Muslim fears. They soon found that the two parties were intransigent. The Congress was unwilling to agree to anything which might open the way to a Pakistan partition, and still doubted the strength of the mass support behind Jinnah; Jinnah on his part was determined to agree to nothing which would shut the door to Muslim claims. He saw in consistent obstruction his best hope of ultimate success and was well aware that he was treading a razor-edge path between violence and destruction. The Mission then prepared an ingenious plan generally credited to Cripps. It was in two parts. The long term part envisaged a federal union of two 'tiers'. The first tier would consist of the British Indian provinces which the Indian states could join after negotiation. The second 'tier' would consist of individual provinces which might form subordinate unions of their own, each deciding which of the provincial powers they would vest in the regional union. The centre for its part would have powers reduced from those of the Cripps proposals in 1942, controlling only defence, foreign affairs, and communications. By strengthening the federating units at the expense of the centre and by providing for subordinate unions it was hoped to allay Muslim fears of Hindu domination while preserving the unity of all India. Both sides in fact accepted this plan, but they then fell out over the second part or interim plan. This provided for an interim government which would call a consituent assembly to draw up a constitution on the agreed basis of part one. Breakdown occurred over the allotment of cabinet seats, the Congress still claiming to represent the whole of India and therefore to be entitled to appoint a Muslim member, and the League claiming to represent all Muslims and therefore to have a monopoly of all their appointments.

It was inevitable, perhaps, considering the tenseness of the atmosphere and the stakes involved, that the breakdown should have been accompanied by recriminations. Since these led on directly to the mounting violence which finally decided the issue I think it can be said that the Cabinet Mission formed the point of no return after which partition was inevitable. Congress rejection of the interim plan concealed their suspicion of Muslim intentions and disbelief in the League's power of invoking the necessary degree of force to achieve partition. Jinnah believed obstruction to be correct because time was on his side. Every week that passed in the existing atmosphere increased the commitment of reluctant middle-class Muslims and stimulated the mass support which was the ultimate sanction of his policy. The results of the Mission's visit were not all negative, however. During this period of intense negotiation the Congress leaders at last became convinced of the sincerity of the declared British intention to hand over power as soon as possible. A new note crept into their relations with the British leaders which had an important bearing on the final settlement in the following year. There is another reason why India may now be grateful for the failure of the Mission's proposals. The price of unity was to have been a weak centre, only partially set off by the device of subordinate unions. There were several dangers inherent in this plan. One was that the Centre would have been so weak and so harassed by communal jostlings for power, that the big developments which have occurred in both India and Pakistan since partition would have been impossible. The other was, given a weak and wrangling centre, that power would have tended to accumulate in the subordinate unions leading to a division of India, not into two but several independent units. There are times when no amount of constitutional ingenuity can cover the stark realities of power contests.

From this time on India slid steadily towards a civil war of the most frightful kind punctuated by communal killings when each community in turn wreaked vengeance on the other. First came the recriminations. Jinnah charged the government with bad faith because it had not entrusted the League only with the administration when Congress refused to join the interim plan. Then Nehru declared at a Congress meeting in July that the Congress would go to the Constituent Assembly uncommitted to any plan. This sounded the tocsin for Jinnah who declared a Direct Action day for 16 August. Bloody riots broke out in Calcutta which the Muslim League government was unable or unwilling to control until British troops were brought in. Here the Hindus suffered chiefly. Soon after the Hindus in Bihar turned on the Muslim minority and there were further outbreaks in East Bengal and the United Provinces. With fury aroused and passions unleashed each outbreak involved hideous excesses.

Sobered by the events of August, the Congress took office in early September, and Jinnah, in fear of isolation, joined in October. But the League came to fight rather than cooperate and its next step was to boycott the Constituent Assembly in December. A worried Viceroy found that he could only remonstrate with men who would not listen to reason. The Cabinet now called the leaders to London and when this had no effect determined on shock treatment as a last resource. On 20 February 1947 it announced that power would be handed over not later than June 1948 and that Lord Mountbatten would succeed Lord Wavell to prepare a plan for the hand over. At last the leaders were sobered. With the Muslim League, in the words of Jinnah, 'not yielding an inch in its demand for Pakistan', and with the British pledged to withdraw by a specific date, they saw a spreading vista of civil strife of a very horrible kind leading to chaos if no settlement was reached by the appointed date. With the collapse of the Khizr ministry early in the year the Panjab was locked in virtual civil war which destroyed Amritsar and Multan. The Congress hope of securing the levers of power in time to prevent partition had now faded with the new time limit. If no settlement was reached the governmental machine would be handed over in parts and these parts very possibly in disrepair. Fragmentation rather than partition was now the most pressing danger. In fact Jinnah's intransigence had won the day. He had already paid a big price and was to pay a bigger. He had succeeded in presenting the Congress with the choice of Pakistan or chaos. Only Gandhi was willing to face chaos.

Events now moved to a climax. After both sides had rejected a last attempt by the new Viceroy to obtain an agreed settlement, the Congress leaders determined that a partition was inevitable. At last Nehru broke with Gandhi on this issue. The veteran Mahatma returned to his reconciling work in Bengal and did not even attend the Independence Day celebrations in August. Mountbatten now produced a plan which owed much to the tireless energy of the Reforms Commissioner, V. P. Menon, and which was accepted alike by Congress, League, and the Sikhs on its publication on 3 June. Two states, India and Pakistan, were to be set up to whom the British government would hand its assets and they would draw up their own constitutions. The independence or handover date was advanced to midnight of 14 August. The states would be released from British paramountcy and treaty obligations on that date but would be encouraged to accede to either India or Pakistan before that date. Provinces would determine their new allegiance by vote of their legislatures. But in the Punjab and Bengal, where communal numbers were nearly equal, there would be division by means of a boundary commission,* and in the Frontier province, where a Red Shirt ministry held office by a precarious majority, there was to be a referendum. The two main parties professed dis-

* This later became the Radcliffe award.

satisfaction but accepted the proposals; so did the Sikhs though they had far greater cause for discontent since their population was divided in half by the probable line of partition in the Punjab.

Once the partition had been agreed the final arrangements were carried through by Lord Mountbatten, a master of rush tactics, with lightning speed. He was much helped by his lack of commitments, by his fresh and direct personal approach which made the aura of royalty surrounding him all the more fascinating, and by Lady Mountbatten who, by her unaffected concern for the Indian people, her energy and sagacity as well as her charm, did much both in public and private to smooth ruffled feelings. The two formed an irresistible team for the occasion. The magic worked and when the moment of independence arrived, Nehru too rose to the occasion. Addressing the Constituent Assembly just before midnight on 14 August he said:

Long years ago we made a tryst with destiny, and now the time comes when we shall redeem our pledge, not wholly or in full measure, but very substantially. At the stroke of the midnight hour, when the world sleeps, India will awake to life and freedom. A moment comes, which comes but rarely in history, when we step out from the old to the new, when an age ends, and when the soul of a nation, long suppressed, finds utterance. It is fitting that at this solemn moment we take the pledge of dedication to the service of India and her people and to the still larger cause of humanity.

(ii) Consolidation

The new government was inaugurated on 15 August. Lord Mountbatten became the first Governor-General of the new Dominion and he and Lady Mountbatten were greeted with enthusiasm in the tumultuous celebrations that followed. Anti-British feeling seemed to vanish overnight, and it was now seen to have been largely built up by suspicion of British intentions and fears of some last minute *volte-face*. Official and personal friendliness has been the general rule since then, punctuated only by temporary ruffling of tempers on occasions like the Suez incident. The Indian friendliness to their late 'oppressors' was a source of puzzlement to outside observers, particularly

Americans and even to Mrs Eleanor Roosevelt herself. A régime which evoked such kindly feelings towards its late representatives could not have been wholly bad.

But the new government had still to show its ability to govern and was soon to be under greater strain than it had expected. This period of strain and adjustment belongs logically to the whole independence period and forms the necessary prelude to the first chapter of the new India. The first strain, which threatened the very existence of the government, was that of the migrations which followed the Punjab massacres. The Radcliffe Boundary award was announced on 17 August, dividing the Sikh community, as anticipated, into two almost equal groups. The Sikh leaders had accepted the award in advance but a large section was determined to resist. To meet this contingency a Boundary Force of 50,000 Indian troops had been constituted under Major-General Rees, but when fighting began it was soon found to be useless. The sympathies of the various units were too engaged with one or other of the three groups (Hindu, Muslim, Sikh) for their action to be effective. In fact, only South Indian troops could be trusted, and these were not immediately available. Within days of the award Sikhs and Hindus were falling on the Muslims of the East Punjab and Muslims on the Sikhs in the west. There was general fighting accompanied by every kind of atrocity; convoys were waylaid, refugee trains held up and their passengers slaughtered, men, women, and children. Within days long convoys were marching east and west seeking shelter in the other dominion. The tide of refugees caused an explosion of communal strife in Delhi in early September. The Muslim community was uprooted and for a time the stability of the government was threatened. The exact number of the dead will never be known and estimates have differed widely. But we shall probably be somewhere near the mark with Judge G. D. Khosla's conclusion, after a very judicious analysis, of about 500,000.* Apart from this holocaust there was a huge involuntary exchange of population. It is reckoned that about five and a half millions travelled *each way* across the new India-Pakistan border in the Punjab. In addition

* G. D. Khosla, *Stern Reckoning*, p. 299.

about 400,000 Hindus migrated from Sind and well over a million moved from East Pakistan to West Bengal.

With the massacres ended the new government was faced with the settlement of the refugees. In the Punjab there was at least the land belonging to the departed Muslims available; in Delhi there were far more incoming refugees than outgoing Muslims. During the autumn this built up a fresh crisis. The refugees not only occupied many of the enclosures which surround Delhi – some like the Purana Qila contained Muslims waiting to be expatriated – they spilled over into the streets and occupied many mosques. Communal feeling began to rise again and it looked as though a pogrom of the remaining Muslim minority might soon start. Gandhi came to Delhi from Bengal in October and now directed his reconciling mission from there. This time it was the Muslims he was championing and he found he was opposed by some elements within the government itself. It was the noblest and most courageous moment of his life. He had quelled the last outbreak of communal rioting in September and in January 1948 the inner voice spoke again. This time the issues were twofold, the payment to Pakistan of her agreed assets which had been withheld owing to the Kashmir dispute and the restoration of peace in the capital. Only when the money had been paid and a peace pact, including the evacuation of the mosques, had been signed, did he give up his fast, on 18th January. Twelve days later, while proceeding to his daily prayer meeting, he was shot by a young Hindu fanatic. The effect of his death was electric. After the lamentations had died down it was seen that the Hindu political extremists were discredited. They were saddled with the responsibility for the plot and have not as yet recovered their political influence. Even Sardar Patel was blamed for failing as Home Minister to guard the Mahatma effectually.

The loss of Gandhi had the paradoxical effect of strengthening Nehru's hand. The government was really a duumvirate between him, who represented the idealism and left wing tendencies of the party, and Sardar Vallabhbhai Patel, the realist and party boss from Gujarat who leaned to authoritarianism, orthodoxy, and big business. He had twice deferred his claims to leadership at Gandhi's instance but now that Gandhi was dead and he had the party machine in his control, he might be a formidable rival. But the shadow of the Mahatma's death had fallen upon him. Friction there was, but no open breach or palace revolution. Instead he carried through the integration of the states with his accustomed vigour and skill. His last throw was to secure his right-wing nominee P. Tandon for the Congress presidency in 1950. But Patel died in December of that year and when Tandon tried on his own to act independently of Nehru he was promptly removed from office and disappeared from the political scene. From that time Nehru reigned without a rival.

The end of the year 1948 thus found the Congress government securely in office, the crises of partition and the refugees surmounted, and internal discord largely eliminated. But with these emergencies dealt with there still remained the two problems inherited from the British period, whose solution was necessary before a forward step could be undertaken. There were the integration of the Indian states and the drawing up of a constitution. That of the states was the most urgent and was tackled first. There were 362 states * from Hyderabad with its seventeen million people to states of only a few square miles in extent. The British had renounced their treaty rights and recommended all to join one or other of the new states. For a time there was some coming and going and an attempt to form a 'third political force' revolving round the Nawab of Bhopal and certain political officers. But it foundered on the usual rock of princely jealousies. By Independence Day all had acceeded to one or other state with the three exceptions of Kashmir, Hyderabad, and Junagadh. But what was to be their place in the new Indian state? Sardar Patel and his agent V. P. Menon set themselves to persuade, cajole, or compel the princes to join or become the nucleus of federal units in the Indian Union. The mail on the government's fist was Patel's, the velvet glove which hid it Menon's; the inducements dangled before the princes were personal privileges and pensions free of income tax. By these means within a few months all the states except the three mentioned had been incorporated in the new federal Union. Some, like Baroda, the Kathiawar and

* The exact number depends upon a distinction between states and 'estates' which in some cases was very fine.

the Rajput states, were thrown together to form the new federal units of Saurashtra and Rajasthan; Travancore and Cochin united to form Kerala, while Mysore became a federal unit on its own. The hundreds of small states simply disappeared in larger units. A few of the princes, such as the Rajahs of Mysore and Travancore were allowed to remain as titular leaders of new states entitled *Rajpramukhs*. But their power was gone and the new states all received a uniform democratic structure. Some members of the princely order faced the new situation by undertaking public service, civil or military, and some have gone into business. As a class and a historical relic they remain; as a political factor they have disappeared.

The three exceptions to the pre-independence accessions were Kashmir, Hyderabad, and Junagadh.* Junagadh was a small seaport state on the coast of Kathiawar with a Hindu population and a Muslim nawab. The Nawab opted for Pakistan but after a few weeks Indian troops occupied the state and a plebiscite declared for Indian union. Pakistan protested but took no action since such an accession was clearly of no value to her. Hyderabad was in a different category. Though it possessed a large Hindu majority (eighty-five per cent) it had a Muslim government going back to Mughal times and had always claimed to be the ally rather than the subordinate of the British. But the state was completely surrounded by Indian territory, and no Indian government could afford to have a block of land so placed independent and perhaps hostile. The Nizam dallied with shifts and evasions, he refused tempting terms of accession negotiated for him by the British, and then allowed an extremist organization, the Razakars, to seize control. This gave India an excuse for a 'police action' in 1948. Hyderabad became an Indian state unit to be later (1956) partitioned among the linguistically-organized states of the Deccan.

There remained Kashmir which was in a class by itself. It was a fringe state, adjacent to both the new states, and could reasonably have joined either. It was also a mixed or conglomerate state, a state as it were by accident, formed through the chances of recent political history. It had a Hindu ruler; to the east it had

* Travancore held out for a few days and then came in voluntarily.

a Hindu majority centre at Jammu, in the Vale of Kashmir itself the population was overwhelmingly Muslim while to the north and west were mountain regions partly controlled by Muslim hill chiefs and partly Buddhist–Tibetan in character. Geographically, racially, and politically it was a ramshackle state. The Hindu ruler played for time and had still not acceded to either side in October when a Pathan irregular force from the old frontier burst in and raced towards the capital Srinagar. In a panic the ruler acceded to India whose airborne troops saved the situation in the nick of time. From that time India has stood on the legal ground of accession, branding Pakistan an aggressor since the Pathans came from her territory. Pakistan called for a plebiscite to which initially Nehru agreed in principle. But he was never able to accept any proposals for carrying it out. A brief war flared up between the two dominions, settled by a United Nations truce in 1948.

The final achievement of the transition period was the new constitution. This was drawn up by the existing Constituent Assembly with remarkable smoothness and implemented from 1950. The 1935 Act was used as a working model and its influence is witnessed by the long passages from its text inserted in the new constitution. In essence the new constitution described a western model federal state with a parliamentary type of democratic government. It had, however, some special characteristics and its chief features are as follows. The federal structure is notable for the strength of the centre. The centre has sole control of defence, foreign affairs, railways, ports, and currency. In addition there is a 'concurrent' list of legislative subjects on which the centre can override the states, together with a reservation of residuary powers to the centre. The President has reserve powers for taking over state administration which he has already exercised more than once. It is this strong centre which made it possible for Nehru's government to carry its programmes of development. The central legislature has two houses, the *Lok Sabha* representing the people and the *Rajya Sabha* the states. Parliamentary responsibility prevails. But we may note two interesting features. One is the reserve powers of the President. These have so far only been exercised on the advice of a Prime

Minister backed by a large parliamentary majority. But suppose that majority did not exist and the ministry depended upon a number of shifting groups? The President's powers would then become a reality and the President might be as powerful as Hindenburg became in republican Germany. The other feature is the absence of a true party system, which adds point to the preceding reflection. Apart from the Communists, whose numbers are small, the real opposition to the government has so far come from within the Congress ranks. The suffrage is universal which gave India, with an initial 175 million voters, the largest electorate in the world.

The new constitution has involved the development of the Federal Court whose independence and acumen have given dignity to its working. There are also certain features not to be found in the old constitution. One is the definition of fundamental rights on the American model, and another the insertion of constitutional directives, or goals of endeavour, which have come from Eire. Throughout the constitution has a pronounced western flavour, which is only increased by its references to traditional Indian institutions. The only one of these institutions mentioned with approval is that of the *panchayat* or village committee. But 'untouchability is abolished and its practice in any form forbidden' (Art. 17) and caste distinctions are ignored (Arts 15(2) and 16(2)). Indeed, the fundamental rights, universal suffrage, and the constitutional directives and the nature of the political machinery all assume western political and ethical principles. Finally, the constitution was rounded off by the conversion of the Indian dominion into a republic within the Commonwealth. The reasons for this were emotional; India wanted to feel independent as well as to be so in fact and law. In this evolution India has led the way to later Commonwealth practice and has perhaps stumbled on a way of providing the Commonwealth with a more realistic as well as more flexible form in its current period of development.

20

NEHRU'S INDIA

By about 1950 it may be said that India had closed a chapter in her long history and opened another. The British had gone, the new régime had been successfully established, and outstanding questions left over from the past had been dealt with. The Congress had, with the exception of the loss of Pakistan, completed its programme, and the way was clear for India to chart a new course into the future. The events and developments since 1950 are therefore still contemporary rather than historical, since they relate to processes still under development and to policies not fully worked out. The historical approach is thus no longer satisfactory since the materials for a considered historical judgement as yet exist only partially. Neither will a mere catalogue of events serve the purpose, since it would leave the reader bemused with information without any enlightenment on the trend of events. For there is obviously a trend even though it cannot be assessed with the rigour of historical analysis. The form proposed for this chapter is therefore that of an essay on contemporary India. This form is particularly convenient in the present case since the years 1947–64 have a unity not often to be found in India's past. That unity was provided by the figure of Jawarharlal Nehru. By a combination of circumstances he had a freer hand in moulding Indian policy than anyone since some of the great Mughals. Along with this opportunity went the ideas as to what should be done, the energy to do it, and the magnetism to maintain his hold over the country to an unprecedented extent. This chapter will therefore be an essay in the assessment of Nehru's India.

The personal supremacy of Nehru at first needs some explanation. Apart from his personality he enjoyed certain other advantages. He was the son of a brilliant father in the select circle of major leaders during the twenties and he came from the heartland of northern India and core of the modern national movement, the middle Ganges valley. He was successively the disciple, favoured son, and lieutenant of Gandhi, the patron saint of the movement, so that much of the veneration attached to the Mahatma descended to him. He was the idol of the younger left wing Congressmen for many years. Finally, he had graduated with flying honours in the Congress school of national distinction, political imprisonment. He was, after the death of Patel, the only surviving founding father of the nation. He carried with him something of the magic aura of the Mahatma for the masses and all the prestige of a forward-looking nationalist for the classes. He was thus, after 1950, the master of the Congress and so the master of India. His national prestige made him indispensable, a fact underlined by occasional threats of resignation, and his indispensability increased as the patriotic ardour of Congress decreased and abuses crept in. He might be the King who had evil advisers or the King who was deceived or wrongly informed, or the King who misunderstood, but he remained the King.

This unique position was supported by a striking personality. The slight spare figure with mobile face and Gandhi capped head contained an abounding energy which constantly astonished observers and a magnetic personality which attracted while it commanded. Though an intellectual and an aristocrat to his fingertips his eloquence could move the masses and he derived strength as well as pleasure from contact with them. His lightning tours made him known throughout the country and his impatience was regarded as a kind of divine discontent. Even his short temper was relished by those who did not suffer from it. His integrity was outstanding and a matter for awe. His catholic interest in all sides of life, from gliding contests to trekking in the hills, increased the sense of identification with the people. A westerner in outlook, in taste, a secularist who disclaimed the name of Hindu and disliked the title of Pandit, he remained acceptable both to the orthodox and the peasant because of his burning patriotism. Thus Nehru not only had the national stage virtually to himself; with his antecedents and his gifts he was able to dazzle and dominate the national audience that watched him.

With such gifts and such latitude of action, Nehru's views became vital in judging his government's policies. With few first ministers could the gap between personal desires and government policy have been so small. Nehru's outlook was essentially that of a democratic socialist of the nineteen-thirties. He proclaimed himself a socialist in the twenties but equally firmly rejected Marxist communism after a visit to Russia. Authoritarianism offended his sense of individual freedom; that and the secret police were to him an aggravated version of the British imperialism and the C.I.D. which he was fighting in India. His sense of personal rights and values led him to oppose Hindu orthodoxy almost as vehemently as the foreign government. Equal rights for all meant not only the outcasts or Harijans as Gandhi taught, but the regular castes as well and women as well as men. He saw socialism as the control of capital in the national interest rather than as the imposition of authority on private enterprise. He was thus an enemy of privilege of every kind and a believer in social control rather than dictation. His ideal was a society Indian in sentiment and social habit, secular in its outlook, and democratic in its working. An essential element in his outlook was a war on poverty. The effect of his first contact with starving *kisans* of Uttar Pradesh as a young man never left him. His insistence on raising living standards prevented him from accepting Gandhi's belief in village democracies loosely knit in a non-industrial society because he believed that the introduction of modern mechanized industry was the only way by which this could be done.

In foreign affairs, in which he was the chief Congress expert from the early thirties, he was a democratic internationalist. He believed in self-governing nationalities, and in an international order to bind them together. He was naturally an opponent of imperialism and had a deep suspicion of the designs of European powers in Asia and Africa. His ideas in this sphere may be said to have been influenced by President Wilson's Fourteen Points.

While Nehru had unusually clear ideas as to what he wanted to do and an unusually clear field for putting them into practice, it must not be supposed that he was an unfettered autocrat, a kind of nationalist archangel. A threat of resignation would give him his way with Congress and even lead to deputations of dissuasion, and a bang on the table would secure assent in the cabinet. But there were powerful vested interests, social and financial, which distrusted some of his policies and practised more subtle methods of opposition than open dissent. Since to be outside the Congress was to be branded as anti-Nehru the conservative groups in particular carried on their opposition from within by means of obstruction at all levels. It is only recently that a conservative as distinct from a communal party has appeared under the name of the Swatantra party. They could take advantage of his multifarious interests and lack of administrative flair, which inhibited sufficient delegation to trustworthy agents, quietly to undermine his decisions on one subject while his attention was occupied with another. On occasion public opinion itself would stir, as in the matters of linguistic provinces and China. But in general the opposition to his policies was covert in form and obstructive in character.

It is in the extent of Nehru's fortune in dealing with this obstruction that the general success of his administration must be judged. On the first issue of a strong central government he enjoyed general support. Text book stories of anarchy and the spectre of partition were too fresh in every mind for localism to raise its head. Under this impulse the new constitution gave the centre wide powers and the princes were integrated into the new state structure. Thereafter occurred a development which is an interesting commentary on the extent of Nehru's power. In Andhra an agitation sprang up for a state on a linguistic basis (of Telugu) separate from Madras. Nehru preferred non-linguistic states in the interests of a strong centre. He feared that a linguistic state, giving political expression to a regional patriotism, like that of the Telugus or Marathas, might generate an emotional force which would jump constitutional limits and threaten the centre's authority. For some time he resisted, but when in 1952 Potti Sriramulu died by hunger strike in the cause of Andhra he gave in. In 1956 there was a radical reorganization on linguistic lines, the two exceptions being the Punjab and Bombay states. But when Marathas and Gujaratis demonstrated he gave in again and recognized a division into the two states of Maharashtra and Gujarat. Later (November 1966), his daughter agreed to a division of the Punjab into the Punjab (Sikh *Subah*) and the Haryana (Hindu) states.

Democracy was another issue on which there was general agreement at least in the open. Thus we find the principle enshrined in the new constitution with the two features of parliamentary responsibility and universal adult suffage. With the general dominance of the Congress in the state legislatures the principle of responsibility has not yet been seriously tested; the greatest struggles have been internal faction fights within the Congress parties. But it is now clear that universal suffrage has had an effect as the low income groups became more aware of their power of electing or rejecting candidates. High caste monopoly of office has suffered a severe blow, for no Brahmin can receive election today without low caste votes. Caste groupings are in many areas being exploited as ready-made political machines with the result that the massive electorate of mainly illiterate voters has been showing unexpected life. The process has been helped by the revival of *panchayats* or village committees which Nehru championed. But he showed curiously little enthusiasm for proceeding to the logical next step in democratic practice, from a mass electorate to mass education. Seventeen years after independence seventy per cent of the population were still illiterate. But here again one suspects that it was not Nehru's desire but performance which fell short. If, conservative interests might argue, we can't prevent every peasant and low caste man having a vote we can at least hinder his getting education and so make it easier to fool him.

The attack on privilege extended from the princes, who were generally agreed to be moribund, to the *zamindars* of northern India, who enjoyed large proprietary rights in return for collecting the land tax for the government (and keeping some of it for their trouble). They were a classic example of the working of the principle of unearned increment in land and had long been the target of criticism. But unlike the princes they had influential friends. The great *zamindaris* were ended but terms of compensation were such that it has been maintained that the tenants derived little benefit. In the sphere of industry Nehru was at first more radical, beginning with threats of nationalization which alarmed foreign business. But in practice socialist theory found expression mainly in heavy taxation, comparable with that of Britain, and in a division of industry into public and private sectors. The great new industrial enterprises were under state control while existing industries went on much as before with a greater degree of control. With foreign business enterprise the government was stricter but this took the form of insisting on a dilution of foreign with Indian capital and management. Foreign enterprise has complained but the extent of its continued activity does not suggest that the restrictions have been penal.

We now come to the subjects perhaps closest to Nehru's heart, the modernization, welfare, and social programmes. The grand object was to bring the country materially on to a level with the western world, by radically raising the standard of living, and by bringing into her social system the principle of individual personal rights. The first process was a material one and its aim generally approved, while the second was moral and intellectual, involving ancient social conceptions. No one but Nehru would have dared to attempt both at once. We will take each in turn. The project of raising the standard of living was a gigantic one, for it was complicated by the rapid and continuous rise in the population. In 1941 it was 389 millions. In 1951, after seventy millions had gone to Pakistan, it was 356 millions, and in 1961 it was 434 millions. It is now over 500 millions. The means of the rise of standards was to be a double movement of increased agricultural output and large-scale industrialization to increase production significantly. This in turn involved the use of foreign capital if an already poor country was not to be subjected to intolerable hardship. The year 1950 was a key one in this respect for in this year Nehru set up the National Planning Commission. Without this body and the constitutional powers allotted to the centre the progress so far made would have been impossible. The first plan, launched in 1951, placed special emphasis on agricultural production to free India from dependence on overseas supplies. This part of the programme was a great success, production increasing by twenty-five per cent over the five-year period. At the same time the great power and irrigation projects of the Damodar valley scheme and the Hirakud dam were undertaken.

Along with these three new steel plants were started, sponsored respectively by Great Britain, West Germany, and Russia. All these were retained in the public sector, but the private sector of industry also made a meaningful contribution. The claimed rise in the national income was eighteen per cent, which, even allowing for the concurrent rapid increase in population, was a substantial advance. A second and more ambitious plan was launched in 1956, in which the emphasis was on large-scale industrialization. The aim was to increase the national income by twenty-five per cent. The cost was nearly double that of the first plan, some four thousand million in the public and two thousand million pounds in the private sector. This involved raising two thousand million pounds abroad, with resultant credit difficulties. These were overcome by outside loans, in particular from the United States. The plan was completed with some trimmings and shortfalls; though its success was less spectacular than that of the first plan the achievement was greater because of its larger scale. India's third five-year plan outlived Nehru. This called for an outlay of about eight thousand million pounds, of which nearly five thousand millions would be in the public sector. This great project aimed at raising the national income by five per cent per annum, at radical expansion of the basic industries, and at making India self-sufficient in foodstuffs. It is claimed that during the decade 1951–61 the national income (at constant prices) rose by forty-two per cent, income per head by twenty per cent and consumption by sixteen per cent. These are impressive figures and there can be no doubt of the magnitude of the achievement. They represent Nehru's bid to reduce poverty and meet the challenge of an exploding population. There is no doubt that he was aware of the seriousness of this latter problem, but so far no serious measures had been taken to meet it.

We now come to the social programme. Nehru's concept of the individual was that of the western liberals and he wished to extend to the people of India legal rights on those lines. This involved, though few perceived it, a direct clash with the existing social system, with its deep roots and religious sanctions. The groundwork of attack on social tradition had already been carried out by Ghandi, with his attack on outcastism and the stricter

caste observances. There was already a widespread disregard of
caste practices among the upper classes, and there was no open
opposition to the abolition of untouchability and of the legality of
caste restrictions in the constitution. But behind this lay the fabric
of Hindu personal law still largely based on the age-old Laws of
Manu, nearly as ancient and as deeply rooted as caste itself. In
Hindu social law the group matters more than the individual, the
woman is subordinate to the man. Nehru hoped to alter all this
in a single session with his Hindu Code Bill. But in fact it took
six years to pass the two most important measures, the Hindu
Succession Act (1955) and the Hindu Marriage Act (1956). The
former gives women equal rights with men in the matter of succession to and holding of property. The latter gives monogamy a
legal basis and provides for divorce with alimony and maintenance. Another Act provides for the maintenance of the Hindu
widow and of separated wives. Such was the obstruction from
within the ample Congress majority that the whole process of
revision is not yet complete. But what has been so far accomplished is nevertheless a major achievement.

Education is an essential part of modernization and here Nehru
was more successful at the top than lower down. There has been
a great proliferation of universities and technical institutes; they
have more than doubled since independence and now number
about seventy. Standards of course vary but in sum this must be
adjudged a major effort. Less progress has been made in primary
education. Some fifteen per cent of the population were literate
before independence. The present claim is thirty per cent. The
matter of the official language is also one on which Nehru encountered opposition. Himself an Urdu or Hindustani speaker,
he was willing for Hindi to be made the official language in spite
of the difficulties this produced in the south. But he wished to
retain English along with it. This involved him in a long-drawn-
out contest with the Hindi enthusiasts. Nehru considered that
their success would both tend to isolate India from the outside
world at a critical time and seriously alienate the south. The disturbances early in 1965 in South India suggest that there was substance in his view.

In foreign affairs Nehru enjoyed almost complete freedom of

action until the Hungarian crisis of 1956, and to a large extent after. The country wanted India to play a full part in international affairs and to be treated on equal terms by the great powers: the details they left to Nehru. His guiding principles may be summarized briefly as national independence, anti-colonialism, internationalism, and neutralism or non-involvement towards the great powers. The doctrine of national independence was relevant to the sub-continent, for it was Nehru's view that the physical limits of India should be coterminous with the national state. France and Portugal had colonial enclaves at Pondicherry and Goa respectively. The French voluntarily withdrew but the Portuguese held on until forcibly ejected in 1961. This act was the product of natural impatience, but it was a unilateral breach of international law and dimmed somewhat the Indian image in the western world. In this same context Nepal has been in a difficult position as being geographically part of India but politically independent. India has respected this independence but has sought to influence her internal affairs, with the result that relations, as with Ceylon and Burma, were not always happy. Since Nehru's death they have improved in all cases.

As an anti-colonialist Nehru tended to be suspicious of the ex-imperialist powers. They were, he seemed to say, at best ticket-of-leave men while communist or eastern powers were at worst first offenders. Thus he worked for the ejection of the Dutch from Indonesia and the French from Indo-China, he was more severe with Britain at Suez than with Russia over Hungary, and his peaceful patience was finally exhausted by the Portuguese foothold in India at Goa. It was China which has ended this phase. As an internationalist India took an active part in United Nations affairs and served with credit and distinction in a number of places including the Congo.

In high politics, as it were, Nehru had three preoccupations, Pakistan, relations with the great powers, and his position in Asia. With Pakistan relations were at first very complicated indeed. There were disputes over the sharing of the old government's assets, the settlement of refugee property, the supply and use of canal water, and of course Kashmir. Underlying them was the bitterness engendered by the massacres and mass migrations. The payment of the assets to Pakistan was secured by Gandhi just before his death in January 1948. The dispute about refugee property went on for years but has now been settled, or perhaps we should say the matter closed. The canal water issue arose from the Indian control of headwaters supplying water to Pakistan canals as part of plans innocently made in the past for irrigating the undivided Punjab. The water being vital for Pakistan, this question might have led to war at any time if India had cut off the supply. The issue became more tense when India announced new plans which would take virtually the whole of the Sutlej outfall for use in India. In this matter the World Bank came to the rescue; in an agreement signed in September 1960 a scheme was accepted by which Pakistan could construct transverse canals to supply the old system with water from the Pakistan-controlled Indus.

There remains Kashmir. The original Indian case was the legally watertight one of accession by the prince. But India's weakness was that she had already rejected this ground in the small case of Junagadh and was soon to do the same in the large state of Hyderabad. Here the people's will was to prevail. To bridge the gap between the two positions Nehru offered a plebiscite but was never able to find any terms proposed by successive U.N. mediators acceptable. He later proclaimed the union of Kashmir with India and resisted Anglo-American attempts to find a compromise. Patel might have given up Kashmir on the principle of the fewer Muslims in India the better, but Nehru was adamant. Why? He was not interested in the Muslim fringe to the north-west. His heart, it can almost literally be said, was in the lovely and fatal Vale of Kashmir. His motives were partly strategical (defence against China), partly those of prestige, but mainly his care for secular democracy in India. A Muslim state voluntarily adhering to the Indian Union is a living witness to secular democracy. The other argument used was that cession would let loose Hindu communal feeling to the destruction of the large Muslim minority still remaining in India. One can only observe that Nehru here maintained his position with great tenacity and at heavy cost; no one can know whether the remedy of independence or Pakistan union would be worse than the present disease of troubled relations.

In the world at large Nehru's policy was the now famous one of non-alignment or non-involvement with the great power blocs. It was invented under the shadow of the threat of nuclear war and for a number of years served India well. The more states, thought Nehru, who were uncommitted, the more careful would the power blocs be before committing themselves to war. This policy was undermined by two developments. The advent of the hydrogen bomb gradually brought the realization that nuclear war cannot now be, and China upset Nehru's balancing trick of relations with both power blocs. This leads on to his relations with Asia. For a time he toyed with Asianism, but the idea was too nebulous to win much support. But he certainly hoped for the moral leadership of Asia outside China and for this he cultivated good relations with that country, expressed in the *Panch Shila* or Five Principles of co-existence agreed in 1954.

In Africa, Nehru's natural sympathy with anti-colonialism led him into sympathy with and encouragement of African aspirations. At one time it began to look as though he was to be the tacit leader of an Afro-Asian group. But hesitancy on his part, due perhaps in some measure to disillusionment and perhaps to some degree of African disenchantment, caused this dream to fade also.

Nehru's fortunes were at their zenith in the mid-fifties, when he seemed to be successfully modernizing and liberalizing his country and exercising an increasing influence in Asia and Africa. About then the first wisps of cloud drifted across his sun; gradually the shadows lengthened and darkened until night fell with gathering clouds. A decade later all India's ills were being attributed to his mistakes, not least by those who had done much to frustrate his designs. The blazing rocket of the fifties became the fallen stick of the sixties.

It was, as nemesis so often decrees, the field in which the victim seemed strongest that Nehru suffered the cruellest blows. A fore-taste was his haste in judging the British action in Suez while showing reluctance to condemn the Russian action in Hungary. Non-involvement for all, said the critics, but more so for some

than for others. A more serious matter was the flight of the Dalai
Lama to India. Nehru had advised him to live on terms with the
Chinese and welcomed him with muted enthusiasm. But while
Suez might have been a misjudgement, the Dalai Lama was an
embarrassment. His presence both soured relations with China,
and stimulated a public response in India. Though the Dalai
Lama was a Buddhist of a distinctly unorthodox kind, many
Hindus regarded him as a sort of extension of Hinduism in a
Buddhist monk's robe. For them he was an *avatar* (incarnation of
a god) from the Himalayas, the abode of the Holy ones. Henceforth Nehru was not a wholly free agent in the conduct of Indian
affairs. There followed the occupation of Goa, already mentioned, which suggested an ageing Nehru, amenable to internal
pressure.

The sourness of the Chinese led on to the China incident of
1962. Mutual suspicions led to counter charges and an aroused
public opinion allowed no private settlement behind closed doors.
Nehru's former dexterity and firm grasp of essentials faded into
alternate defiance and procrastination. The nub of the problem
was the discovery of a Chinese highway from Tibet to Sinkiang
built across the desolate Aksai Chin plateau, which British
foreign maps in the nineteenth century had alternately included
and excluded from the Indian empire. The road involved prestige
and this made settlement difficult. To this was added an unnecessary advance beyond the Macmahon line near the Sikkim border
which precipitated the actual fighting in impossible conditions
for the Indians. Nehru never recovered from the rout which ensued and the revelations of cross purposes and incompetence
which followed. Like Napoleon after Moscow, he recovered
enough agility to fend off western demands for a Kashmir settlement and American urgings for the conversion of military aid
into an alliance. But policy he had none, and soon after he had
released Sheikh Abdullah for what might have been his independent bid for a Kashmir settlement, he died.

As with Gandhi, men said that the light had gone out, but they
felt that it had gone, not in the first glimmerings of dawn but in
the gathering shadows of night. For this there was some justifi-
cation. Diplomatically, India was alone in the world, with a

hostile China and Pakistan, an aloof Russia, a critical western world and a disenchanted third world. Internally, the third five-year plan had run into difficulties, both of finance and achievement. Industrial expansion was flagging while the unexpectedly rapid increase in the population had overtaken the increase in the national product. Development had given way to marking time, and hope to disillusionment and anxiety.

Any attempt to appraise Nehru's achievement must fall somewhere between the extremes of success and failure. His rule, notable both for length and achievement, had neither the heroic note of success against odds nor the doleful one of stark failure. If there has been more dexterity than conflict, a tendency to compromise rather than fight to a finish, there has nevertheless been solid achievement. Has it been the success for which he had been striving; is the present India the India of his ideal?

In most areas of endeavour we find an air of half-achievement, of a process stopped short. In the field of democracy we have a shiny machine on a western model but no party system to oil its working parts. In education there is an impressive expansion of higher education and a distinct lag in the primary field. Industry has expanded in a big way, but not sufficiently to raise materially the standard of life in the country as a whole. The middle class has greatly grown with this expansion, but as between them and the peasant mass it is still a question of 'we' and 'they'. In the secular field good progress has been made with the reform of the Hindu Code, but there are distinct signs of an orthodox reaction; Hindus cannot be restrained from blaming Muslims whenever relations with Pakistan are specially strained. In the control of population there was little progress, but where else has anyone done any better? In foreign affairs India played a distinguished part but gradually lost the halo of superior moral virtue which Gandhi bequeathed her.

Looking back on this survey I should say that Nehru's greatest success was his social legislation, because achieved with the greatest effort, and likely to influence the future most. His greatest failure was his inability to set up an educated social democracy above the poverty line. Instead he established an India with all the appurtenances of a modern state. New industry called forth an enlarged middle class. The enlargement and enrichment of this class took up most of the increase in the national income produced by the five-year plans, leaving the remaining eighty per cent much as before. When we compare the state of modern India with its condition in only 1940, the achievement was great, but it was not the achievement on which Nehru had set his heart.

21

POST-NEHRU INDIA: EPILOGUE

THIRTEEN years have passed since this book was completed, a period long enough to demand some addition, but too brief for more than a short attempt at contemporary historical writing. Yet such an effort is needed because India has changed radically during this time. Nehru's India has become Post-Nehru India; the political balance has been disturbed; new factors have emerged and a turning point, it would seem, has been reached.

Contemporary history is necessary, but it is at best a tentative record. It lacks knowledge and it lacks proportion. It possesses, indeed, a massive supply of public record, but it necessarily lacks the inner knowledge of politicians' minds, of planners' proposals, of scientists' discoveries, of technicians' break-throughs. There is the even graver matter of proportion. It is impossible, over just a few years, to estimate accurately the significance of the various events. Some portentous events can be seen to be so from the moment of their occurrence, like the discovery of the New World; others of equal moment are hidden in obscurity. What Roman writer in A.D. 40, for example, would have realized the import of events in Judaea, during the previous decade? Contemporary history is a fickle mistress, apt to change colour and shape as she recedes with the years. Yet partial understanding is better than none at all. For this reason a survey of the last thirteen years is called for, even if it is only a sketch rather than a finished picture.

Nehru's death in May 1964 at first seemed to confirm the strength of the Congress party. The succession of Lal Bahadur Shastri was smoothly managed and unanimously agreed in public. Yet two incidents were telltales for the future. The appointment had been arranged by a group of party leaders and managers known as the 'Syndicate', and the claims of Mr Morarji Desai, if not defeated openly, had been smothered in private. Mr Shastri, a short man coming from a small town environment, had been a life-long Congress worker dedicated to the national cause. His dedication, his fair-mindedness, his flair for conciliation, had aroused general respect. He had even been to Kashmir and returned with an enhanced reputation. He had within him some of the qualities of Gandhi which in time might have converted respect into veneration.

Mr Shastri believed in consensus as the Gandhian way of arriving at decisions. As each of the many problems was considered there were conferences and discussions, but it seemed, after a year of office, that the general upshot was postponement. But he was not long allowed to proceed on his chosen way. The proclamation of Hindi as the national language in January 1965 sparked off disturbances, especially in Madras, which threatened national unity. In March hostilities with Pakistan troops in the Rann of Cutch suggested that the Indian army had not yet recovered from the China incident. But this man of peace was to be saved by war. Pakistani infiltration into Kashmir in August followed by an armoured thrust towards Jammu billowed into a full scale war during which the Pakistani armour was halted and Lahore threatened. It was a traumatic experience for India, calling out a latent unity obscured by recent perplexities, and for a time Shastri became a national hero. This image seemed likely to be dimmed by the controversy surrounding the Tashkent Peace Conference of January 1966 until critical voices were hushed by his tragic death at its conclusion.

Shastri's death was followed by Mrs Indira Gandhi's appointment as Prime Minister, believed to have been her father's secret wish. The 'Syndicate' showed the same expertise but this time Mr Desai's claim was more openly pressed. The appointment was really a temporary one, to carry the Congress over the general election of 1967. Mrs Gandhi was on trial, the relationship between the Prime Minister and the party managers, which Nehru had settled for his lifetime in his clash with Purshottamdas Tandon in 1951, being still undecided. During this interim year a drastic devaluation of the rupee was carried through.

The general elections of early 1967, all-India and State, expressed in electoral terms the end of the Nehru era. Congress retained its overall majority in the central Parliament, but only with a margin of about forty seats; it lost control of eight of the sixteen States. Congress supremacy was broken. At the centre the opposition was split into opposing groups, but in the States there were signs of effective alternatives. In Madras there was the D.M.K.,* which achieved a majority, in Madhya and Uttar Pradesh there was the Jan Sangh, in Gujarat the Swatantra party, and in Kerala the Communists. The swing from the Congress was both to the Right (Jan Sangh and Swatantra) and to the Left (P.S.P. and Communists). However, the sequel suggested that some of these labels were more easily fixed than retained. Where no overall party majority existed coalition governments proved unstable and subject to an epidemic of floor-crossing or defection, suggesting that politics might be dissolving into faction, with individuals as their nuclei and office as their object. Mid-term elections in some states failed to halt the process.

A third succession crisis confirmed Mrs Gandhi in office, but not before Mr Desai had carried his claim to an open vote. She managed Mr Desai as Deputy-Premier deftly but still had the 'Syndicate' to reckon with. For the next two years, while the two wings of Congress tended to draw apart, she played the role of conciliator and national figure, steadily growing in stature in the process. Her foreign tours enhanced the Indian name abroad. A food crisis of near famine in north India in 1967 was surmounted. But the tension within the party remained unresolved. Was it to become an office-gaining body on the American model, with Mahatma Gandhi as the presiding deity and the 'Syndicate' as its party bosses, or was it to retain some kind of ideology, and if so, of what kind? The showdown, which was perhaps inevitable, came in the summer of 1969, and when it came, began as a clash of personalities. How far there were really ideological overtones, as claimed by both sides, had yet to be seen. It began with the election of the right-wing Mr Nijalingappa as President of Congress, to Mrs Gandhi's distaste. Then came the sudden death of President Zakir Husain. An impartial and respected Congress veteran, his departure brought the Presidency into politics because its reserve powers might prove crucial in the event of the Congress losing its overall parliamentary majority at the general election of 1972. The Congress committee chose the right-wing Mr Sanjiva Reddy as their candidate. Mrs Gandhi, it may be suggested, saw herself becoming the prisoner of the party mana-

* Dravida Munetra Kazagham

gers. She struck back. She supported Vice-President Giri, a veteran left-wing Congressman, for the Presidency. She nationalized the banks, an election promise, over the head of the Congress Committee. She dismissed Mr Morarji Desai from the Finance ministry. Mr Giri was in fact elected President of India and from that moment the division between the groups widened until it became an open breach in November. Mrs Gandhi was supported by about two-thirds of the Congress parliamentary party and opposed by a majority of one in the Congress Working Committee. There were then two Congress bodies, the one claiming to uphold the Nehru gospel of reform and moderate socialism, and the other the cause of democratic freedom against personal autocracy. The actual facts are still difficult to discover. Cynics might say that the Congress (R) (Mrs Gandhi's) consisted largely of hopeful men who thought her a good bet for office, and the Congress (O) of displaced party managers with links with big business and the orthodox. They certainly looked for allies towards the orthodox Jan Sangh and the capitalist Swatantra parties. In fact both factions had men of principle as well as of opportunity. It may be suggested that Indian parties are largely what their leaders, when charismatic, make them. When leaders lack leadership they lapse into faction, as with the Communist and Socialist groups and many a state Congress party. In this sense politics since Nehru's death may be described as India looking for a leader like Tibetans searching for a reincarnation, and, in 1971, their discovery of one.

This uneasy situation, with Mrs Gandhi depending on Communist votes for a majority in the Lok Sabha, and the various groups too divided to unite against her, lasted for over a year. Then, encouraged by Congress success in the Kerala elections, she went to the country at the beginning of 1971, a year before the statutory limit of Parliament. There followed a landslide victory in February–March, with the near extinction of Congress (O). Only the D.M.K. stood its ground in Madras, and even in radical Bengal the left-wing parties were sufficiently eroded to bring the Congress back into a coalition ministry. In the Lok Sabha Congress, with 353 seats, had an overall majority of 185. The Congress had found a leader, the successor to Nehru, in his daughter, who in the next few months was to be the acclaimed of all India. The Nehru dynasty had found its second ruler.

The reasons for this success, unexpected by many to the last moment, were various. There was much dissatisfaction with the old party managers and much bewilderment as to the future. On this troubled sea of opinion sailed Nehru's daughter, whose relationship profited as her father's latter discredit faded into the general memory of his greatness. Her frequent tours, her concern with the people's ills, both familiarized and endeared her to the country at large. Before the election campaign began, she was virtually the only national figure known to the masses. This was an advantage far outweighing the suggestion of irresolution and ineffectiveness circulating in the lobbies of New Delhi. Her stand against the managers pleased them and her nationalizing measures, with promise of more to come, delighted them. India craved a leader, and now, it appeared, they had found one.

Mrs Gandhi was now mistress in her own house. But immediately she was faced with a wholly unexpected challenge from outside. The elections in both wings of Pakistan at the end of 1970 seemed to presage happier relations for both countries. In West Pakistan Mr Z. A. Bhutto, who was reputed to be both anti-Indian and a social reformer, had a majority, but Sheikh Mujibur Rahman of East Pakistan, an advocate of better relations with India and autonomy for the east wing, had an overall majority in the national assembly. However, when negotiations with the Sheikh seemed to be on the point of success the Pakistan government, on 25 March 1971, arrested the Sheikh, suppressed the autonomy movement and a spontaneous revolt with violence and severity. World opinion as well as Indian was stirred, but what mattered to India were the human consequences. Before long refugees began to appear at the frontiers, with the usual pitiful tales. It was at first thought that this symptom of any social upheaval in the sub-continent would soon subside. But the trickle became a stream and the stream a flood. By the end of August Indians were talking of a mounting ten millions. Observers generally spoke of nine to ten millions and Pakistan admitted to two. We should perhaps do best to take the figures accepted by the World Bank, which had good reason to seek an accurate estimate without exaggeration. It was nine millions. Of these it was generally agreed that about two millions were Muslims and seven millions Hindus from the resident Hindu minority of ten millions.

Such an exodus of an eighth of the East Pakistan population posed grave logistics problems for India. They had to be fed, sheltered and protected from epidemics. They had come to the most crowded state of a generally crowded country. Their support was a heavy financial drain; their settlement out of the question; they were too numerous for the despairing solution of semi-permanent refugee camps to become a running sore in the Indian body politic. At the same time guerilla warfare was begun by bands known as the Mukhti Bahini (Freedom fighters). The Indian policy was first to convince world opinion that the refugee problem was of such dimensions as to require outside assistance and intervention. It was hoped that international pressure might induce the Pakistan government to promote a political settlement making possible the refugees' return. To this end Mrs Gandhi toured the western capitals. As hope of this faded India increasingly trained, armed and sheltered the guerilla bands. In August an agreement was made with Russia for security and aid, short of armed intervention. This was a turning point, for it countered Chinese professed support for Pakistan and veiled official American hostility. Thus tension increased in a situation in which Mrs Gandhi appeared to move faultlessly, until Pakistan raids on Indian airfields in the west precipitated war on 6 December. It lasted twelve days. Fortunes were fairly evenly balanced in the west, but East Pakistan was overrun and Dacca and the Pakistan army there captured on 18 December. India then announced a cease fire, underlined by the United Nations, hitherto held up by the Russian veto. India recognized the new state of Bangladesh on the outbreak of war.

At the turn of the year India found herself in military occupation of Bangladesh, with about 93,000 Pakistani prisoners of war and with nearly ten million refugees still within her borders. Russia was friendly, China enigmatic and the United States government chagrined by the sudden collapse of her policy of Indo-Pakistan balance. What the summit meeting between President Nixon and the Russian leaders at Moscow would produce had still to be seen, while the real results of the previous year's Peking summit were not yet clear. The situation was therefore full of doubt and uncertainty but India had now acquired a new self-confidence with which to meet it. Since then Mrs Gandhi's government has been moving deftly and cautiously. By the end of March India had returned all the refugees and withdrawn all her troops from Bangladesh except those asked to stay by the Bangladesh government itself. Mrs Gandhi visited Dacca and struck an accord with Sheikh Mujibur Rahman. She then turned to negotiations with Pakistan. A summit meeting at Simla with Mr Z. A. Bhutto in June proved more successful than expected, producing an agreement for the mutual withdrawal of troops from the occupied areas on both sides. But the main settlement was still to come, and there, at the time of writing, the matter rests.

These developments clearly constitute a major event in Indian history. The repercussions are bound to be many and continuing, but the factors involved, both within and without the country, are so various that much speculation would be unprofitable. It is clear, however, that the balance of power within the sub-continent has been altered. India will have to come to terms with a new and struggling Bangladesh as well as with a truncated Pakistan. She will also now, willy-nilly, be involved in the politics of the great powers. It is not often that one state knocks another in half in twelve days and the consequences are bound to be considerable. Mrs Gandhi guided India during the year with a Bismarckian sureness of touch. It was now to be seen if she would display a Cavour-like agility in steering a lesser power through the troubled waters stirred by the rivalries of the three super-powers. It can be said that in success India has found a new resilience and self-confidence while her leadership united moderation with firmness, and humanity with resolution.

The period 1971–77 has been one of crisis and controversy, of clamant problems which will not be denied and of dramatic reversals of fortune. In the foreshortened perspective of the immediate past the historian can be little more than the chronicler of apparently significant events, hoping that his shots of interpretation may pass through the multitude of changing circumstance and jostlings of people to find some sort of mark on the target of truth.

At the beginning of 1972 Mrs Gandhi was at the height of her reputation, a goddess Durga in conflict, a Kautiliya in counsel. Surely now those social reforms, postponed with the onset of the Bangladesh crisis, could be implemented? But once more fate intervened. The economic crisis of 1966 had been eased, though not solved, by the drastic devaluation of the rupee in that year, whose effect was to enable India to recover lost ground in Asian markets and so stimulate home industries. In 1970 a fourth five-year plan had been launched after several revisions, with the emphasis again on industry and communications, and the public sector taking two-thirds of the outlay. Behind the plan, however, lurked the old problem of the money supply for the planned expenditure, and with it the spectre of inflation. But for the moment these fears were stifled by the 'Green Revolution' which replaced agricultural anxiety with a short-lived euphoria. This was brought about by the introduction of new strains of wheat and rice together with the heavy use of fertilizers and a mass sinking of tube-wells. Grain production increased dramatically and rice production less so. Grain production, which was 74·2 tonnes in 1966–67, recently approached the 120 million mark. The problem of production to feed all the people became one of storage of surpluses. It was hoped that food production could be doubled in twenty years against a possible population double in twenty-eight years. Hope and buoyancy, strangers to India since the later Nehru years, reappeared briefly.

But it soon became apparent that these were but shafts of sunlight glinting through gathering clouds. Inflation had been kept in line with the figures elsewhere – of 3–4 per cent – until the Bangladesh crisis. But then refugee and war expenditure, on top of the calls of the fourth five-year plan, began to swell the rate. When, beyond this, came the O.P.E.C. quadrupling of oil prices in late 1973, the rate jumped to the near crisis level of 25 per cent. India's consumption is not large by Western standards (22·6 million tonnes in 1972) and she herself produces nearly a third of this. But consumption is increasing with industrial expansion; the economy was so poised that from being 11 per cent of total imports, the cost of oil now shot up to 45 per cent of the total import bill.

Apart from these new economic factors there was the continuing problem of population. The annual increase of twelve to thirteen millions could not, it seemed, be stemmed. In spite of strenuous efforts by persuasion and education a recorded total of over a million fewer births quite failed to meet the target of ten millions by 1974. India was eating up her prosperity by producing too many mouths. This prosperity, it seemed, was a stone of Sisyphus which plummeted down to the valley of despair whenever it was painfully pushed nearly to the summit of achievement.

This was the background to the Emergency. Inflation meant fast-rising prices, stagnation of trade, mounting unemployment. It seemed bitter to a public expecting a good time just round the corner after several expectant turns and disappointments. It was like dashing a cup from the lips of a parched and expectant sufferer. Through late 1974 and early 1975 the discontent and unrest gathered. The opposition leaders naturally made what play they could of the situation and they found a ready response. The leaders were the eighty-year-old Morarji Desai, the austere Gandhian, ex-Bombay Chief Minister, thrice contender for the premiership, and the elderly and frail Gandhian socialist from Bihar, Jai Prakash Narayan. There was rising criticism of governmental inefficiency and corruption; there were demonstrations; there was some loose talk by Jai Prakash about the loyalty of the police and the armed forces. Tension rose. The flashpoint came with an Allahabad court's decision on an electoral petition against Mrs Gandhi from the last election. The full penalty was imposed for a technical offence on one item of the indictment, and there were immediate cries for her resignation.

From now on we are in a field of continuing controversy, so that anything said must be provisional. The full story can only be unfolded much later when greater information is available. This discussion will therefore be confined to two main points: why was the Emergency imposed in the first place, and why was Mrs Gandhi defeated when it was lifted? Let us first be clear that the declaration was in itself a legal action provided for in the Indian constitution when the safety of the state was judged to be in danger (Part XVIII). It gave power to override constitutional guarantees such as freedom from arrest without trial, freedom of speech and discussion, and to legislate by ordinances having the power of law for six months. It was validated by Parliament where the Congress had a two-thirds majority in both Houses. This leaves of course the question: was the declaration sufficiently justified by necessity and what was done under it?

On the first count it seems probable that Mrs Gandhi feared some sort of conspiracy to be hatching. A cabinet minister had been assassinated and she was said to believe her own life to be in danger. The election case sentence may have seemed to provide proof of some such scheme. This may have inclined her to listen to the activist group of her son Sanjay. It seems likely that the opposition went beyond the guidelines of constitutional custom or democratic propriety, though they did nothing overtly revolutionary. She may have been talked into it by Sanjay and his friends when faced with the prospect of resignation. Be this as it may, the remedy seemed to liberal opinion both within and without India too drastic for the actual symptoms of unrest. There were cries of dismay as though a stark military dictatorship had been imposed overnight. Nevertheless, it has to be said that at first the move appeared to have been successful. Helped by two good harvests prices steadied, profiteers disgorged, smugglers went out of business, production improved and the public services and commerce received an injection of vigour. Many welcomed the new regime for its order, its economic stability and its purposefulness.

But there was of course another side, the price in liberty which was exacted. There were many arrests and much detention without trial, apart from the house detention of Morarji and Jai Prakash. In addition to what may be called traditional police high-handedness, there was a degree of surveillance which made the urban classes especially afraid to speak freely and to feel themselves to be under pressure. Constitutional changes curbed the independence of the judiciary, and there was the birth-control campaign which was officially stated by the new Health Minister, Mr Raj Narayan, to have secured the sterilization of nearly eleven million people.

As soon as the Emergency was lifted in early 1977 for a General Election which many thought would be little more than a formality, it became clear that there was a great volume of pent-up feeling in the country. The first sign was the defection of Mr Jagjivam Ram with his millions of Depressed class voters; it was a Mughal style changeover of a big political *omrah* to what was thought to be the winning side. Opposition groups rapidly joined to form a loosely knit 'Janata party' led by Morarji and Jai Prakash. Mrs Gandhi, flitting indefatigably from political rally to rally, was reduced to an apologetic defensive. It remains to explain both the dramatic result and its extent. Groups with special grievances like the lawyers, the journalists, and liberals of all kinds, naturally saw in it a vindication of their own principles. But the cause of democracy or of personal liberty does not explain why the rural masses of North India went to the polls as to a religious fair or *mela*, decked out in their festival garments. For them the price of rice and grain loomed larger than personal rights.

At this stage explanations can only be suggested rather than asserted. It would seem that there were two overriding factors. The first was police high-handedness or *zulum* : inquisitions, arbitrary arrests, often brutal actions, the rule of the big stick – *danda raj*. This alienated the urban classes and also affected the rural ones. The second was the birth-control campaign as developed by Sanjay Gandhi and his associates. It was this which aroused the villagers of North India – the south was much less affected. The sterilization project, a delicate issue anywhere, but specially so in an ignorant and rumour-prone population, was brashly pushed with Punjabi vigour, shooting tremors of suspicion, alarm and resentment throughout the northern countryside. Sanjay Gandhi, as the organizer, became the scapegoat for the excesses of many minor agents and officials.

The Janata party government has been too briefly in office (at the time of writing) for any considered judgement on its performance. It is a loosely-knit coalition with a hard core of the former Jan Sangh or pro-Hindu party. The immediate future will show whether it is to become, like the Congress before it, a mainly power-seeking and office-holding organization, or whether India is on the threshold of a new political development. This would be a switchover from a single ruling party with peripheral groups to two major parties, each competing, with programmes as well as persons, for the vote of the Indian masses.

Prophets of doom speak of the centrifugal tendencies in Indian society. These are strong but they have always existed and have to be balanced against the countervailing centripetal ones. There is the degeneration of politics into factions, there is the divisive language issue, separating south from north by a wall of suspicion, there is the increasing assertiveness of the linguistic states and signs of regional nationalisms within them. There are community pressures as with the Sikhs and the Tamils of South India. The comparison is sometimes made with the latter days of the Mughal Empire, when provincial governors intimated to the Centre what 'orders' they were to receive. A formidable list, but against these must be set forces unknown in Mughal days. Tribalism, caste, regionalism, community selfishness, opportunism all exist, it is true, but in nearly all cases they are weaker than before. There is the rapidly expanding industrial–technical class, the managers and technicians, whose interest is unity as a condition of development. There is the largely augmented commercial class, increasingly outward looking, whose interest is the same. There is the cementing force of fear of interference from outside, especially from Pakistan and China, and also the United States, and there is the steadily mounting pressure from the outside world, economic, social and ideological. The mental isolation of historic Hinduism from the days of Albiruni in the eleventh century, a prime factor with caste in Hindu divisions, is being over-run in volume and undermined in content.

India is steadily moving forward into the great world community of nations. Indian society was overlaid by the Perso-Turkish world of the Middle East through the Mughals, and by the western world through the British. These covers removed, she is now taking her place in the new world society into which the west itself is merging. In that world of the future she will be a giver as well as a receiver. With the western intrusion she is using her genius of absorption to fashion something neither wholly traditional nor wholly modern. In the new world society she will not only receive from the east as well as from the west, but will give out in return her treasures of the spirit which at the moment are largely hidden. And so, with haunting doubts and quickening hopes, we take leave of India and wish her well.

Cambridge
September 1977

I HAVE thought it best to leave chapter 21 (Post-Nehru India: Epilogue) as written in September 1977, which recorded the events leading to the traumatic political change of the General Election early in that year. I also adhere to my final reflections on pp. 269–70. What has followed has been two years of controversial politics without decisive results. There are, however, one or two developments significant enough to mention; but since they are contemporary, involving speculation as much as judgement and record, it seems best to touch on them in a separate note.

The new Janata government began its career in a mood of euphoria. But the enthusiasm soon waned, the momentum for change slackened. The government has become a virtual coalition of three main parties with divergent ideologies, held together so loosely as to be widely described as a departmental *raj*. One can therefore only note some tendencies. The first is the revival of Mrs Gandhi's Congress and leadership. She has held the south, moved into the Deccan, but not breached the Janata's grip of the northern Hindi belt. Within the Janata party itself there seems to be a strengthening of its Jan Sangha wing, with the R.S.S. hovering in the background. Its symptoms have been some instances of casteism. The Swatantra party seems to have virtually disappeared. But there has been a notable growth in the influence of the Bharatiya Lok Dal (B.L.D.) of the vigorous Uttar Pradesh septuagenarian, Charan Singh, The party (founded in 1967) has grown dramatically. It stands for the propertied peasant and the introduction of capitalism into agriculture in place of the old *zamindari* feudalism. The Janata government is now an uneasy partnership of Morarji Desai, Charan Singh and the Jan Sangha party, a provisional situation which might either solidify into semi-permanence or break up in confusion.

May 1979   PERCIVAL SPEAR

BIBLIOGRAPHY

General

There are few general histories which cover the Mughal and British periods together. They either cover the whole range of Indian history or confine themselves to the British period only. It is to be hoped that this gap will soon be filled for the two periods, as this book has endeavoured to show, are closely interlinked. Of the wide ranging histories mention may first be made of K. M. Panikkar's *Survey of Indian History* (London, 1960), brief but wide-ranging and abounding in acute observation : B. G. Gokhale's *The Making of the Indian Nation* (Bombay, 1958) is also stimulating and original. For the Mughal period only there is H. L. O. Garrett and S. M. Edwardes's *Mughal Rule in India* (London, 1930), which still has value, specially Edwardes's contribution. I have attempted in *India, a Modern History* (Ann Arbor, 1961), chs. 10–15, a rounded sketch of the Mughal empire.

For the British period there are a number of works. The connoisseur should read J. Mills's *History of British India* continued to 1835 by H. H. Wilson (10 vols., London, 1858). It was compared by Macaulay to Gibbon's History and, while this seems now far-fetched, it remains outstanding. It is opinionated but has the spice of H. H. Wilson's notes of protest at some of Mills's statements. Among more modern works the most lively is E. Thompson's and G. T. Garratt's *Rise and Fulfilment of British Rule in India* (London, 1934). P. E. Robert's *History of British India* (3rd edition, London, 1952) is readable, scholarly, and mildly liberal in tone. And there is now the *Oxford History of Modern India* by the author (Part III of the third edition of the *Oxford History of India*). Coming to the general histories we have in the third section of the Cambridge *Shorter History of India* (1934) a very able treatment from the imperialist point of view by H. H. Dodwell, and there is a comprehensive presentation in the *Advanced History of India* by Drs R. C. Majumdar, H. C. Raychaudhuri, and K. K. Datta (London, 1946 et seq.). Finally there is a valuable study of *Modern India* (London, 1957) by Sir Percival Griffiths. A further reference book is the *Cambridge History of India*, Vols. IV, V, and VI. A documentary work of great value is *The Evolution of India and Pakistan 1858–1947* edited by C. H. Philips (London, 1962).

A good introductory book is H. Tinker's *South Asia, A Short History* (London, 1966).

The Mughals

Surveys of the Mughal period as a whole are still rare but many scholarly works on aspects of the period, specially by Indian authors, are now available.

The coming of the Mughals is still best dealt with in L. F. Rushbrook-Williams's *An Empire Builder of the Sixteenth Century* (London, 1918). Alongside this the reader should not forget Babur's own classic *Memoirs*, in the Oxford edition (2 vols., London, 1921). The reigns of Babur and Humayun are covered in another classic, W. Erskine's *Babur and Humayun* (2 vols., London, 1854). For the Afghan interlude of Sher Shah there is Qanungo's *Sher Shah* (Calcutta, 1921).

Akbar has so far failed to find a biographer worthy of him. The best character sketch is Lawrence Binyon's *Akbar* (London, 1932), and the best general study still Vincent Smith's *Akbar the Great Mogul* (Oxford, 1927). There is a detailed factual record by Wolseley Haig in the *Cambridge History of India*, Vol. IV (Cambridge, 1937). Jahangir is well covered by Beni Parshad's *Jahangir* (London, 1922) and also his own *Memoirs* (transl. by Rogers and Beveridge, 2 vols., 1909 and 1914) and Shah Jahan by B. P. Saksena's *Shah Jahan of Delhi* (Allahabad, 1932) while K. R. Qanungo has contributed a study of *Dara Shukuh* (Calcutta, 2nd ed., 1952). The long reign of Aurangzeb is covered by the great work of Sir Jadunath Sarkar, one of the most distinguished of modern Indian historians. The *History of Aurangzeb* (5 vols., Calcutta, 1916–25) is virtually a history of India during the second half of the seventeenth century. There is also an abridged version in one volume.

The story of the decline is carried on by William Irvine's very learned but rather congested work, the *Later Mughals* (2 vols., London, Calcutta, 1922) and then by Sir J. Sarkar's second great work the *Fall of the Mughal Empire* (4 vols., Calcutta, 1932–50). A shorter and still valuable account for the last stages is H. G. Keene's *Fall of the Moghul Empire* (London, 1887).

The Marathas

For the Marathas we may start with H. G. Rawlinson's sketch *Shivaji the Maratha* (Oxford, 1925). For a full scale treatment there is S. N. Sen's *Siva Chhatrapati* (Calcutta, 1920) and N. S. Takakhov and K. A. Keluskar's *Shivaji Maharaj* (Bombay, 1921). For Maratha history the classic Grant Duff's *History of the Marathas* (3 vols., 1826, and reprints) has been followed by G. S. Sardesai's *New History of the Mahrattas* (3 vols., Bombay, 1946). Justice M. G. Ranade's pioneer work *The Rise of the Mahratta Power* (Poona, 1900) is still valuable. For administration there are S. N. Sen's two important volumes, the *Administrative System of the Marathas* and the *Military System of the Marathas* (1925 and 1928).

ADMINISTRATION, ETC.

Dr I. H. Qureshi's new work *Administration of the Mughal Empire* (Karachi, 1966), is authoritative. S. M. Edwardes in *Mughal Rule in India*, mentioned above, gives a useful sketch and Sir J. Sarkar an introduction in his *Mughal Administration* (2nd ed., Calcutta, 1924). On particular aspects there are now some admirable works: Ibn Hasan, *Central Structure of the Mughal Empire* (Oxford, 1936) describes the central and P. Saran, *Provincial Government of the Mughals* (Allahabad, 1941) the provincial administration. Then there is Irfan Habibh's *Agrarian System of Mughal India* (London, 1963), a brilliant achievement in breadth and depth by a still young scholar. For economic life there are the two standard works of W. E. Moreland: *India at the death of Akbar* (London, 1920) and from *Akbar to Aurangzeb* (London, 1923).

Europeans in India

For the Portuguese see the still standard work by R. S. Whiteway, *The Rise of the Portuguese Power in India* (London, 1895). Sir W. W. Hunter in Vol. 1 of his *History of British India* (London, 1899) provides a readable account. The best modern summary is by C. R. Boxer in *The Portuguese Seaborne Empire* (London, 1969). Short accounts of the English, French, and Dutch Companies are to be found in the *Cambridge History of India*, Vol. V, chs. II–IV. For more on the English Company, see Hunter's two volumes already mentioned, while for the early French S. P. Sen in *The French in India* (Calcutta, 1946) gives an admirable account.

There are many European accounts of India in the sixteenth and seventeenth centuries of which the greatest by common consent is François Bernier's *Travels in the Mogol Empire*, edited by V. A. Smith and A. Constable (Oxford, 2nd ed., 1934). He covers incisively court, country, and Hinduism. Then there is the account of the jeweller, J. B. Tavernier, transl. by V. Ball, 2nd edition, edited by W. Crooke (2 vols., London, 1925). The *Indian Travels of Thevenot and Careri* (*New Delhi*, 1949) have been learnedly edited by Surendranath

Sen; they cover the second half of the seventeenth century. The Venetian Niccolao Manucci lived in India throughout Aurangzeb's reign and his memoirs the *Storia do Mogor* have been brilliantly translated and edited by W. Irvine (3 vols., London, 1907–8). An abridged version entitled *A Pepys of Mughal India* is also available. A selection from early travellers in the reigns of Akbar and Jahangir has been made by Sir W. Foster in *Early Travels in India 1583–1619* (London, 1921), and there is also his edition of *The Embassy of Sir T. Roe to India 1615–19* (London, 1926).

On art there is Percy Brown's *Indian Painting under the Mughals* (Oxford, 1924) and V. A. Smith's *History of Fine Art and Architecture in India and Ceylon* (revised by K. de B. Codrington, Oxford, 1930. There is an excellent chapter in the *Cambridge History of India*, Vol. IV, by Percy Brown.

The Rise of the British 1740–1818

I still think the best general work on this period is P. E. Roberts' *History of British India*. The other English writer of authority is H. H. Dodwell; both Roberts and Dodwell have chapters in the *Cambridge History of India*, Vol. V.

For the Anglo-French struggle we have Robert Orme's classic work *History of the Military Transactions of the British Nation in Indostan* (3 vols., 4th ed., London, 1803, reprint, Madras, 1861). For modern treatment see H. H. Dodwell's masterly *Dupleix and Clive* (London, 1920) and A. Martineau's *Dupleix et l'Inde Française* (4 vols., Paris, 1920–28). S. P. Sen deals gracefully with the final phase in his *French in India 1763–1816* (Calcutta, 1958).

For the British in Bengal we have Robert Orme as a near contemporary author on the British and the contemporary *Siyar-ul Mutaqherin* on the Indian side. There are good biographies by A. M. Davies of *Clive of Plassey* (Oxford, 1939) and *Warren Hastings* (London, 1925). Keith Feiling's study *Warren Hastings* (London, 1954) is a standard work and there is a good character sketch by Penderel Moon, *Warren Hastings and British India* (London, 1954). Good Indian monographs are now appearing of which may be mentioned A. C. Roy's *Mir Jafar* (Calcutta, 1953), N. L. Chatterji's *Mir Kasim* (Allahabad, 1935), and B. K. Gupta's *Sirajuddaullah and the East India Company* (1962). See also A. Majed Khan, *The Transition in Bengal, 1756—1775* (Cambridge, 1969), an important work. For the economic side see N. K. Sinha, *The Economic History of Bengal* (Calcutta, 1956), and W. W. Hunter, *Annals of Rural Bengal* (Lon-

don, 1871), and for the English background of intrigue the great
work of Lucy Sutherland, *The East India Company in 18th Century
Politics* (Oxford, 1952).

For the Hastings era, apart from works already mentioned, M. E.
Monckton-Jones covers the early reforms in her *Warren Hastings in
Bengal* (Oxford, 1918). A. Aspinall deals with Cornwallis in *Cornwallis in Bengal* (Manchester, 1931) and there is the *Cornwallis Correspondence* (ed. C. Ross, 3 vols., London, 1859). An admirable
general work is Holden Furber's *John Company at Work* (Cambridge, Mass., 1948).

For contemporary Calcutta there is H. E. Busteed's *Echoes of Old
Calcutta* (4th ed., London, 1908) and for social life H. H. Dodwell,
The Nabobs of Madras (London, 1926) and T. G. P. Spear, *The
Nabobs* (Oxford, Paperback, 1963). C. H. Philips in his great *East
India Company* (2nd ed., London, 1962) provides the London back-
ground, and Sir C. Ilbert, *The Government of India* (London, 1916)
the constitutional.

The military and political events of the final phase are covered in
the general histories. To these may be added H. G. Keene's *Hindustan under the Freelances* (London, 1907) for the European adventurers, E. Thompson *The Making of the Indian Princes* (Oxford,
1943) – a vivid book which catches the spirit of the times – and H. T.
Prinsep's contemporary *History of the Political and Military Transactions in India of the Marquess of Hastings* (2 vols., London, 1825).

The Completion of Dominion 1818–58

The best description of India about this time is Bishop Heber's
Narrative of a Journey, etc. (2 vols., London, 1828, etc.) and V. Jac-
quemont's *Letters from India* (2 vols., London, 1834) are vivid and
individual. The best of the measured surveys are Sir J. Malcolm's
Memoir of Central India (2 vols., London, 1832) and M. Elphinstone's
Report on the Peshwa's territories (London, 1822).

The Abbé J. A. Dubois, *Hindu Manners and Customs* (3rd ed.,
Oxford, 1906) describes in detail the Hinduism of the South while
G. A. Herklot's *Islam in India* (new ed., Oxford, 1928) gives an
account of popular Islam in the North. For the Thugs see Sir W. H.
Sleeman's *Report ... on the Thug gangs* (Calcutta, 1840) and Mead-
ows Taylor's classic *Confessions of a Thug* (World's Classics, London,
1933).

For the political side of this period there is, in addition to general
works, J. W. Kaye's *History of the War in Afghanistan* (3 vols., Lon-

don, 1851) and P. Sykes's *History of Afghanistan* (2 vols., London, 1940) may be consulted. There is also Sir O. Caroe's *The Pathans* (New York, 1958). For Sind see H. T. Lambrick's *Sir C. Napier and Sind* (Oxford, 1952).

For the Sikhs, J. D. Cunningham's *History of the Sikhs* (new ed., Oxford, 1918) is an accepted classic. But the important modern works of K. Singh should now be consulted. These are *The Sikhs* (London, 1953), an introduction, *Ranjit Singh* (London, 1962), a spirited biography, and the *History of the Sikhs*, 2 vols. (London, 1964–6). For origins see the important work of W. H. Macleod, *Guru Nanak and the Sikh Religion* (Oxford, 1969).

The development of the administration is well described in *The Montagu–Chelmsford Report*, Vol. 1 (London, 1918) with the Cambridge History, Vols. V and VI, for a more detailed treatment. On land questions there is W. K. Firminger's great edition with commentary of the *Fifth Report to the House of Commons . . . 1812* (Calcutta, 1917). The work of the civil service is well described by P. Woodruff, *The Founders* and *The Guardians* (London, 1953–4). For the Indian states see K. M. Panikkar's *The Evolution of Indian Policy towards Indian States 1774–1858* (London, 1929). For the change of policy see first, apart from the general works, S. E. Stokes's striking *The English Utilitarians and India* (Oxford, 1959) and K. A. Ballhatchet's *Social Policy and Social Change in Western India* (London, 1957). R. Coupland's *Wilberforce* (2nd ed., London, 1945) and K. Ingham's *Reformers in India* (Cambridge, 1956) trace Evangelical influence. There is no full study of Bentinck yet, but for a general treatment of the subject see L. S. S. O'Malley's *India and the West* (London, 1941). The best study of Ram Mohan Roy is S. D. Collet's *Life and Letters of Raja Rammohun Roy*, 3rd ed., edited by J. K. Biswas and P. K. Ganguly (Calcutta, 1962). See also his *Collected English Works* edited by K. Nag and D. Burman (Calcutta, 1946) and S. N. Mukherjee's chapter, 'Class, Caste and Politics in Calcutta, 1815–38', in *Elites in South Asia*, eds. E. Leach and S. N. Mukherjee (Cambridge, 1970).

For the mutiny period we have a two-volume study of Dalhousie in the *Life* by Sir W. Lee Warner (London, 1904) and an edition of his *Private Letters* (London, 1910) by J. A. Baird. For the Punjab see the *Life of Lord Lawrence* by S. B. Smith (2 vols., 3rd ed., London, 1883) and *The Life of Henry Lawrence* by J. L. Morrison (London, 1934). For the Mutiny itself there is now the admirable work of S. Sen, *1857* (Delhi, 1957), scholarly, judicious, and humane. E. Thompson, *The Other Side of the Medal* (London, 1925) helps to correct perspective. S.

Ahmad Khan's *The Indian Revolt* (Benares, 1873) is an acute contemporary Indian judgement. Canning's part is described by M. Maclagan in his *Clemency Canning* (London, 1926), a general work of great value.

Imperial and Renascent India

Reorganization is most conveniently treated in the *Cambridge History*, Vol. VI. T. R. Metcalf in the *Aftermath of Revolt* (Princeton, 1964) gives a good study of the reconstruction period. There are a series of viceregal studies of which may be mentioned S. Gopal's *Lord Ripon* (London, 1953) and Lord Ronaldshay's *Life of Lord Curzon*, Vol. II (London, 1928). The main histories give the general trend. H. H. Dodwell is good on foreign policy in the *Cambridge History*, Vol. VI, and this work is also good for administration. S. Gopal's *British Policy in India, 1858–1905* (Cambridge, 1965) is an able general review. New work in this period, based on recently released material, is now in progress.

For economic development the standard works are Vera Anstey's *Economic Development of India* (3rd ed., London, 1949) and R. C. Dutt's *Economic History of India* (2 vols., London, 1901 etc.). For railways see L. C. A. Knowles's *Economic Development of the British Overseas Empire* (London, 1924); for industry D. R. Gadgil, *The Industrial Evolution of India* (London, 1934) and D. H. Buchanan's *Development of Capitalist Enterprise in India* (New York, 1934), an American work.

For the mind of the new India see A. Mayhew's *Education of India* (London, 1926), a sober study. L. S. S. O'Malley's *India and the West* (London, 1941) is invaluable for all development. For religious movements there is an unsatisfactory compendium in J. N. Farquhar's *Modern Religious Movements in India* (New York, 1918). For the Brahmo Samaj see P. K. Sen, *Biography of a New Faith* (2 vols., Calcutta, 1950), for Ramakrishna and Vivekananda the works of Romain Rolland and Sister Nivedita. J. C. Smith in his *Modern Islam in India* (2nd ed., London, 1946) deals with the Muslim side, as does S. M. Ikram's and P. Spear's (editors) *Cultural Heritage of Pakistan* (Karachi, 1955). There is no good work on the Arya Samaj in English yet. N. C. Chaudhuri's *Autobiography of an Unknown Indian* (London, 1951) is a moving, brilliant account of thought processes.

For the new class a basic work is B. B. Misra's *The Indian Middle Classes* (London, 1961). See also A. Seal's *The Emergence of Indian Nationalism* (Cambridge, 1968). S. N. Bannerjea's *A Nation in the Making* (London, 1925) is valuable for the early days. See also Sir

W. Wedderburn's *A. O. Hume* (London, 1913), H. P. Mody, *Sir P. Mehta* (London, 1927), and B. C. Pal *Memories of my Life and Time* (1932).

For Congress the basic work is P. Sitaramayya's *History of the National Congress* (2 vols. Allahabad, 1946). A useful compendium is C. F. Andrews and A. Mukerjii's *Rise and Growth of Congress* (1938). S. Gopal's book on Ripon has already been mentioned. S. A. Wolpert's comparative study *Tilak and Gokhale* (California, 1962) is excellent, and there are separate studies of *Lokamaniya Tilak* (London, 1956) by D. V. Tahmankar and of *G. K. Gokhale* (Calcutta, 1933) by J. S. Hoyland.

National India 1905–64

THE PRELUDE 1905–14

For the Morley–Minto period see J. Morley's *Recollections* (2 vols., London, 1917) and *Speeches on Indian Affairs* (London, 1909) and for Minto, Mary, Countess of Minto, *India, Minto and Morley* (London, 1934), a valuable documentary. A new and balanced study of the two is S. R. Wasti's *Lord Minto and the Indian Nationalist Movement* (Oxford, 1964). For the Congress side there is Sitaramayya's book, for Gokhale his *Speeches* (Madras, 1900), and for Tilak his *Writings and Speeches* (1922). Lord Hardinge's papers are now fully available and there is his own rather brief *My Indian Years* (London, 1948). The Congress split of 1908 is dealt with from various points of view by Wolpert (*Tilak and Gokhale* above), Tahmankar (*Lokamaniya Tilak*, above), and S. N. Bannerjea (*A Nation in the Making*, above). The spirit of the old administration can be sensed in Lord Beveridge's *India Called Them* (London, 1947), with a liberal bias, and Sir M. O'Dwyer's *India as I knew it* (London, 1925), with a Punjab and imperialist twist. See also S. A. Wolpert's *Morley and India, 1906–10* (California, 1967).

A description of India's contribution to the First World War may be found in Sir C. Lucas's *The Empire at War*, Vol. V (London, 1920) and Sir J. Willcock's *With the Indians in France* (London, 1920). For internal history we have V. Chirol, *India* (London, 1926), A. Besant, *How India wrought for Freedom* (London, 1915), S. N. Bannerjea's book, and Tilak's *Writings and Speeches*. Sitaramayya gives the Congress viewpoint while the Montagu mission is covered by E. S. Montagu's vivid *An Indian Diary* (London, 1930). We now also have S. D. Waley's *Edwin Montagu* (London, 1964) with long extracts from his letters, etc.

Bibliography

THE INTER-WAR YEARS

For the events leading up to Amritsar see the two government reports, the *Rowlatt Report* (London, 1918, cmd. 9190) and the *Hunter Committee's Report* (London, 1920, cmd. 681). The *Montagu-Chelmsford Report* (London, 1918, cmd. 9109) is a state-paper of great importance giving both a view of the past and a *rationale* of future development. For the idea of Dyarchy see L. Curtis, *Dyarchy* (London, 1920).

We now come to the reign of Gandhi. Read first his autobiography, *The Story of my Experiments with Truth*, first published at Ahmadabad in 1927. Then there is D. G. Tendulkar's *Mahatma* (Bombay, 1952, etc.) in eight volumes. The best concise *Life* is the joint work of H. S. L. Polak, H. N. Brailsford, and Lord Pethick-Lawrence (London, 1949). Louis Fischer has provided an American interpretation in his *Life* (New York, 1950) and there are thoughtful studies by J. Bondurant, *The Conquest of Violence* (Princeton, 1959), and E. Morton, *The Women behind Mahatma Gandhi* (London, 1954).

For these years the *Indian Annual Register 1920–47*, edited by N. N. Mitra, is very valuable. On the British side there are lives of Lords Reading and Birkenhead, Lord Birkenhead's *Life of Lord Halifax* (London, 1965), Lord Halifax's *Fullness of Days* (London, 1957), Lord Templewood's *Memoirs*, and S. Gopal's study of Lord Irwin (Oxford, 1957). On the Indian side we have Azim Husain, *Fazli-Husain* (London, 1946), N. D. Parikh's *Sardar Vallabhbhai Patel* (Ahmadabad, 1953), President Rajendra Prasad's *Autobiography*, Abul Kalam Azad's *India Wins Freedom* (New York, 1960), Jawarharlal Nehru's *Autobiography* (London, 1936, etc.). and Michael Brecher's authoritative *Nehru, a political biography* (London, 1959). M. R. Masani in his *Communist Party of India* (London, 1954) gives a valuable account of its rise.

The documents to notice are the *Nehru Report* (1928), the Congress reply to the Simon Commission's appointment, and the *Simon Commission Report* (London, 1930, cmd. 3568–9). Most valuable is M. Gwyer and A. Appadorai's *Speeches and Documents on the Indian Constitution, 1921–1947* (2 vols., London, 1957). See also *The Evolution of India and Pakistan* mentioned in the general note to the bibliography.

THE SECOND WORLD WAR AND TRANSFER OF POWER

An official history is under production directed by Professor Bisheshwar Prasad (New York, 1960–). G. Tyson in *India Arms for Victory* (Allahabad, 1944) provides a useful summary.

The first two volumes of R. Coupland's *Constitutional Report* (London, 1942) gives a useful summary up to 1942. Vol. II contains the Congress constitution of 1939 and its Declaration of Fundamental Rights. The *Annual Register* continues to be valuable. The lives and memoirs mentioned above are all valuable and Brecher's *Nehru* is now indispensable. C. A. Cook's *Life of R. S. Cripps* should also be seen. Lord Glendevon in *A Viceroy at Bay* (London, 1971) has provided a defence of his father, Lord Linlithgow.

The chief documents covering the transfer of power will be found in Gwyer and Appadorai's *Speeches and Documents* above mentioned. E. W. R. Lumley's *Transfer of Power in India* (London, 1954) is an excellent summary, while V. P. Menon's personal account in his *Transfer of Power in India* (Princeton, N.J., 1957) is both fascinating and authoritative. For the Mountbatten Mission see A. Campbell-Johnson's *Mission with Mountbatten* (London, 1951), and for a description from the military angle *While Memory Serves* by Sir F. Tuker (London, 1950). Brecher's *Nehru* continues to be vital. The latest study is H. V. Hodson's *The Great Divide* (London, 1969). There is also an important symposium, edited by C. H. Philips and M. D. Wainwright, *The Partition of India* (London, 1970), and the great documentary, *The Transfer of Power*, edited by Nicholas Mansergh and E. W. R. Lumby (London, 1970-). It covers the years 1942–7 and so far three volumes have been published.

Pakistan

For the rise of Pakistan I. H. Qureshi's *Muslim Community of the Indo-Pakistan Subcontinent* ('s Gravenhage, 1962) should be consulted. Other studies are W. C. Smith's *Modern Islam in India* (London, 1946) and the *Cultural Heritage of Pakistan* (Karachi, 1958), editors Ikram and Spear. A. H. Alberuni in *Makers of Pakistan* (Lahore) has contributed studies of leaders. There are *Lives* of Jinnah by H. Bolitho (London, 1945), a character-study, and by M. H. Saiyyed (Lahore, 1945), a detailed record. For ideas read M. Iqbal's *Secrets of the Self*, transl. R. A. Nicholson (London, 1920) and the *Reconstruction of Religious Thought in Islam* (London, 1934). On the separation there is a dispassionate study by R. A. Symonds, *The Making of Pakistan* (London, 1950). See also P. Moon's *Divide and Quit* (London, 1961), a personal record.

THE NEHRU ERA 1947—64

The books by and about Nehru have already been detailed. For the integration of the Indian States see V. P. Menon's first-hand and valuable *Integration of the Indian States* (Princeton, 1956). There is a good general study by Sir P. J. Griffiths in *Modern India* (London, 1957).

The text of the constitution is available in an official publication. For comment see G. N. Joshi's *Constitution of India* (3rd ed., London, 1954) and Sir A. Jennings's *Some characteristics of the Indian Constitution* (London, 1952). W. H. Morris Jones has made a valuable study of its working in his *Parliament in India* (London, 1957). See also G. Austin's *The Indian Constitution* (Oxford, 1966).

For the reorganization of the States see the *Report of the States Reorganization Committee* (Delhi, 1955) and on language the *Report of the Official Language Commission* (Delhi, 1957).

The five year plans are covered in the Planning Commission's two reports, *The First Five Year Plan* (Delhi, 1953) and *The Second Five Year Plan* (Delhi, 1956) and their statement *The New India* (New York, 1958).

On the social sphere see Taya Zinkin *Changing India* (London, 1958), and D. E. Smith, *India as a Secular State* (Princeton, 1967).

For foreign affairs the publications of the Indian Council of World Affairs should be consulted. For Kashmir there are studies by M. Brecher, *Struggle for Kashmir* (New York, 1953) and Sisir Gupta, *Kashmir, A Study in Indian-Pakistan Relations* (London, 1966). Works on 'the China incident', like those on Kashmir, are apt to be deemed controversial, and none of the next three titles escape this label altogether. They are: A. Lamb's *The McMahon Line, 1904–1914*, 2 vols. (London and Toronto, 1966) and *The China-India Border: the Origins of the Disputed Boundaries* (London, 1964), and N. Maxwell's *India's China War* (London, 1970).

For Communism see G. A. Overstreet and M. Windmiller's *Communism in India* (California, 1959).

For the post-Nehru succession see M. Brecher, *Succession in India* (London, 1966).

Finally, two general books may be recommended. They are C. E. Heimsath's *Indian Nationalism and Hindu Social Reform* (Princeton, 1964) and T. R. Metcalf's interpretative anthology *Modern India* (London, 1971).

Addenda: books published mainly between 1972 and 1977

General

A. L. Basham (ed.), *A Cultural History of India*, Oxford, 1975.

The Mughals

J. F. Richards, *Mughal Administration in Golconda*, Oxford, 1975.

M. Athar Ali, *The Mughal Nobility under Aurangzeb*, New York, 1966.

The Rise of the British, 1740–1818

N. C. Chaudhuri, *Clive of India: A Political and Psychological Essay*, London, 1975.

P. Spear, *Master of Bengal: Clive and his India*, London, 1975.

P. J. Marshall, *East Indian Fortunes: The British in Bengal in the 18th century*, Oxford, 1976. A study in depth of the British in Bengal.

P. J. Marshall, *The Impeachment of Warren Hastings*, Oxford, 1965. A searching critical analysis of the case.

Iris Butler, *The Eldest Brother*, London, 1973. A vivid study of Lord Wellesley, based on new material.

J. Pemble, *The Invasion of Nepal*, Oxford, 1971. Newly researched, dramatic and illuminating.

The Completion of Dominion, 1818–58

J. Roselli, *Lord William Bentinck: The Making of a Liberal Imperialist*, London, 1974. A subtle and important study.

W. H. Mcleod, *Evolution of the Sikh Community*, Oxford, 1976. An excellent introduction.

R. E. Frykenberg, *The Guntur District, 1788–1848*, Oxford, 1965. A vital grass-roots study, opening up new vistas.

Imperial and Renascent India

O. Caroe, *The Pathans*, Karachi, 1975. A study by a leading authority.

S. Chakravarty, *From Khyber to Oxus*, New Delhi, 1976. An able study in nineteenth-century imperialism.

National India, 1905–64

THE PRELUDE, 1905–18

P. G. Robb, *The Government of India and Reforms, etc, 1916–21*, London, 1976. A new and original examination of Lord Chelmsford's Viceroyalty.

Judith M. Brown, *Gandhi's Rise to Power, 1915–22*, Cambridge, 1972. A searching study in depth by a leading authority.

Bibliography

INTER-WAR YEARS

J. M. Brown, *Gandhi and Civil Disobedience, 1928–34*, Cambridge, 1976. Another searching study by this authority on Gandhi.

R. Iyer, *The Moral and Political Thought of Mahatma Gandhi*, New York, 1973. A philosophical study of depth and subtlety.

Ved Mehta, *Mahatma Gandhi and his Apostles*, London, 1977. An original and searching personal study.

THE SECOND WORLD WAR AND TRANSFER OF POWER

N. Mansergh (ed.), *The Transfer of Power*, London, 1970–. Three more volumes of this great work have appeared. They are:

   IV. *The Bengal Famine and the new Viceroyalty*, June 1943 to August 1944.

   V. *The Simla Conference, etc.*, September 1944 to July 1945.

   VI. *The Post-War Phase: new moves etc.*, August 1945 to March 1946.

P. Moon (ed.), *Wavell: The Viceroy's Journal*, London, 1973.

L. Collins and D. Lapierre, *Freedom at Midnight*, London, 1975. Notable for personal insights; a study of Gandhi's last days and of the conspiracy to assassinate him.

G. D. Khosla, *Stern Reckoning*, New Delhi, 1950. A study by a judge of the post-Independence massacres in northern India.

Pakistan

P. Hardy, *The Muslims of British India*, Cambridge, 1972. A notable survey by a recognized authority.

THE NEHRU ERA

M. Edwardes, *Nehru: A Political Biography*, London, 1971. An attractively written work with original views.

N. Maxwell, *India's China War*, London, 1970. A detailed study of the events leading to the Indo-Chinese clash in 1962, with some controversial views.

POST-NEHRU INDIA, 1964–

Much of the writing here is polemical, and much of the information still confined to articles in journals and the press.

F. L. Frankel, *The Green Revolution*, U.S.A., 1971. A useful study of the agricultural revolution in India.

K. Bhatia, *Ordeal of Nationhood: A Social Study*, London, 1971. Mr Bhatia is a publicist of standing and insight in India.

K. Bhatia, *Indira: A biography of Prime Minister Gandhi*, London,
1974. A perceptive study of Mrs Gandhi before the Emergency.
Dilip Hiro, *Inside India To-day*, London, 1976. Perceptive and in-
formative.

INDEX

Abdur Rahman, 156

Abu'l Fazl, 11, 37

Adham Khan, 30

Afghans, 110, 112; their empire in northern India, 16–17, 53, 129, 132; and the Mughal invaders, 22, 27; Sher Shah and, 28; and the decline of the Mughals, 71–2, 74; and the Marathas, 74–5; their annexations, 132; their wars, 156

Afghanistan, 22, 72, 74, 174

Afzal Khan, General, 59

Age of Consent (Sarda) Act, 151

Agra, 16, 27, 65; the Mughals and, 20, 23, 27, 28, 29, 30, 50, 54

Ahmad Shah Abdali, and Delhi, 74, 75, 83

Aix-la-Chapelle, Treaty of, 78

Akbar (1542–1605), 26; his birth, 27; debt to Sher Shah, 28; early years, 29–30; character and achievement, 30, 31, 34 ff., 37–8, 52, 54; conquests, 30–31; nature of his rule, 31, 34, 41; his imperial service, 34–5; restores the idea of imperial India, 36; his 'Divine Faith', 36; his eclectic cult, 36–7, 57; his army, 44; compared with Aurangzeb, 55, 56; his revenue, 109

Albiruni, on the Hindus, 158–9

Albuquerque, Affonso de (1453–1515), 62, 63

Ali Ibrahim Khan, 95

Aligarh College, 226, 228

Alivardi Khan, ruler of Bengal, 81, 82

Amboyna, Massacre of, 65

Amherst, William Amherst, Earl (1773–1857), Governor-General of India, 131

Amir Khan, 105

Amritsar, Golden Temple of, 134; massacres of, 139, 191, 235

Andhra, 247

Arabs, traders in India, 19, 31, 61, 62, 221

Architecture: Hindu-Muslim, 20; the Mughals and, 46–7, 54; Persian influence on, 48–9; its decline by 1818, 119–20

Army, the, under the Mughals, 44, 46; Europeanized by Cornwallis, 98–9; and revenue collection, 112; under British rule, 118; reformed after the Mutiny, 145–6; its Indianization, 194–5; and Second World War, 215, 230

Asaf Jah, Nizam-ul-mulk, 70, 71

Asia, national movements in, 181; Nehru and, 254

Asoka (264–223 B.C.), 38

Asquith, Herbert Henry, Earl of Oxford (1853–1928), 181–2

Assam, 129, 131, 176, 210, 215, 216

Ataturk, Kemal, abolishes the Caliphate, 194, 227

Aurangzeb (1618–1717), 34, 36, 69; his fame, 40, 52; and annexation, 53–4; personality and reign, 55–6 57; and the Sikhs, 58, 134; and the Marathas, 60; his policy and the Mughal decline, 71

Ava, kingdom of, 129, 130, 131, 132

Azad, Maulana, 233

Babur (1483–1530), 16, 50; his dynasty, 21; early life, 21–2; invade India, 22–3; his empire, 23, 116; character, 23–4, 40; condition of his state, 24–5; and Homayun, 26; *Memoirs*, 23 and n., 24

FOR THE BEST IN PAPERBACKS, LOOK FOR THE 🐧

In every corner of the world, on every subject under the sun, Penguin represents quality and variety – the very best in publishing today.

For complete information about books available from Penguin – including Pelicans, Puffins, Peregrines and Penguin Classics – and how to order them, write to us at the appropriate address below. Please note that for copyright reasons the selection of books varies from country to country.

In the United Kingdom: For a complete list of books available from Penguin in the U.K., please write to *Dept E.P., Penguin Books Ltd, Harmondsworth, Middlesex, UB7 0DA*

In the United States: For a complete list of books available from Penguin in the U.S., please write to *Dept BA, Penguin, 299 Murray Hill Parkway, East Rutherford, New Jersey 07073*

In Canada: For a complete list of books available from Penguin in Canada, please write to *Penguin Books Canada Ltd, 2801 John Street, Markham, Ontario L3R 1B4*

In Australia: For a complete list of books available from Penguin in Australia, please write to the *Marketing Department, Penguin Books Australia Ltd, P.O. Box 257, Ringwood, Victoria 3134*

In New Zealand: For a complete list of books available from Penguin in New Zealand, please write to the *Marketing Department, Penguin Books (NZ) Ltd, Private Bag, Takapuna, Auckland 9*

In India: For a complete list of books available from Penguin, please write to *Penguin Overseas Ltd, 706 Eros Apartments, 56 Nehru Place, New Delhi, 110019*

In Holland: For a complete list of books available from Penguin in Holland, please write to *Penguin Books Nederland B.V., Postbus 195, NL–1380AD Weesp, Netherlands*

In Germany: For a complete list of books available from Penguin, please write to *Penguin Books Ltd, Friedrichstrasse 10 – 12, D–6000 Frankfurt Main 1, Federal Republic of Germany*

In Spain: For a complete list of books available from Penguin in Spain, please write to *Longman Penguin España, Calle San Nicolas 15, E–28013 Madrid, Spain*

A HISTORY OF INDIA VOL I
Romila Thapar

The first volume of this history traces the evolution of India before contact with modern Europe was established in the sixteenth century. Romila Thapar is the Reader in History at the University of Delhi: her account of the development of India's social and economic structure is arranged within a framework of the principal political and dynastic events. Her narrative covers some 2,500 years of India's history, from the establishment of Aryan culture in about 1000 B.C. to the coming of the Mughuls in A.D. 1526 and the first appearance of European trading companies. In particular she deals interestingly with the many manifestations of Indian culture, as seen in religion, art and literature, in ideas and institutions.

THE GREAT MUTINY
India 1857
Christopher Hibbert

'By far the best single-volume description of the mutiny yet written'
– *Economist*

'A good book can always be expected from Christopher Hibbert, but this time he has excelled himself' – *Sunday Telegraph*

'A first-rate book, well researched, beautifully written and so exciting that I had difficulty in laying it down' – Philip Magnus in the *Sunday Times*

AN AREA OF DARKNESS
V. S. Naipaul

Coming from a family which left India only two generations ago, V. S. Naipaul felt that his roots lay in India. But the country and its attitudes remained outside his experience, in an 'area of darkness', until, with some apprehension, he spent a year there. He arrived at Bombay, then travelled as far north as Kashmir, east to Calcutta and south to Madras. Here he shares his experience of India generously and gives the reader deep insight into a country and a writer's mind.

'Tender, lyrical, explosive . . . excellent' – John Wain

'Most compelling and vivid' – V. S. Pritchett

THE PENGUIN TRAVEL LIBRARY – A SELECTION

Hindoo Holiday   J. R. Ackerley
The Flight of Ikaros   Kevin Andrews
The Path to Rome   Hilaire Belloc
Looking for Dilmun   Geoffrey Bibby
First Russia, then Tibet   Robert Byron
Granite Island   Dorothy Carrington
The Worst Journey in the World   Apsley Cherry-Garrard
Hashish   Henry de Monfreid
Passages from Arabia Deserta   C. M. Doughty
Siren Land   Norman Douglas
Brazilian Adventure   Peter Fleming
The Hill of Devi   E. M. Forster
Journey to Kars   Philip Glazebrook
Pattern of Islands   Arthur Grimble
Writings from Japan   Lafcadio Hearn
A Little Tour in France   Henry James
Mornings in Mexico   D. H. Lawrence
Mani   Patrick Leigh Fermor
Stones of Florence and **Venice Observed**   Mary McCarthy
They went to Portugal   Rose Macaulay
Colossus of Maroussi   Henry Miller
Spain   Jan Morris
The Big Red Train Ride   Eric Newby
The Grand Irish Tour   Peter Somerville-Large
Marsh Arabs   Wilfred Thesiger
The Sea and The Jungle   H. M. Tomlinson
The House of Exile   Nora Wain
Ninety-Two Days   Evelyn Waugh

The Second World War (6 volumes)   Winston S. Churchill

The definitive history of the cataclysm which swept the world for the second time in thirty years.

1917: The Russian Revolutions and the Origins of Present-Day Communism
Leonard Schapiro

A superb narrative history of one of the greatest episodes in modern history by one of our greatest historians.

Imperial Spain 1496–1716   J. H. Elliot

A brilliant modern study of the sudden rise of a barren and isolated country to be the greatest power on earth, and of its equally sudden decline. 'Outstandingly good' – *Daily Telegraph*

Joan of Arc: The Image of Female Heroism   Marina Warner

'A profound book, about human history in general and the place of women in it' – Christopher Hill

Man and the Natural World: Changing Attitudes in England 1500–1800
Keith Thomas

'A delight to read and a pleasure to own' – Auberon Waugh in the *Sunday Telegraph*

The Making of the English Working Class   E. P. Thompson

Probably the most imaginative – and the most famous – post-war work of English social history.